X

The Natural History of

ANTELOPES

The Natural History of

ANTELOPES

C. A. SPINAGE

Facts On File Publications
New York, New York ● Oxford, England

First published in the United States by
Facts On File, Inc.
460 Park Avenue South
New York, New York 10016

Library of Congress Cataloging-in-Publication Data

Spinage, C. A. (Clive A.)
    The natural history of antelopes.

    Bibliography: p.
    Includes index.
    1. Antelopes.   I. Title.
QL737.U55S68   1986   599.73′58   86–11508
ISBN 0–8160–1581–3

Printed in Great Britain
10 9 8 7 6 5 4 3 2 1

Contents

Colour plates

Figures

Acknowledgements

I am grateful to the following for permission to reproduce material: Figures 1.1 and 11.2 from Blackman, A.M. (1914) *The Rock Tombs at Meir Mem* 23, The Egypt Exploration Society; Figure 2.1 after Grassé, P-P. 1955 ed. Traité de Zoologie, Tome XVII part I, Masson et Cie; Figures 1.3 and 6.5, African Journal of Ecology, Blackwell Scientific Publications; Figure 9.2, Macmillan and Co.; Figures 8.12 and 8.14, Academic Press; Prof. F. Walther for Figure 8.5; colour plate 18, bongo, Alan and Joan Root. Also to Russell Kyle for providing me with Figure 11.1.

Series editor's foreword

In recent years there has been a great upsurge of interest in wildlife and a deepening concern for nature conservation. For many there is a compelling urge to counterbalance some of the artificiality of present-day living with a more intimate involvement with the natural world. More people are coming to realise that we are all part of nature, not apart from it. There seems to be a greater desire to understand its complexities and appreciate its beauty.

This appreciation of wildlife and wild places has been greatly stimulated by the world-wide impact of natural history television programmes. These have brought into our homes the sights and sounds both of our own countryside and of far-off places that arouse our interest and delight.

In parallel with this growth of interest there has been a great expansion of knowledge and, above all, understanding of the natural world—an understanding vital to any conservation measures that can be taken to safeguard it. More and more field workers have carried out painstaking studies of many species, analysing their intricate behaviour, relationships and the part they play in the general ecology of their habitats. To the time-honoured techniques of field observations and experimentation has been added the sophistication of radio-telemetry whereby individual animals can be followed, even in the dark and over long periods, and their activities recorded. Infra-red cameras and light-intensifying binoculars now add a new dimension to the study of nocturnal animals. Through such devices great advances have been made.

This series of volumes aims to bring this information together in an exciting and readable form so that all who are interested in wildlife may benefit from such a synthesis. Many of the titles in the series concern groups of related species such as otters, squirrels and rabbits so that readers from many parts of the world may learn about their own more familiar animals in a much wider context. Inevitably more emphasis will be given to particular species within a group as some have been more extensively studied than others. Authors too have their own special interests and experience and a text gains much in authority and vividness when there has been personal involvement.

Many natural history books have been published in recent years which have delighted the eye and fired the imagination. This is wholly good. But it is the intention of this series to take this a step further by exploring the subject in greater depth and by making available the results of recent research. In this way it is hoped to satisfy to some extent at least the curiosity and desire to know more which is such an encouraging characteristic of the keen naturalist of today.

Ernest Neal
Taunton

Introduction

'Antelope' is a term which covers a wide range of mammals distinguished by chewing the cud, found in such far-flung regions as Russia, the Far East, India and, above all, Africa. Of the 111 species known to exist, two-thirds live in the latter continent alone. Because of this, and because Africa is the country with which I am most familiar, where I have lived and worked among the wildlife for the past 30 years, including a three-year field study of the waterbuck in Uganda, this book has been limited to the African antelopes, enabling them to be viewed as a whole. It is impossible to understand the wide range and complexity of forms by jumping from one country to another where, in most cases, antelopes are now represented by only one or two species with fragmented distributions. By limiting this natural history to Africa, the greater number can be covered coherently.

When Dr Ernest Neal asked me to write this book, he spoke of the great amount of research that had been done on antelopes in recent years, and which needed presenting to a wider audience. But as I proceeded with the task, I became more and more aware of how little we know about antelopes. There are species known to science since the eighteenth century of whose habits, social organisation, breeding or physiology we are still completely ignorant. One example is the diminutive royal antelope of West African forests, known since 1705!

Many preliminary surveys have been conducted on the commoner species since the 1960s, but very few full, detailed studies; so that we still need to know a great deal more even of some of the most common species. Unfortunately many antelopes are becoming rare almost daily, so that regretfully we never *shall* know more about their lives. For the several now rare species of Somalia, we have only a few hunters' anecdotes of 60 or more years ago, and seemingly little hope of ever learning more before such species as the dibatag, Swayne's hartebeest, Pelzeln's and Speke's gazelles, for example, become extinct.

This century has already seen the disappearance of the northern hartebeest and the red gazelle. Last century saw the disappearance of the bluebuck in South Africa, while although the bontebok and the black wildebeest were reduced almost to the point of extinction by 1865, reasonable numbers of these two species still exist today, showing that it is not always too late to take steps to save a species.

In spite of their interest, the antelopes have always been a rather neglected group. I know of only three previous books in English that have been devoted to them; one now a very expensive rare collector's item, Sclater and Thomas's *The Book of Antelopes* (1894–1900), one a simple introduction and the other a book of plates. While one standard university zoological text dismisses antelopes in only three out of its 786 pages! Perhaps the reason, apart from a previous lack of knowledge, lies in the fact that they are such a large and complex group. This book is by no means intended as an exhaustive account, but simply attempts to draw together some of the results of research that have appeared in recent years, and to present them in a way which emphasises the interest of this remarkable and neglected group of mammals.

*To
Roseline*

1 Antelopes and their origins

Perched on the lofty rim of Tanzania's Ngorongoro Crater to watch the ant-like movements of untold thousands of wildebeest milling about on the distant crater floor, is to me one of the unforgettable experiences of Africa. Here, captured in this vast amphitheatre like some gigantic fishbowl, one can see at a glance the character of wild Africa, with its antelopes – antelopes in countless numbers. Antelopes which once roamed all over this vast continent; through its woodlands, its plains, and even its deserts; in an exuberance of forms that have been with us for over fifteen million years. God may have had an inordinate fondness for beetles, as J.B.S. Haldane, one of England's great biologists once remarked, but luckily for us, when it came to Africa He was equally fond of antelopes. At least 74 different species greet the eye, ranging in size from the 4 kg pygmy antelope to the giant eland weighing almost a tonne; and with some species reaching concentrations which make those of the American bison look impoverished in comparison.

Who could fail to be captivated by this vast assemblage; their colours, their graceful forms and soft brown eyes, and, above all, their striking horns, twisting and curling in a baroque extravaganza of shapes. Their horns long ago earned them a special place in man's perverse psychology as trophies of the hunt. But the early Dutch settlers in South Africa slaughtered these graceful antelopes in their thousands for their meat and skins, or to make way for their cattle. It was not until British Indian Army officers started to take their furloughs in Africa a century ago, to hunt in imitation of the Indian princes, that the antelopes became a sought-after symbol of the chase, their horns becoming an essential part of the macabre furnishings of the mausoleums of every aspiring Nimrod.

Antelopes had been favoured animals of the chase in ancient Egyptian times; but only in the past century, since the first descriptions by such naturalists as Buffon, were they seen simply as things to hunt in Western eyes. Books told you how to identify them, where to find them, and how to shoot them; and almost nothing about how they lived. But times have changed, and in recent years we have seen a tremendous awakening of interest in the real lives of animals. Nevertheless, when I first started to study African antelopes 20 years ago, I think it is true to say that most of us were still in that stage of thinking that believes they all behaved like

1

sheep, whose stupidity at that time was proverbial. This benighted approach was engendered in part by the fact that most of our knowledge of the behaviour of mammals stemmed from the observation of activities of laboratory rats. I well recall telling an American colleague how the water-buck doe, upon coming to the edge of a piece of high ground, would stand for a long time searching the plains below before venturing down. 'Ah!' my colleague exclaimed, 'the edge effect.'

'The edge effect?' I queried.

'Yes,' was the reply, 'when a laboratory rat reaches the edge of a plat-form, it always investigates the edge first before climbing down.'

Is there then a connection between a rat in a laboratory not wishing to throw itself over the edge of a potential precipice, and a waterbuck doe looking for predators (looking for disturbances caused by the predators rather than actually expecting to spot the predators themselves)?

You do not have to watch antelopes for very long to discover, as I did, that they do have real lives – that they have characters of their own and a complex and intriguing behaviour. I do not believe that their activities are so stereotyped that we can liken them to the activities of a laboratory rat. Nevertheless the danger is always to anthropomorphise – that is, to endow our subjects with human qualities – which is seen as a cardinal sin in zoological behavioural research. But yet antelopes seem to have many emotions which we regard as human. Watching a herd of stolidly munch-ing does of the Uganda kob, who would believe that they could exhibit jealousy? Yet when a rather small and scruffy dog of the mistress of a tame doe dared to sit on the mistress' lap, the kob would angrily butt it off and try to sit there itself! A somewhat incongruous sight if you have ever had the good fortune to see a Uganda kob and could appreciate its clumsy, flailing spidery legs and hard hooves; graceful enough on the plains, but not on a lady's lap!

In the past two decades considerable research has been carried out on African antelopes and, although we are still far from understanding much of the story, we can at least begin to appreciate something of their complex lives. To do this it is necessary to start at the very beginning, with a brief look at their origins.

Some 20 million years ago, a population of a small, horned ungulate,

Figure 1.1   Ancient Egyptian natural history and hunting scenes from the tomb of Ukht-Hop, 2000 to 1780 BC. 'A': A beisa oryx left, and an ibex right, being seized by hunting dogs. Ibex, left, and gazelles, right, mating. 'B': Top row, left, an ibex being seized by a hunting dog, and right, a gazelle with young suckling. Centre, left to right, a gerenuk seized by a hunting dog, ibex, oryx with a calf and lion attacking a buffalo. Bottom left to right, a hunting dog, hedgehog and a hare, an ibex brought down by a hunting dog, a jackal or fox struggling with the arrows in it, a dog bringing down a Barbary sheep, while another brings down a hartebeest as two leap away

which has been named *Eotragus*, popularly rendered as 'the dawn deer', became a fount of a succession which developed into a thousand million descendants, divisible into hundreds of non-interbreeding populations which covered the greater part of the earth. In today's Africa, their numbers swarming on the great open plains, bizarre hartebeest, comic wildebeest and the jolly Thomson's gazelle, helped to give rise to Theodore Roosevelt's epigrammatic description of 'a railroad through the Pleistocene'. A relict memory of what life on earth must have been like some 50,000 years ago.

The zoologist calls these remarkable animals the *Bovidae*, or 'hollow-horned ruminant artiodactyla'. This means that they have, at least in the males, bony cores which are covered with a horny sheath; that they chew the cud, and that they have cloven hooves. This distinguishes them from the other cloven-hoofed ruminants, the deer and the giraffe; and from the non-ruminants such as the pigs and their allies. What are popularly known as 'antelopes' form a part, if not the majority, of this vast assemblage of bovids: but the word 'antelope', although in common use, is not a zoological term. The *New English Dictionary* tells us that the meaning of the word is unknown, and although mediaeval bestiarists referred to an animal called the 'antalops', from its description – 'long horns shaped like a saw' – this seems to have been the fallow deer. The dictionary definition of a 'hoofed ruminant, notable for its graceful and agile movement' leaves us none the wiser. Strictly speaking, as far as the zoologist is concerned, there is only one 'real antelope', and that is the Indian blackbuck *Antilope cervicapra*; although it is allied with ten other genera in the sub-family *Antilopinae*. So most zoologists avoid the uncertainty of the term by simply referring to 'bovids', or 'hoofed ungulates'.

Classifying Antelopes

But although 'antelope' may be a vague term, we do little better when we look at divisions within the somewhat large family *Bovidae*. This is because, as has been pointed out by one authority, the family is still at the height of its development, making classification very difficult. We cannot point to a member of this family and say: 'This is an antelope, that a cow, and this other a sheep.' But popularly we think of antelopes as all bovids other than deer, buffaloes, sheep and goats.

Within this diverse and highly successful family, there exist today some 49 genera and about 111 species. Distribution ranges from the north-western coast of Greenland (musk ox), south in the New World through North America into northern Mexico (mountain sheep); north-eastern Mongolia, Kaliura, Volga, Ural and Emba steppes (saiga antelope); the French Alps (chamois); southern Poland (bison); throughout Africa; India, Sri Lanka; Malaysia; Japan (Formosa serow); Philippine Islands (serow) and Indonesia. Of this wide range, it is in the Old World tropics that the family has become the most successful in terms both of variety and of numbers. The African continent has taken pride of place as the centre for development, because there the bovids have adapted best to the grasslands and open woodlands which this continent has provided in the geologically recent past. Although in the sub-continent of India two centuries ago, the numbers of some species there may have been as numerous as those of some African species are today, it is, above all, in Africa south of the Sahara where the bovids have reached their pinnacle, with representatives of 27 genera and 74 species of antelope; compared with India's 18 genera and 20 species.

An early zoologist, Dr Hartwig, wrote of the antelope in 1873: 'The great peculiarity of the zoology of South Africa is the predominance of antelopes. Here no species of deer, roe, stag or elk greets the eyes of the sportsman: their place in nature is taken by the hollow-horned ruminants, which have been created in an unusual number and variety of specific forms, constituting a series that fills up the wide hiatus between the goat and the ox.'

Africa being the home *par excellence* of the antelopes, this book has been confined to the African species alone; but also because more studies have been conducted there. Studies upon their anatomy, physiology, reproduction and behaviour; which provide a better understanding of how this kaleidoscopic exuberance of forms adapts each to its particular way of life – the niche of the ecologist.

In conformity with the popular, and Hartwig's, idea of what constitutes an antelope I will restrict my account to the tribe *Tragelaphini* and the sub-families *Cephalophinae, Reduncinae, Hippotraginae, Alcelaphinae, Aepycerotinae*, the African *Antilopinae* and the *Peleinae*; omitting the *Caprinae*, the sheep and goats, which are not represented in Africa south of the Sahara; and also the *Bovini*, as one could hardly regard the African buffalo as 'notable for its graceful and agile movement'.

The Classification of the *Bovidae*

The following table will make the divisions of this complex family clear, but I must stress that not all zoologists are agreed upon the arrangement – for the reasons that have already been given. The appendix gives fuller details of all of the African antelopes.

Family *Bovidae*
  Sub-family *Bovinae*
    Tribe *Bovini* – bovids, oxen and buffaloes.
      Genus *Bubalus* water buffalo. Asia.
          Anoa anoas. Asia.
          Bos cattle. Eurasia.
          Bibos gaurs. Asia.
          Syncerus African buffalo. Africa.

Bison. bison, wisent. North America, Europe.
Tribe *Tragelaphini* – tragelaphines, spiral-horned antelopes.
  Genus *Boocerus* bongo. Africa.
      Tragelaphus nyalas, sitatunga, bushbuck, kudus. Africa.
      Taurotragus elands. Africa.
Tribe *Boselaphini* – boselaphines.
  Genus *Boselaphus* bushcow. Asia.
      Tetracerus four-horned antelope. Asia.
Sub-family *Cephalophinae* – duikers.
  Genus *Cephalophus* red and blue duikers. Africa.
      Sylvicapra common duiker. Africa.
Sub-family *Reduncinae* – reduncines, kobs, waterbucks and reedbucks.
  Genus *Redunca* reedbuck. Africa.
      Kobus kob, waterbuck, lechwes. Africa.
Sub-family *Hippotraginae* – hippotragines, oryxes and allies.
  Genus *Addax* addax. Africa.
      Hippotragus roan and sable antelope, bluebuck. Africa.
      Oryx oryxes. Arabia, Africa.
Sub-family *Alcelaphinae* – alcelaphines, hartebeests and gnus.
  Genus *Connochaetes* wildebeest. Africa.
      Alcelaphus hartebeest. Africa.
      Damaliscus topi, blesbok. Africa.
      Beatragus Hunter's antelope. Africa.
Sub-family *Aepycerotinae* – impala.
  Genus *Aepyceros* impala. Africa.
Sub-family *Antilopinae*
Tribe *Antilopini* – antelopes and gazelles.
  Genus *Antilope* blackbuck. India.
      Antidorcas springbok. Africa.
      Litocranius gerenuk. Africa.
      Gazella gazelles. Eurasia, Africa.
      Procapra black-tailed gazelle. Asia.
Tribe *Ammodorcadini* – dibatag.
  Genus *Ammodorcas* dibatag. Africa.
Tribe *Neotragini* – neotragines, pigmy antelopes.
  Genus *Oreotragus* klipspringer. Africa.
      Madoqua dik-dik. Africa.
      Dorcatragus Beira antelope. Africa.
      Ourebia oribi. Africa.
      Raphicerus steenbuck, grysbuck. Africa.
      Neotragus pygmy antelope, suni. Africa.
Sub-family *Peleinae* – rhebuck.
  Genus *Pelea* rhebuck. Africa.
Sub-family *Caprinae* – caprines, sheep and goats.
Tribe *Saigini*
  Genus *Panthalops* Tibetan antelope. Asia.
      Saiga saiga antelope. Eurasia.
Tribe *Rupicaprini*
  Genus *Naemorhedus* goral. Asia.
      Capricornis serow. Asia.
      Oreamnos mountain goat. North America.
      Rupicapra chamois. Eurasia.

Tribe *Ovibovini*
   Genus *Budorcas* takin. Asia.
         Ovibos musk ox. North America, Eurasia.
Tribe *Caprini* – sheep and goats.
   Genus *Hemitragus* thar. Asia.
         Capra goat, ibex, markhor. North Africa, Eurasia.
         Pseudois blue sheep. Asia.
         Ammotragus barbary sheep. North Africa.
         Ovis sheep. North America, North Africa, Eurasia.

Contrary perhaps to the taxonomist, the person who classifies animals, the ecologist and the behaviourist are interested by not what unites this vast assemblage, but what differentiates its components in terms of their different lives. When, for example, an animal gives rise to descendants with a different horn shape, then the behaviour of those descendants must change also – they must fight differently, for we will see that horns are not mere decorations. How differently they fight may determine their future success. We must not think of evolution solely in terms of change in form, any change in form must be accompanied by a change in function. Even physiological or bodily changes will be accompanied by changes in behaviour. Unfortunately the fossil record shows us only change in form, and when we come to the bovids, only a part of that. Horn sheaths, for example, do not fossilise; and so we can only speculate from the bony core which remains what the external shape may have been like. Nevertheless it is instructive to see how real our Pleistocene panorama is by looking at some of the fossil antelope antecedents.

Our history of antelopes in Africa does not go back very far (other animals, such as the forerunners of the mammals, the mammal-like reptiles, go back to the Late Permian age, over 225 million years ago), and most of the fossils that have so far been found are identifiable with present-day groups.

In Africa fossil bovids have been found in the north, in East Africa at the world-famous Olduvai Gorge in Tanzania, and in South Africa. There are none from the ancient weathered surfaces of West Africa and the forested Congo basin. Some major East African sites are of Pliocene age, about three million years ago, although an early bovid fauna from Fort Ternan in Kenya dates back for 14 million years, but only comprises four species. There are only a few bovids from sites older than this.

Fossil History

The *Bovidae* first appear, fully developed, in the Miocene era, 20 million years ago. These were characterised by bearing horns consisting of a simple, unbranched core of bone (unlike the bizarre branching processes of many other prehistoric ungulates) and covered, we assume, with a horny sheath. The best known of these is *Eotragus*, whose remains have been found in Libya and Namibia; but there are a few other rare, less well-known ones, as well.

One school of thought believes that the bovids developed in Asia, with Eurasia as the centre of their dispersal, for many primitive genera have been described from the Pliocene beds of the Siwalik Hills in India. But although Siwalik bovids bear more resemblance to those from Africa than they do to Eurasian forms, it has been suggested that this similarity may have been acquired only some hundred thousand years ago, possibly due to the success of the deer in Europe which replaced the bovids there. A link with the Arabian peninsula is however provided by the presence in the latter of the oryx, and formerly a hartebeest (or a type of hartebeest), as well as possibly the lesser kudu.

Whatever their origin, by the time of the Pleistocene era most of the bovids had disappeared from Europe due to the increasing cold, which the deer were able to withstand. Africa and Asia thus became major refuges, particularly the former which had seven times the land area of the Indian sub-continent at the bovid's disposal. Here they displaced the formerly abundant horses, rhinoceroses and their kin.

By the time of the Pleistocene, we can already identify elands and kudus. Species of greater kudu are the most frequently found tragelaphines at Olduvai Gorge and one, considered to be only a race of the modern form, known as *Tragelaphus strepsiceros grandis*, must have been a magnificent beast, ten to twenty per cent larger than today's animal. But for the bushbuck, the most common living tragelaphine, virtually no fossils have been recovered. A reedbuck *Redunca darti* existed in Ethiopia which could be ancestral to, or related to, the two living species, the common and the southern reedbucks; but no ancestor has been found for the mountain reedbuck, which is thought to have a separate lineage. Likewise we have fossils of the ancestors of the kobs and the waterbuck, but not for the Nile lechwe. Reduncines were common in the Pliocene to later Pleistocene in Ethiopia, but are rather rare at Olduvai. Some, from the Siwalik Hills, with kob-like characters, could be ancestral to *Kobus sigmoidalis*, a kob from Olduvai which was probably evolving into the waterbuck; but they could equally be primitive survivals isolated already from the African forms. Other species suggest a near contemporaneous occurrence of similar primitive reduncines in both Asia and Africa during the earliest Pleistocene.

Among the *Hippotraginae* we have fossils of animals related to the living oryx and roan, and also an extinct line of roan antelope. There are also fossils of the recently exterminated South African bluebuck which lived side by side with an extinct roan. *Hippotragus gigas* was a giant roan antelope with horns bigger than all but the biggest living giant sable antelope. Although abundant in South Africa it was extinct by the Holocene period, 10,000 years ago. These hippotragines were not in the direct line of ancestry to our living species and may have originated from a Siwalik line together with the ancestor of the oryx, also found at Olduvai.

Fossil alcelaphines assignable to all living, and several extinct, lines are abundant. These range from a giant named *Megalotragus priscus* of the late Pleistocene in South Africa, which had long downward-curving horns, to an earlier, smaller form from Olduvai, *Megalotragus kattwinkeli*.

The wildebeest survived in North Africa until the late Pleistocene, and perhaps into Neolithic times. From South Africa we have an extinct sub-species of the black wildebeest, indicating the long presence of this species there; while at Olduvai there was a race of the blue wildebeest.

Hartebeest are known only from very late sites in both northern and southern Africa, less than a million years old, and thus, we suppose, appeared very quickly. This is supported by the great variety of living forms, for about 70 different sub-species, or races as we call them, have been described on the basis of slight differences in horn shape and coat colour. Other than the more ancient gazelles, this is more than for any other antelope. These are generally reduced to about 26, of which there are 6 principal races and about three full species. They illustrate a gradual change in space, or cline in the evolutionist's term, from one form to another. We are not sure in this particular case which way the change is taking place, from north to south or south to north, although the former seems the more likely. But had the hartebeest been an ancient form we would have expected those forms which are the furthest apart not to be able to interbreed anymore. Had evolution run its full gamut none of the intervening forms would be able to breed with each other and we would regard each as a distinct species. The fact that they do all interbreed suggests that they have not been changing for very long.

Both the topi and the south African bontebok have ancestors from Olduvai, as does also the Hunter's antelope, which seems to have a separate lineage from the topi. The impala also stems from a separate line, with fossil remains occurring in Ethiopia, well north of its present range. Thus the wildebeest, the Hunter's antelope, the topi-hartebeest group, and the impala, all seem to have had separate lines of evolution going back to well over 4 million years ago.

The springbok, one of a distinct line for over 15 million years, today

Figure 1.2 Species and some races of the hartebeest

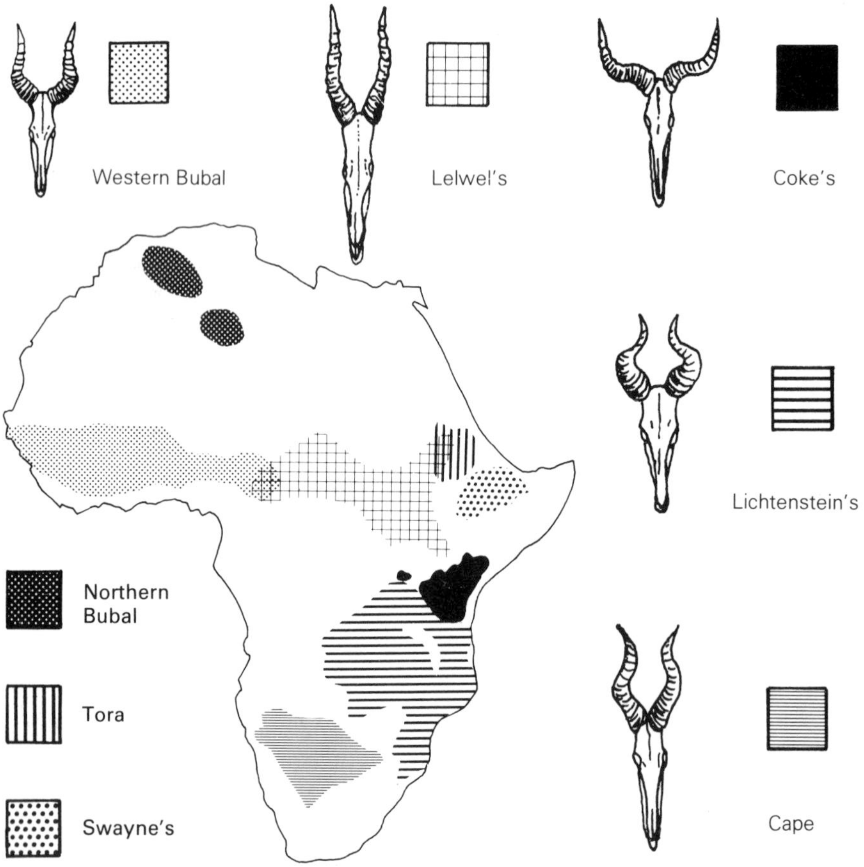

8

restricted to South Africa, had a Pleistocene ancestor at Olduvai, as well as in its present homeland; and others also in northern Kenya, Ethiopia, Tunisia and Algeria. Fossil gazelles are common in the Pleistocene of North Africa and represent a very early bovid which survived in arid areas of the Palaearctic, Indian and African regions. There are also South African fossils believed to be of the same species which were present at Olduvai, close to the modern Thomson's and the red-fronted gazelle, showing that the gazelles once had a much wider distribution well south of their present limits. Some 72 living forms have been described from northern Africa of which about ten are regarded as distinct species (some consider only eight to be distinct); and in this case they do not interbreed, even though they may live side by side like the Grant's and the Thomson's gazelle (or tommy). Together the hartebeest and the gazelle provide a beautiful illustration of evolution in action, the more ancient gazelles have separated to the point where they no longer interbreed, while the hartebeest has yet to achieve this differentiation.

Many genera today show a shrinkage of their former ranges, a wave of Pleistocene extinctions having led to much speculation as to its causes. After the early Miocene, when 57 genera vanished from Africa, extinctions of large mammals declined to their lowest in the Pliocene, when 17 per cent of those known in the fossil record disappeared. But during the Pleistocene era extinctions rose to 33 per cent, and of the 56 genera which this represented, 33 disappeared in the early Pleistocene, 12 in the middle and 11 towards the end. But this should be looked at as a high replacement rate rather than as a disappearance, for 53 *new* genera appeared in the fossil record in the early Pleistocene, followed by another 24 in the middle. Thus more were gained than had been lost.

Figure 1.3   Species differences in gazelles. The Grant's gazelle, Kilimanjaro region, Tanzania

Figure 1.4 Robert's gazelle, a race of the Grant's, Ngorongoro Crater, Tanzania

Among the bovids it is the more generalised forms that seem to have been the most successful in surviving the vicissitudes of changing climate; too much specialisation, as we might expect, leading to extinction. One example that has been given is that of the waterbuck ancestor, *Kobus sigmoidalis*, whose premolar tooth row appears to have been shorter than that of the living waterbuck. Assuming that this was not accompanied by an increase in molar height, then the animal must have either had a shorter life span (its teeth wearing away more quickly than would a larger set), or it must have had a softer diet.

We should thus visualise the extinctions as being a weeding-out process, rather than a loss of viable species. We are not able to identify any species in Africa today which does not seem to be eminently adapted to its habitat, but clearly if, for example, the arid Horn of Africa became wet, then the specialised gazelles which are restricted to it today would disappear. But the majority has shown a remarkable tenacity to survive in the face of man's irruption. Fleetness of foot and extreme alertness save them from the hunter, while a varied diet buffers them against habitat change. Those species most at risk in Africa today are those with the most specialised diets, few in number and widely dispersed, which cannot suffer a reduction in their habitat. Some are dangerously near to extinction, and two, perhaps more, have been lost since the end of the nineteenth century. But one thing is clear, that Roosevelt's epigram was no exaggeration. In spite of the extinctions, the antelopes of Africa today form a panorama of life that provides us with a true peep into the Pleistocene.

2 Antelope adaptations

Antelopes range in size from the diminutive royal antelope weighing only 4 kg, to the huge giant eland which can reach 900 kg in weight. Yet the same basic structure is retained throughout. The general form of the body is always similar, a box-like shape varied by deepening the chest, heightening the shoulder, and lowering the hindquarters in forms where sudden acceleration is important. Shorter hind legs act like low gears on a car, permitting a quick start before launching into the high gear of the larger stride provided by longer front legs. Most species show a sex difference in size, the male often, but not always, being larger than the female; a notable exception being provided by the neotragines.

Coat colour is very variable, but based upon arrangements of white, grey, brown (from bright chestnut red to dark chocolate), and black; and may be related to camouflage, heat control, social communication, or combinations of these factors. Being colour blind (in the sense that we see colours) antelopes have no need of the bright colours of birds. The hair of the coat is usually short, but some species have a mane, rarely there is a beard. Body shape, coat colour and hair developments, are all brought in to play a role in social communication.

The Horns

In all males, and in some females, there are paired horns situated on the frontal bones of the skull. In their simplest form they are mere spikes, as in the rhebuck; but in larger species, where they become potentially more dangerous by virtue of the weight of the thrust that can be put behind them, they may adopt complex spiral developments related to social behaviour, as in the kudu. This is not an invariable rule, as the eland still basically has simple spikes, the twists of which are probably related to strengthening rather than having any combat or social meaning. North and south of the equatorial region seasonal checks to growth are apparently portrayed in annulations or rings at the base of the horn, which in southern Africa have been related to age in species such as eland, kudu and bushbuck; just as they can be in temperate zone species.

Some years ago a publication appeared on the fauna of the then Belgian Congo which contained an illustration of the profuse variations of shape of antelope horns. This led to speculation that evolution did not always lead to the most efficient form, otherwise why do not all antelopes have the same shape of horn? But of course one could equally portray pictures of the variety of antelopes without their heads, and then ask why is there not just one shape and size of antelope? But there is no paradox, for just as there are many antelopes, each one adapted to fill its own particular niche, so will these adaptations be reflected, not only in body size and colour, but also in horn shape and social behaviour.

Antelope Success

A world of cow meadows would require only a world of cows: but the fundamental reason for the variety of antelopes in Africa, is the variety of habitats available to them for exploitation. They have indeed exploited nearly all of them, from freshwater aquatic to desert, as exemplified by the sitatunga and the addax; and from steaming tropical forest to freezing,

Figure 2.1   Horn shapes in the principal African antelope species. 1 Eland; 2 Bongo; 3 Greater kudu; 4 Bushbuck; 5 Common duiker; 6 Blue duiker; 7 Yellow-backed duiker; 8 Bohor reedbuck; 9 Rhebuck; 10 Kob; 11 Waterbuck; 12 Lechwe; 13 Addax; 14 Sable antelope; 15 Beisa oryx; 16 Southern hartebeest; 17 Bontebok; 18 Hunter's hartebeest; 19 Black wildebeest; 20 Blue wildebeest; 21 Impala; 22 Dibatag; 23 Gerenuk; 24 Dorcas gazelle; 25 Springbok; 26 Klipspringer; 27 Oribi; 28 Steenbok; 29 Suni; 30 Pygmy antelope; 31 Salt's dik-dik; 32 Günther's dik-dik; 33 Beira antelope. Not to scale

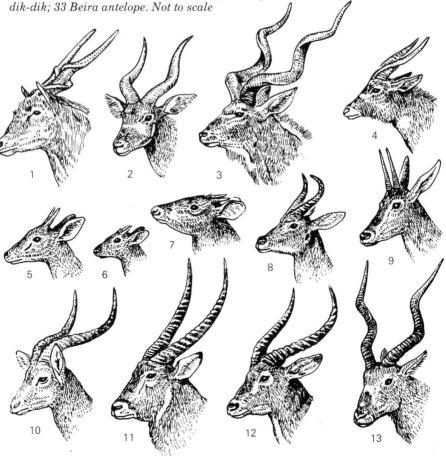

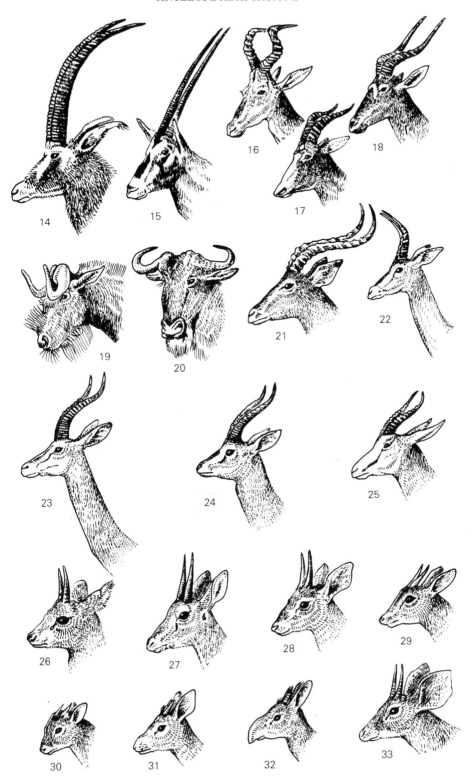

high altitude moorlands, as shown by the forest duikers and the mountain nyala. Only the marine habitat has been omitted: there is no species which feeds along the littoral or willingly enters salt water.

It seems to have been an eminent professor of anatomy who first postulated that one of the reasons for the success of the antelopes was their development of rumination, or chewing the cud. The professor suggested that this process allowed them to snatch their food rapidly, and then retire to digest it in security. This is rather reminiscent of the Victorian view of nature 'red in tooth and claw', with the gentle ungulate seizing a hasty mouthful of food before the savage predator has a chance to bear it down. It is perhaps easier to visualise such a reason in small forest species like the tiny suni, which creeps quietly about the forest floor in the evening dusk, lying hidden during the daylight hours. It is less easy to visualise rumination as important in this respect in the species of the open plains (and the zebra, which is not a ruminant, seems to manage just as well); even though it has been suggested that the plains ruminant, standing erect with head up while ruminating, is more alert to predators. To give the professor his due, he only suggested it as a contributing factor to the bovid's success, but it is now often taken to mean that the group owes its success to this habit alone.

It is just as easy to find alternative, and to my mind, more plausible, propositions. The cloven hoof could be a much more important factor, allowing its possessor to exploit a wide range of environments from loose sand to swamps. It is not much good having an efficient digestive system if you cannot get at the food to eat it first! Horses and zebras, which balance

Figure 2.2   The antelope forelimb

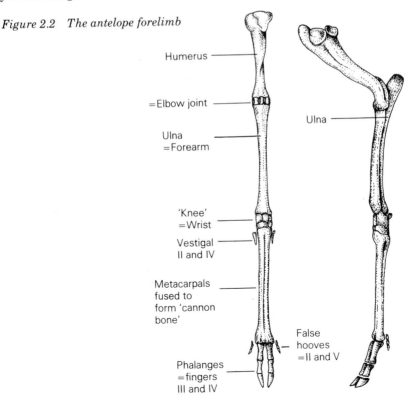

14

on a single toe like a stiletto heel, are restricted to a hard, non-slippery terrain; while the awkward, three-toed extremity of their ancestors, still found in the rhinoceros, does not permit of the same turn of speed.

The Limbs

In the antelopes, the bones equivalent to those which we can feel in the back of our hand (which shows the primitive state), have become extraordinarily elongated, and also reduced in number. The third and fourth have become fused to form the 'cannon bone', while the second and fifth are reduced to fine splints or disappear altogether, just as the first has. The antelope's 'wrist' is thus halfway up its leg, these bones forming an interlocking series so that the limb is restricted to a backwards and forwards movement, and cannot move sideways. This gives stability in speed.

The extremities of the two digits are each covered in a horny hoof, always larger in front than behind because it is the forelegs which take the weight of the body when the animal runs. The hoof is very pointed in the smaller species of antelope, which do not have the weight to sink into the ground, and they can use the point for digging up tubers, grooming, or even fighting. It becomes rounded in the larger species where the balancing of weight on a point without sinking into the ground can become a problem. Thus when an antelope runs, it does not keep the points of its hooves together, but splays them apart so that they do not dig into the ground. Each antelope has a characteristic shape to its hooves, whose impression on the ground is exploited by hunters. The most extreme developments are seen on the one hand in the rock-dwelling klipspringer, which stands on the tips of its hooves like a little ballerina. The hooves being rounded and

Figure 2.3   Adaptability of the cloven hoof: left to right, sitatunga, hartebeest and klipspringer

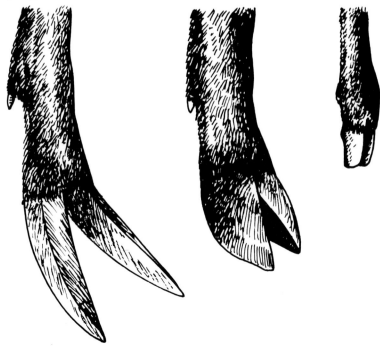

stubby, of a hard rubber-like consistency which does not slip, permit the klipspringer to leap from rock to rock with great agility. At the other extreme is the aquatic-dwelling sitatunga whose elongated hooves when splayed out allow it to walk over floating vegetation.

Figure 2.4   A range of African antelope footprints. The male forefoot is shown, the hindfoot is usually more elongated, but there is great variation in the form of the footprint, a divided print (22) being left on hard ground. 1 Eland; 2 Bongo; 3 Greater kudu; 4 Lesser kudu; 5 Sitatunga; 6 Bushbuck; 7 Lechwe; 8 Yellow-backed duiker; 9 Blue duiker; 10 Red duiker; 11 Common duiker; 12 Bohor reedbuck; 13 Kob; 14 Puku; 15 Impala; 16 Waterbuck; 17 Roan antelope; 18 Sable antelope; 19 Oryx; 20 Blue wildebeest; 21 Kongoni; 22 Topi; 23 Gerenuk; 24 Thomson's gazelle; 25 Dik-dik; 26 Steenbok; 27 Grant's gazelle; 28 Klipspringer; 29 Oribi; 30 Suni. Not to scale

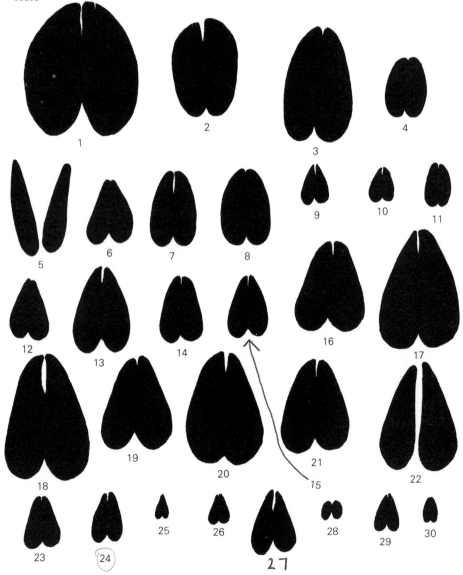

Sleep and Vision

This universal limb pattern amongst the antelopes testifies to its success, but success does not depend upon one factor alone. In the context of the watchful predator may be the antelope's lack of necessity of deep sleep. The longest that I have timed a waterbuck in deep sleep, when its head flops over onto the ground and it lies as if dead, is four minutes. Most of the time an antelope only dozes, alert to the slightest sound with eyes half-closed. More important also to my mind, than standing alert while ruminating, is the fact that antelopes have a horizontal pupil to the eye. They can thus see just as well out of the corner of the eye as they can straight to one side. This is of course related to the fact that the eyes are usually on the sides of the head; but they become more forwardly placed in a species like the klipspringer, which must be able to judge distances precisely when leaping from rock to rock.

Dentition

Adaptations of the teeth are closely related to the ruminating habit, for a grass eater can either have the tall teeth of the horse, with its massive jaw accommodation, long length of the teeth being necessary to accommodate the wear which they must undergo caused by grinding open the cell walls of plants; or it can first chop its food lightly into suitable lengths for swallowing, and then soften it up by the action of the rumen, before chewing it properly. This would mean less wear and shorter teeth. Since the teeth were the first to evolve, before the ruminant stomach, let's look first at them.

As in most mammals there are two sets of teeth, the deciduous or 'milk' teeth which the animal loses early on in life, although not until it is already weaned and has been using them for hard foods; and the permanent teeth. The deciduous teeth comprise on each side of the lower jaw, three incisors or cutting teeth, one canine or stabbing tooth and three premolars or chopping teeth. They are replaced by the permanent teeth which push up under the incisors, canine and premolars, but the three molars grow forward from the rear. The forward movement continues throughout life creating a constant pressure from behind so that a united tooth surface is maintained.

Ruminants possess a very specialised dentition in that the incisor and canine teeth are absent from the upper jaw, although rarely vestigial canines may occur. In the lower jaw of grazers these teeth have all become broad and spatulate in form, while in browsers they are more pincer-like. They bite against a horny pad in the upper jaw, which can be constantly renewed, while its relative softness means that the incisors are subjected to much less wear. If they were to bite against other teeth, as in the horses and zebras, then they would need to be very long or continuously growing to accommodate the wear. Some species take the process a step further and use the tongue to tear off grass or select leaves. My studies have shown that the incisor teeth of grazers wear down at a fairly constant rate, until in old age there is no crown left; while in browsers wear is irregular, the teeth generally showing little change in height with age.

Primitively there were four premolars, but the first is usually lost, and sometimes even the second. They are not 'molarised', that is, they have not developed broad, complex surfaces for grinding, and rather than this being because they are not needed for grinding, it may be that their function is

Figure 2.5   The teeth of an antelope (kongoni)

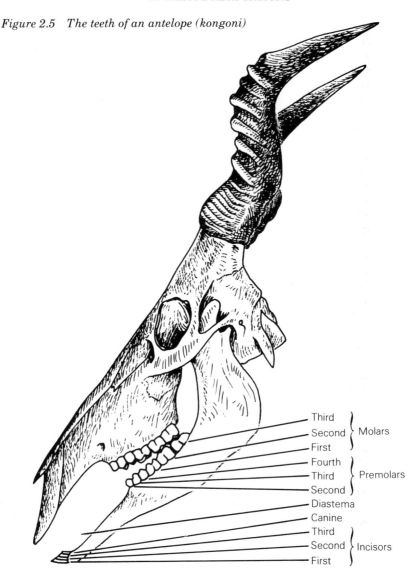

the preliminary chopping of the food before it is ruminated. The molars form the grinding battery and have developed longitudinal, crescentic-shaped crests, formed by the fusion of primitive cones (which were rather like the teeth of a crocodile). This has given rise to their name of selenodont or 'moon-shaped teeth'. It is obviously a successful pattern as there is very little difference in the appearance of antelope teeth from one genus or species to another – to the casual glance they all look much alike. Whether in fact, such differences as the fusion of the paraconid and metaconid of the fourth premolar, which is found in the impala but not in the *Antilopinae*; or the presence or absence of basal pillars, etc., have any functional impor-tance, has yet to be demonstrated; but the teeth of the alcelaphines approach more to the form of a grass-grinding tooth, with intricate cavities providing more of a grinding area, than do the teeth of other groups.

According to one authority, the most generalised antelope tooth row is found in the small neotragine, the grysbok; in contrast to the oribi, the only partially grazing neotragine, in which species the molars have broadened and deepened and the premolars reduced in size, while grinding edges have increased. Where the action of the tooth row is to slice or chop, as in the browsers, the premolars retain their importance. An example is the pygmy antelope, in which the tooth rows have been likened to long, narrow 'saw-edged' blades. But the subject of tooth structure in antelopes still awaits detailed study.

The Tongue

The tongue may be used to select food, and in all antelopes it is long and relatively prehensile. In order to find room for it in the mouth the jaws have lengthened between the incisor teeth and the molars to form what is called the diastema. Thus teeth, tongue and diastema are all part of the ruminant's adaptation, and influence the shape of the muzzle. A coarse grazer like the wildebeest, which simply mows the grass, has a broad, cow-like muzzle. In contrast, a more selective grazer like the topi has a pointed muzzle suitable for picking rather than mowing. Browsing species of course have the most pointed muzzles of all, the most slender being that of the gerenuk.

Rumination

Chewing the cud, or rumination as it is more properly called, is a process familiar to most of us who have spent a day in the country. Its mechanics are less well known. The ruminant stomach has four chambers: the 'S'-shaped rumen; the reticulum, popularly known as the 'honeycomb' on account of its lining of hexagonal ridges; the omasum, called the 'prayer-book' due to its leaf-like arrangement of skin folds; and the abomasum which acts like an ordinary stomach.

The rumen, lined with tongue-shaped protuberances or villi to provide a dense absorptive surface as well as trapping particles of food, is the most capacious. It is into this chamber that the food, hastily chewed, is first swallowed. Here it is mixed with mucus and acted upon by bacteria which can break up the walls of the plant cells with their chemicals. There is also

Figure 2.6   A diagrammatic exploded view of the ruminant stomach

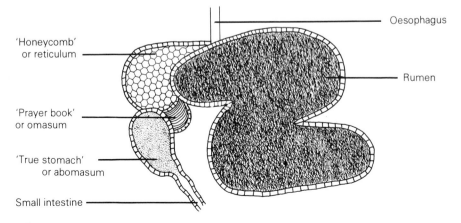

Oesophagus

'Honeycomb' or reticulum

Rumen

'Prayer book' or omasum

'True stomach' or abomasum

Small intestine

a rich fauna of microscopic single-celled animals known as ciliate protozoa, which propel themselves along through the fluids by waving batteries of tiny hairs or cilia. These strange creatures digest the cellulose of the plant walls and are themselves later digested by the host. The remarkable thing about mammals is that they have not themselves evolved the production of a chemical which will break down cellulose, and the ruminants are thus dependent upon this arrangement with bacteria and ciliate protozoa. Field studies of the gorilla, which is entirely herbivorous, have revealed that it eats its own faeces first time round, a process well-known in hares and rabbits, probably because double-digestion is the only way that these non-ruminant animals can get sufficient nourishment from an entirely herbivorous diet.

Little is known of the ruminant's strange protozoan fauna, but the numbers, which occur in countless millions, are less in grazers than in browsers. There are two distinct groups: one which splits up the cellulose and another which is unable to do this and has to rely on the bacteria to help it. Yet others are carnivorous, so we have carnivores and herbivores within the rumen of the herbivore itself. All multiply rapidly by simple division, living only about 24 hours. After they die they are then digested by the host, supplying an astonishing fifth of its total protein requirements from their dead bodies.

Of the few studies that have been conducted on antelopes, those on the greater kudu in South Africa and Zimbabwe revealed a total of 18 different species of these protozoa in the rumen. Some of these were found everywhere, while others were specific to the areas in which the kudu were obtained; and eight were found to occur also in the bushbuck. In the sable antelope 11 species have been found.

We will leave out the actual and complex mechanics of rumination: suffice to say that after the food has been softened by the cellulose-splitting bacteria and protozoa, and then fermented, it is regurgitated and thoroughly ground, to be swallowed into the reticulum, or mixing chamber. It then passes through the other chambers where water is extracted and various nutrients are absorbed, final digestion taking place in the abomasum before it enters on its long journey through the intestines; nearly 43 m long in the wildebeest but only 14 m in the gerenuk, where the major absorption of nutrients and water takes place.

This system has a significant effect upon its possessors, because their activity must now be divided into three distinct phases: feeding, ruminating and digestion. Smaller, more primitive antelopes, feed and ruminate intermittently, as they have a rapid food passage time. The Günther's dik-dik is said to ruminate for 5 to 15 minutes, alternating this with feeding; whereas the larger antelopes spend longer periods at a time on each activity. Although I found in my studies on the waterbuck that this species can show a very intermittent pattern of activity in the morning, when an adult buck might pass periods of anything from 4 to 48 minutes' duration in grazing, and 4 to 40 minutes in ruminating, interspersed with other activities. Rumination was usually preceded by lying still for a while, often 20 minutes or less, but periods of as long as 40 minutes were recorded. Examples of grazing-ruminating sequences during the day were: grazing 84 minutes, ruminating 48 minutes, grazing 72 minutes, lying still 28 minutes. On another occasion the sequence was: ruminating 56 minutes, grazing 52 minutes, ruminating 40 minutes. At night activity was much more continuous: ruminating 3 hours and 44 minutes, grazing 3 hours and 8 minutes, ruminating 3 hours and 32 minutes.

Thus the timing of these activities was not balanced alternately, but on average over a period of 24 hours, the time spent in feeding and ruminating was approximately equal. Lying still, presumably digesting, is an important part of the sequence, for rumination alone is not digestion.

Such a complex activity as rumination has attracted other proposals as to its purpose besides that of avoiding predators, and notable among these is nitrogen cycling. When protein is fermented in the rumen it produces poisonous ammonia which is either used directly by the bacteria and protozoa for their body-building, or it is absorbed through the wall of the rumen into the bloodstream to be extracted by the liver and converted into urea, which is then returned once more to the rumen. The urea is then taken up by the bacteria to make protein which, when the bacteria are digested provides protein for the host. Thus instead of the urea being excreted in urine, which requires water, it is fed into a cycle which uses it as food. But rather than being a means of conserving water, it may simply be a necessary means of neutralising the very poisonous ammonia by-product which is produced in the rumen; but nevertheless one which the animal can turn to good advantage.

Studies have shown that, complex enough as the process is, the ruminant stomach must also be structurally adapted to different diets. Thus it is possible from the appearance of the rumen to classify antelopes into one of three classes according to their diet. These classes are: selectors of juicy rich herbage or browsers; bulk and roughage eaters, or grazers; and intermediate feeders which are both regionally and seasonally adaptable.

The soft leaves of browse are more easily fermentable than grass, and usually have much higher protein as well as being more juicy. This does not apply throughout the life of a leaf, and there is much less food available to a browser than meets the eye, for as the leaves of woody plants mature they accumulate chemical substances known as tannins and alkaloids which are unpalatable, or indigestible, to herbivores. Grasses are tougher because of their skeletons of lignin and silica and, except in the very early stages of growth, have much lower protein levels than browse. But on the other hand they are much more easily gathered, which is why grazers can occur in large herds. Intermediate feeders can make do with both, depending usually upon seasonal availability, although this is probably an over-simplification. My studies of the Grant's gazelle, for example, which is normally a browser, have shown that grass is apparently important for the production of milk. Mothers which have just given birth will seek it even though it is not in season and therefore not easily found. Selectors of juicy, rich herbage, have been termed concentrate feeders. They have the most primitive type of rumen, relatively small and simple and comprising only 8 to 10 per cent of the animal's body weight, adapted to a quick turnover of food and a high fermentation rate. Specialisation of the rumen allows further division of the group into those which feed on the leaves of trees and shrubs, and those which feed on fruit and the leaves of trees and shrubs as well as forbs, the broad-leaved plants found in the grass layer.

In the first group have been classified such species as the bongo, gerenuk and lesser and greater kudu; while the second group has the duikers, suni, dik-diks, klipspringer and bushbuck. In contrast to the first group, the latter antelopes wander about picking from one plant to another, rarely feeding for any length of time on any one plant. Little or no grass is taken by any of these species.

Bulk and roughage eaters have in common a capacious rumen occupying 14 to 15 per cent of their body weight, which permits the maximum delay of coarse fibrous food. This group can also be divided according to their rumen structure into roughage grazers, fresh grass grazers dependent on water, and dry region grazers.

Roughage grazers all eat grass and are characterised by having long necks which enable them to graze without bending their legs. They include the hartebeest, topi, fringe-eared oryx and the mountain reedbuck. The fresh grass grazers include the kob, waterbuck, wildebeest and common reedbuck; while only one dry region grazer has been identified, the beisa oryx.

The third major division, the intermediate feeders, are sometimes referred to as 'mixed feeders', adapting their diet to changing habitats and vegetation by switching from grass to browse, and vice versa. They are thought to have the most advanced form of rumen. An example of this group is the impala which in overgrazed areas, where it is forced to browse heavily, the rumen shows all the characteristic features of a concentrate selector; while in other areas it resembles that of grazers. This group can also be divided, into those preferring grasses and those which prefer broad-leaved species. Examples of the first group are the impala and the tommy, while in the second category are found the Grant's gazelle, steinbok and Cape eland. There is some doubt as to whether or not the oribi is a fresh grass grazer or a mixed feeder.

Figure 2.7   The basi-cranial axis, or angle of the base of the brain with the tooth row in left, blue wildebeest, a grazer; and right, the gerenuk, a browser. Not to scale

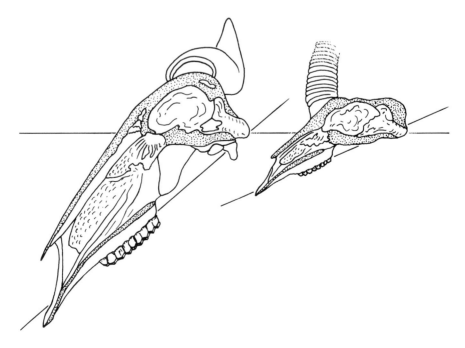

Skull Structure

Feeding habits are thus more complex than a simple division into grazers and browsers, and clearly play an important part in determining the shape as well as the life of an antelope. One might not think that the position of its horns was influenced by feeding habits, but in some measure it is, being reflected in the angle that the base of the brain makes with the tooth row. Just as one can look at the rumen and tell what an antelope's feeding habits are, so can one by looking at a longitudinal section of its skull.

In the primitive vertebrate the jaws, brain and vertebral column are all in a straight line, as in a reptile. In the primitive mammal the brain remains in this position, and we find a tendency towards this arrangement persisting in strictly browsing antelopes; for when feeding the browser holds its head parallel with the ground, due to the right-angled bend that the base of the skull has evolved with the vertebral column. The browser is just as likely to need to reach *upwards* to feed, as downwards. But when we come to the strict grazers, such as the hartebeest and wildebeest, who spend most of their time reaching to the ground to feed, we find that the jaws have now bent down towards a right angle in relation to the brain case. If you look at a wildebeest standing normally, unalert, you can see that its nose points towards the ground. This means that its eyes are maintained in a horizontal position while feeding without the necessity to pivot the eyes. In fact this is one thing that no vertebrate can do, as it would twist the optic nerve. Even the chameleon swivels its eyes, it does not pivot them.

Between the extremes of browser and grazer there are many intermediate forms depending upon the animal's mode of feeding, and the angle of the antelope's horns in relation to the top of its skull is reflected in this. In its turn this has played a part in a whole range of variation in the behaviour of social confrontation.

3 The exploitation of habitats

Africa is a continent with a surface area of some 30 million square kilometres, straddling the equator from 37 degrees north to 35 degrees south. This, a distance of almost 13,000 km, provides a range of climate from desert, with an erratic rainfall of less than 50 mm per year, to equatorial with a rainfall of up to 2,500 mm, approximately double that experienced in Great Britain. This results in a latitudinal arrangement of vegetation types, from the equatorial belt of tropical lowland moist forest found in the Congo basin, to the waterless Sahara desert in the north. In the south is the less extreme Kalahari desert, the aridity of the Cape being ameliorated by its surrounding of oceans on three sides. If there was no other influence, by virtue of this wide range of climate alone, Africa would boast a diversity of vegetation types, and an accompanying wide diversity of mammalian fauna.

But the climate of Africa does not observe such a simple pattern, in spite of the fact that between the tropics is regarded as the best example of the expected arrangement of climatic zones; for large, sub-tropical anticyclones both to the north and to the south of the equator result in vast areas with a very meagre rainfall, but the rainfall does increase in intensity as the equator is approached. However the maximum which is experienced is only 2,000 to 2,500 mm per year, much less than that of some other tropical regions; although certain coastal and mountainous areas may receive much more than this.

Climatic Considerations

The greater part of the African continent receives its rainfall almost entirely during the six months centred on 21 June, the summer solstice; although the forest areas experience a year-round distribution. In the central region of East Africa an anomaly produces two well-defined rainy seasons each year, known as the short rains (November to December) and the long rains (March to May). The south-west extremity of the Cape has a 'mediterranean' climate, with rain falling mainly in the winter half of the year, in contrast to the eastern Cape where it is well-distributed year-round.

The climatic pattern results principally from north-easterly dry air currents (the north-east trade winds); Atlantic or mainly south-west winds bringing moist air from the ocean, and south-east winds (the south-east trade winds), whose moisture content is variable as the airstream is relatively shallow. Where these air currents meet, a zone of turbulence is formed known as the Inter Tropical Convergence Zone. Lacking the moist Atlantic air, eastern Africa is drier than the west, breaking up the latitudinal pattern of the vegetation so that the northern and southern savannas meet around the eastern edge of the tropical forest, which terminates in western Uganda.

Most of the East African game parks are situated in areas where the temperature is equable: the nights are warm and never cold. This tends to give the impression that the fauna is adapted to this type of climate, but the vast majority of the savanna zones north and south of the equatorial forest can experience quite cold winter nights, although temperatures rarely, if ever, fall to freezing at the lower altitudes.

But superimposed on this broad climatic pattern which gives Africa its characteristic vegetation zones, we have a range of altitudes ranging from sea level to, in the case of Mount Kilimanjaro, 6,000 m. Much of the eastern part of the continent is over 500 m in altitude, with a number of significant elevations above this. The Congo basin and the greater part of West Africa is by contrast flat and low-lying, with only occasional isolated high mountains, such as Mount Nimba in Liberia and Mount Cameroun. These elevations also affect the vegetation by producing zonal patterns, the climate generally becoming wetter with increasing altitude, but at the same time colder, so that if one goes high enough, rainfall then decreases. The highest mountain of all, Mount Kilimanjaro, is a very dry mountain; consequently its plant life is less rich than that of the Ruwenzori Mountains, or of the Virunga Volcanoes, which both receive moist Atlantic air.

Where there is high ground then one will find rivers draining it, and in the depressions lakes will form. East Africa is well supplied with lakes on account of the depression formed by the Rift Valley fault which divides it. However, apart perhaps from the sitatunga, these lakes do not of course provide a habitat for antelopes; but they do hold water during the long dry seasons which Africa experiences, and thus enable populations to survive in regions which would otherwise be denied them. Lake Victoria's 75,000 sq km of water surface also significantly affect the climate of the surrounding country, making it wetter than it would be otherwise. Rivers, of which the four major ones, the Nile, Zaïre (Congo), Zambesi and Niger, provide at least 17,000 km of waterway alone, are important for their role in aiding the dispersal of forest species, which use the riverine gallery forest to colonise savanna areas well away from the dense forest. Lakes are of less importance, despite the fact that Lake Victoria and Lake Chad together probably provide some 2,500 km of shoreline. The importance of lakes is more likely to be connected with the formation of new species, their expansion in wet periods serving to isolate populations; although rivers can also play this role.

Moist lowland, gallery and mountain forests all provide a gamut of niches for exploitation by herbivores: but it is above all the savannas, providing the largest single vegetation type in Africa, continuous from north to south of the equator, which have provided the arena for the expansion of the antelopes. It has been estimated that the savannas cover some 50 per cent of the continent, an area of over 14 million sq km; a vast arena indeed.

In western Africa the wooded savannas probably approach nearer to the ancestral type, for in the east they are modified by a drier climate and a much more diverse topography. Western Africa has simply lain and weathered for the past 65 million years, with only isolated spots of rejuvenation created by Pleistocene volcanic activity. Compared with eastern Africa its savannas are characterised by a relatively heavy rainfall, resulting each season in grasses up to 3 m in height, instead of the mere half a metre found in all but the wettest areas of East Africa. This vegetation has probably been modified by frequent fires for the past 180,000 years, and the more fuel the hotter the burn, so that fires are much fiercer in the west than they are in the east.

In East Africa, the paradise of big game, one fails to appreciate the latitudinal zonation in speciation; all of the animals are within one major vegetation type termed the afro-oriental domain. Just as south of the equator the greater part of the continent comprises the Zambesian domain of moist savanna woodland. It is only in western Africa north of the equator, that one is able to appreciate the zonation of vegetation types from forest to desert, and their concomitant changing fauna. Also, although Africa has evolved a number of broad vegetation types which have probably permitted a relatively conservative type of mammalian evolution, the Tertiary to Quaternary geological events in the east, exemplified by rifting and vulcanism, accompanied by significant changes in climate (particularly a number of pluvial or very wet periods), has probably been responsible for the development of a wider range of species than might otherwise have been the case. This could result both from the diversity of habitats which have been produced, and from the interplay of geological events leading to both the isolation and the mixing of animal populations.

Distribution

Opinion generally favours the theory of the ancestral ruminant as a forest creature, and that during the Miocene era a reduction in forest, accompanied by an expansion of grasslands, led to the colonisation of the latter by antelopes seeking emancipation from the forest environment. But these grasslands were unlikely to be like those of the famed Serengeti Plains; more probably they resembled the *Terminalia* wooded savannas of the west, populated by scraggy trees, albeit slender, that would hardly permit the passage of a vehicle between them.

It is not possible from actual mammalian distributions to identify centres of radiation, and insufficient is known of the fossil faunas to aid us. The Congo forest is probably the most ancient tropical forest remaining on the continent (although the west African coastal strip may be older), but it is on Kalahari sands of Miocene-Pliocene age, and thus it probably was not the original forest home.

Not one of the antelopes in existence today can be called truly ubiquitous; the nearest to this is the bushbuck. This species might rightly be termed a 'facultative' antelope, for it is only absent from arid areas, denied to it by its physiological demands. In contrast the common duiker occupies almost as large an area of the continent as does the bushbuck, but it is absent from the tropical forest zone where, one assumes, it is not limited by its physiology, but by competition with the other duikers. Of the total number of species of antelope, equal numbers are restricted to each side of the equator; approximately 31.5 per cent in each case. Only slightly more, 37 per cent, are found on both sides of it.

Vegetation

The climatic regions which form the basis apart, there are two systems of classifying the vegetation. One can consider it as biotic types, based on the form of the vegetation; or one can consider it according to the species which are present. We need not trouble ourselves with the animal, or zoogeographical, classification; for as was realised over a century ago, the whole region south of the Sahara falls within one category known as the Ethiopian Realm.

Six principal biotic types can be recognised in Africa, as well as six phytogeographical regions, sub-divided into seven 'domains'. Antelope distributions are related to the biotic types rather than to the plant species classifications, although the two systems are, in effect, complementary.

The systems are summarised as follows:

Biotic type	Phytogeographic class	Approximate area in km^2
Lowland rain forest	Guineo-Congo region (Congo domain, Usambaro-Zululand domain).	4,213,000
Moist savanna woodland	Sudano-Zambesian region (Sudanian and Zambesian domains).	9,889,000
Dry savanna woodland	Sudano-Zambesian region (Sahelian and Afro-oriental domains).	4,335,000
Sub-desert and desert	Saharo-Sindian and Karoo-Namib regions.	8,048,000
Mediterranean	Mediterranean region (Mauritanian domain), Cape region.	71,000 (Cape)
Montane forest	All regions and all domains except the Usambaro-Zululand domain.	715,000 (includes Afro-alpine)

To these biotic types, for our purposes, I would add gallery forest, the rich vegetation which fringes rivers and streams; aquatic habitats and islands. The former two types occur throughout with the exception of the Saharo-Sindian, Karoo-Namib and Cape regions. Most islands were probably formerly clothed with a vegetation akin to lowland rain forest, but the majority has now been considerably modified by man. The Usambaro-Zululand region comprises only a narrow coastal strip from about Lamu, in Kenya, to the Cape. Phytogeographers divide the domains still further, the vegetation showing considerable susceptibility to rainfall patterns; but for our purposes the concept of the domain is sufficient. If we accept the theory that the antelopes have stemmed from a forest origin, then the relating of species to the different broad vegetational zones is fundamental to understanding their diversity. It is not an evolutionarily haphazard production of different types but has some relation to the size of the vegetation zones:

the biggest zone has the most species. The only exception is the sub-desert/desert type, which has less species than would be expected on size of the zone alone.

A look at these vegetation types will show us how each has a characteristic antelope fauna, adapted to the climatic regime rather than to the actual species of plants available as food.

Lowland Rain Forest

This consists of evergreen, or partly evergreen, lowland moist forest, sometimes termed dense tropical forest, covering the Congo basin. In Pleistocene times it probably covered the Lake Victoria basin also. It stretches westwards along the west African coast, except for a significant gap between Ghana and Benin, well known as the Dahomey Gap and attributed to a diminution of rainfall in this area caused by an upwelling of cool water off the coast. This forest typically experiences year-round high rainfall and humidity, with only minor fluctuations of temperature. The trees are tall, up to 30 m in height, characterised by smooth trunks and a

Figure 3.1   The biotic types of Africa

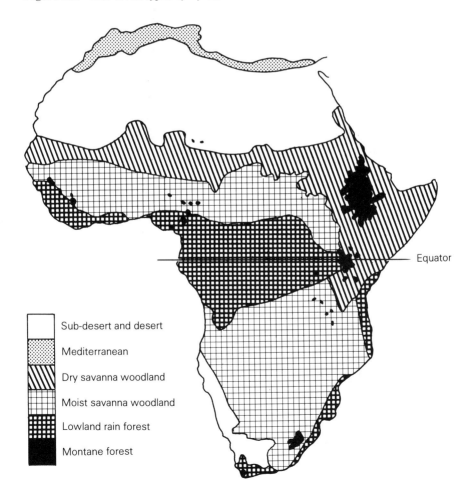

Equator

Sub-desert and desert

Mediterranean

Dry savanna woodland

Moist savanna woodland

Lowland rain forest

Montane forest

closed canopy whose shading causes the forest floor to be relatively open, with few grasses; and shrouds it in gloom, making it dark, dank and mysterious. Most people, including myself, are glad to get out of its endless trees and murky shadows.

The East African coastal strip is not an isolated relic of the Congo forest, but results from the high rainfall and humidity of the coastal climate. Much of it is secondary, the coastal strip having for centuries been cultivated by slaves, owned by the Arab settlers until the abolition of slavery.

The largest antelope inhabiting the tropical forest is the bongo, followed in size by the sitatunga where swamp conditions persist, as is indeed the case in large areas of the Congo forest. The bushbuck is also present. None of these large species is limited to this type of forest alone; the bongo flourishes in the montane forests of East Africa, the sitatunga occurs in swamps in Kenya and in Zambia, while the bushbuck, as we have seen, is virtually ubiquitous.

The rest of the antelope fauna is limited to duikers and pygmy antelopes. Three duikers exist in both the Congo and the west African coastal strip, four are restricted to the Congo forest alone, and five are limited to the west African strip; two of these to the west of the Dahomey Gap.

Common to both the Congo and West Africa is the yellow-backed duiker, which extends its range also to the limits of the Sudanian domain in the Central African Republic, radiating into the savannas by means of the gallery forests; as does also the blue duiker. The bay duiker is common to both the west African and the Congo forests, but restricted to the latter are the Peter's, Gabon and black-fronted duikers; and also the diminutive Bates' pygmy antelope. In the west African coastal strip we find the black, banded, Jentink's and Ogilby's duikers, plus the tiny Royal antelope. Two-thirds of the antelope fauna is thus composed of species less than 55 cm high at the shoulder and weighing no more than 20 kg.

All of these species are concentrate selectors in their food habits, for the forest floor provides little in the way of grasses. The smaller species are all furtive, generally dark-coloured, relying on scent for social contact. All are probably territorial, living the greater part of the year in isolation, but little is known of their habits or their breeding cycles; while that which is known is gained largely from captive specimens.

Only the bongo forms herds, sometimes numbering up to 50 individuals. This anomaly in a forest antelope may be due to the need to search for food in a regular pattern; for example, visiting certain forest glades at regular intervals after regrowth has taken place. It is easy to visualise that, where resources are limited, it would be disadvantageous for an animal to make a journey to a certain spot only to find that another had already been there and eaten everything up. A co-ordinated effort means that they do not make wasted journeys. But this is only speculation and it may simply be a question of seeking safety in numbers, for the bongo's large size is not easily concealed. Its only natural predator found persistently in the forest is the leopard, but herding could be a response to the native method of hunting it with dogs.

The forest harbours only 21 per cent of the antelope species considered here, a relatively low percentage, but if we consider its size in relation to other habitats, then the number of species is not unusual.

Only four species of duiker have evolved outside of the lowland forest: the Abbott's duiker, which inhabits an extremely localised area of montane forest in East Africa; the red-flanked and red duikers which inhabit the moist woodland of the Sudanian and Afro-oriental-Zambesian domains respectively; and the almost ubiquitous common duiker. The yellow-backed and the blue duikers have extended their range well into the moist woodland habitat but do not seem to be really emancipated from a forest life.

Moist Savanna Woodland

This vegetation type covers some 36 per cent of the continent, forming its largest single division. It consists of relatively open woodland formations with grassland of fire tolerant species. Although this woodland is more or less continuous around the eastern limit of the Congo forest block, its composition differs markedly between the north and the south. The northern woodland is less vigorous, the trees in general not attaining the same height that they do in the south; and it is lacking in the two dominant species which characterise the latter, *Brachystegia* and *Julbernardia*. The lack of vigour in the north is probably attributable to the poor nutrient status of the ancient weathered soils; but the species' difference suggests that the connection of the two blocks is geologically recent, and we would not be surprised therefore to find differences between the two in the fauna also.

It is generally considered that these woodland savannas are maintained by the fierce grass fires which sweep throughout the greater part of Africa each year, and that in the absence of fire they would revert to dense thicket. In the higher rainfall areas this is true, but it is unlikely to be true of all woodlands. What is agreed is that they have been much disturbed by man over the greater part of their range, and represent secondary vegetation resulting from shifting cultivation. The vegetation type is predominantly a woodland, and the wide, open treeless plains of East Africa, such as the Serengeti, are not typical, but the result of sub-surface hardpans limiting tree growth. Plains of lesser extent occur in other regions caused by seasonal waterlogging.

In spite of the fact that the limits of distribution in relation to habitat are less clearly defined in the woodland savannas, the northern savanna is greatly impoverished in species by comparison with the southern savanna. The latter boasts some 26 species compared to the north's 15. There are also distinct species' differences among those genera common to both: the giant eland of the north is replaced by the smaller Cape eland in the south, although the latter just breaches the equator in East Africa. The kob, probably the most successful antelope in the north in terms of numbers, is replaced by the puku and lechwe; the common reedbuck by the southern reedbuck; the bubal hartebeest by the red and the Lichtenstein's; the topi by the sassaby; and the red-flanked duiker by the red duiker. Only the roan seems to be universal, for although five races have been named there seems to be little real difference between them. The most notable omissions from the northern savanna are the sable antelope, wildebeest and impala; while also absent, but less conspicuously so, are the neotragine steenbok and grysbok, and the rhebuck.

Several species in South Africa, such as the white-tailed gnu and the bontebok, formerly had a somewhat wider range than they do today, but not greatly so, being relatively unsuccessful species occupying small niches at the extremities of the genera's ranges. Another example is the extinct bluebuck which, although its former distribution is imperfectly known, seems to have been restricted to the mediterranean climatic region of the Cape. It appears unlikely that any species of antelope has been exterminated within recent times in the northern savannas.

Although it has been suggested that the rare western race of the giant eland formerly had a continuous distribution from Cameroon to Senegal, this seems improbable. In the Sudanian zone of the Central African Republic, under a rainfall of 1,100 to 1,300 mm, the giant eland is common. The roan antelope, on the other hand, is about 16 to 33 per cent less numerous. Some 2,400 km to the west in Burkina Faso (formerly Upper Volta), where the principal habitat type is also Sudanian but under a rainfall of 700 to 1,000 mm, the eland is absent but the roan is probably the most common antelope. The belt of rainfall equivalent to that of the Central African Republic is relatively narrow, with the intensity of rainfall increasing rather sharply due to the influence of the moist Atlantic winds. Thus I suspect that the western region of Africa is either too dry, or too wet, for the giant eland to be successful; and indeed the western race is smaller in size than the central one. Its place thus seems to be taken by the more ubiquitous roan.

The antelopes which have colonised these moist savanna woodlands provide a considerable variety of form, their size ranging from the small common duiker to the giant eland, 70 times the duiker's weight; while the number of genera, 13, is indicative of the variety of niches which can be exploited.

We still have concentrate food selectors among the inhabitants of this type of habitat: namely the greater kudu (which is rather atypical in the north); the duikers, bushbuck and the klipspringer. But by far the greatest number is made up by the bulk and roughage eaters; the hartebeest, topi, waterbuck, kob, wildebeest, oribi and common reedbuck. There are intermediate feeders also; the impala, steinbok, eland, and probably the roan and sable antelopes. Thus all facets of the vegetation are exploited.

Social organisation is predominantly of the territorial kind; but whereas the smaller species, the duikers, neotragines and reedbucks, are principally asocial, living singly; among the larger species such as the waterbuck and hartebeest, the males defend territories against other males, and the bachelors and females associate in herds. In the eland, however, a hierarchical system probably holds sway among the males; that is to say, males do not exclude each other, but each one knows its place in relation to each other.

A forest-type niche is still offered by the thickets of the savanna woodlands to be exploited by some species, such as the red-flanked duiker; but in contrast it offers the most open of habitats, the treeless plains, exploitable only by those species completely emancipated from a forest existence, like the wildebeest. Grazer that it is, the hartebeest is more often found in woodland over the greater part of its range than it is in open country; which typifies the majority of species which is best at home where some cover is provided.

Dry Savanna Woodland

Still predominantly woodland but experiencing less rainfall, this type of vegetation covers some 16 per cent of the continent. Less extensive than the moist woodlands it forms the buffer zone between moist and semi-arid conditions. The northern belt consists of the sahelian domain, the region which has suffered such intense exploitation by nomadic herdsmen to the detriment of both wildlife and habitat. It is this region which has experienced increasing dryness during the past 20 years or so, and the destruction of its once viable ecosystem has led to intense suffering of the overpopulated nomads and their stock.

Dry savanna woodland also includes the Somali arid or Afro-oriental domain, whose mountainous nature turns it into a very diverse habitat in many places, despite its low rainfall. The moist savanna and dry savanna ecotone, or zone of change, tends to be much broader than the moist forest–moist woodland ecotone; merging gradually, it often takes a botanist to know when the vegetation has altered, species replacing similar species before the woodland becomes more open in aspect, and the flat-topped acacias and spiny *Balanites* become characteristic. The fauna changes gradually also, but when, in the western zone, the red-fronted gazelle becomes common, then we know that we are in the sahelian domain. In the east the zone forms a block rather than a belt, by virtue of the dry conditions extending southwards, and it is influenced by the high ground of the Ethiopian highlands.

The sahelian zone boasts 13 species representing 11 genera of antelopes, of which 7 species are found also in the moist savanna woodland, although not all of these 13 species are found in the drier parts of the zone. Those which are lost are the giant eland, waterbuck, kob, and red-flanked duiker; but we have gained the red-fronted gazelle. The Afro-oriental domain loses some 6 species but gains about 7. The Cape eland may still be found to a limited extent, able to exist in much drier country than the giant eland; but such species as sable, puku, lechwe, wildebeest, impala and red duiker are absent. The topi is found isolated along the East African coastal strip where conditions are moist, but technically it is absent from the Afro-oriental domain. Several species adapted to dry conditions are gained, notably oryx, gerenuk and Grant's gazelle; but we have also the lesser kudu, Hunter's hartebeest, tommy and dik-diks. These cover all the spectrum of feeding adaptations and although the habitat is one step further from the forest type, concentrate selectors are still present, because they can make use of the abundant and protein-rich acacias, and the many xerophytic succulents. Thus the diminutive dik-dik takes the place of the

Figure 3.2   The topi was formerly one of the most numerous of antelopes

tiny forest neotragines, antelopes of this size being generally absent from the intervening habitat type (the exception being the blue duiker which is really a forest outlier), probably being excluded by the success of the common duiker.

Typical of the sahelian zone is the appearance of the gazelles, the red-fronted and the dama. At one time the west African sahel boasted vast herds of topi, considered to be probably up to 10,000 strong, the range stretching from Senegal to the Sudan. But the topi has now fallen to the status of a rarity in many areas, and all of the fauna is greatly impoverished. The biomass, or weight, of cattle which has replaced it suggests that at one time this region must have equalled what we now associate with the more phenomenal areas of East Africa. Indeed, it was stated in 1935 that if the topi could be counted it would no doubt be shown to have the greatest population of any African antelope.

Sub-desert and Desert

A transitional zone to desert conditions is provided by an impoverished region extending between the sahelian domain and the Sahara desert, and around the edge of the Somali arid zone of the Afro-oriental domain. A distinct type also occurs in south-west Africa classified as the south-west arid zone or the Karoo-Namib region, characterised by such strange succulents as *Welwitschia bainesii* and *Acanthosicyos horridus*.

Rainfall is low and erratic, and the areas support little vegetation, much of it seasonal in occurrence; but both possess a distinctive antelope fauna, very poor in the north but quite diverse in the Horn of Africa. The northern zone was probably once the southern limit of the addax and the scimitar-horned oryx, although both are true desert species well adapted to survive in its most inhospitable parts. The topi seems to have penetrated this far north in suitable localities, but the main species to be met with are the dorcas and dama gazelles.

The Horn of Africa, by contrast, boasts ten species, which include the klipspringer and the gerenuk from the dry savanna woodland region; plus eight new species. There is the beisa oryx, the largest antelope to be found there and very similar to the fringe-eared oryx found further south. Also we find the long-necked dibatag, the Beira antelope, two species of dik-dik and three new species of gazelle. The south-west arid region has the gemsbok, springbok, klipspringer, steinbok and common duiker. This area is not quite as arid as that of the north, and for the gemsbok and springbok it probably represents a refuge from a once much wider distribution in southern Africa.

Most of these arid zone species are probably concentrate selectors, existing mainly on succulents and acacia species; with the exceptions of the oryx, gemsbok, springbok and duiker, which are intermediate feeders. Little is known of their social organisation, but the majority is gregarious.

True desert conditions occur, to any extent, only in the Sahara, floristically classified as the Saharo-Sindian region. Its distinctive antelope fauna comprises the addax and the scimitar-horned oryx, both considered as endangered species; the dama, dorcas and Loder's gazelles. The first European travellers through the Sahara, such as Barth in 1850–1, found a flourishing wild life. In the region of Aïr, Barth met or saw the tracks of, ostrich, giraffe, and oryx; while still farther to the north he had met hartebeest: 'Bare and desolate as the country appears, it is covered, as well as the whole centre of the desert, with large herds of wild oxen (*Antilope bubalis*) ...'

Barth's reference would have been to the now extinct North African race, still found in Morocco until 1933; but by 1937 it had practically disappeared from the northern border of the Sahara, probably becoming extinct about 1940. Barth's observation appears to be the most southerly record of this race.

When he arrived to the west of Lake Chad he saw a solitary Soemmering's gazelle (now only found in the Horn, he may have meant the dama gazelle) but stated: '... indeed antelopes of any species are rare in these quarters, and on the whole road I had seen but a single gazelle ... but it seems remarkable that, from the description of the natives, there can not be the least doubt that the large and majestic variety of antelope called addax ... is occasionally found here.'

The addax appeared to be very common to the north of Lake Chad, where the explorer Nachtigal found it in large numbers in 1871: '... antelopes were to be seen grazing peacefully wherever the eye turned; they had so seldom been pursued by man there that they did not permit even the closest approach of humans to disturb their ordinary activities.' Later he wrote: 'The number of these animals was almost unbelievable. They were to be seen in every direction, singly, or in small groups, or in herds of hundreds.'

Nachtigal found them easy to shoot, and thought that they moved with difficulty because they were so well fed; in fact this is because their broad hooves are adapted to moving on soft sand, and it has a reputation for being fast in the desert. It is possible that what Nachtigal witnessed was a congregation of this species on a good feeding ground, for it is the habit of these antelopes to concentrate on fresh flushes which come on after showers. Nevertheless today they are a rare sight, and their drastic decline is

Figure 3.3   A herd of addax in the desert in 1871. From Nachtigal, G. 1879. Sahara and Sudan, Vol. I. Weidmannsche Buchhandlung, Berlin

generally attributed to the motorised slaughter by oil company and military or other official personnel; but the slaughter had already begun a long time ago. Gautier, writing in 1928 of the Algerian sahara, reported that the addax was 'now represented only by a small number of individuals'.

With their water-independent physiology and their tolerance to heat, these desert antelopes represent the most extreme adaptation that the antelopes have evolved in their radiation from their forest origin, and it is remarkable that today they cannot find refuge from the depredations of man in the Sahara's seven million square kilometres.

Mediterranean Habitat

The Mediterranean region today has no antelopes and so need not concern us here, but a similar type of climatic zone exists at the southernmost tip of the Cape, with a Mediterranean climate and a rich flora of its own. Although the smallest of the floristic regions it has eight species of antelope: the bushbuck and common duiker, the bontebok, klipspringer, steinbok, Cape grysbok, Vaal rhebuck, and also, well beyond its normal limits, the blue duiker. These represent six genera, a high variety for such a small and distantly-sited zone, but illustrative of the antelope's powers of radiation into even the remotest of corners.

Montane Forest

Mountain or montane forest is found on all of the isolated mountains of Africa which rise above 1,000 m, if the conditions are sufficiently moist. Structurally similar to lowland forest, it is marked by a cooler climate and wider variations in daily temperature. Frequently covered in mist and cloud, the all-pervading dampness causes a profusion of lichens and other epiphytes, giving the forest a distinctive character. This reaches its most impressive form in the stands of *Hagenia*, with their twisted trunks and gnarled branches draped in old man's beard. If the climate is wet enough this forest merges into bamboo forest, but this is a different bamboo to that of the west African savannas, covering the ground continuously and not growing in clumps. It terminates in an ericaceous heathland and moorland belt at about 3,500 m. Above this there is the Afro-alpine zone, with its strange flora of giant senecios, giant groundsels and lobelias; but few mammals venture into this zone.

Two species of antelope are restricted to the montane forest; the rare mountain nyala which occurs in a small area of the Ethiopian highlands, and the Abbot's duiker which exists in only six small localities in Tanzania. The forest does of course serve as a habitat for other forest antelopes, such as the bushbuck, the red duiker and the suni; while the bongo, more characteristic of the lowland rain forest, is found in Kenya in the Aberdare Mountains, on Mount Kenya, and formerly in the Cherangani Hills.

In addition to these animals a unique population of eland inhabits the ericaceous or moorland zone of Mount Kilimanjaro. No specimens of this animal seem ever to have been collected and it is rarely seen, although alleged to have a rather long coat. I have myself seen its tracks on the moorland.

Montane forest is very limited in extent and widely separated, so that it is not surprising that it has received few antelopes; nevertheless the two endemic species, and the exploitation of the moorland on Mount Kilimanjaro, are sufficient testimony to the ability of antelopes to colonise this type of habitat. All, with the exception of the eland, are probably concentrate selectors in their feeding habits. The eland's feeding habits have not been studied, but it probably makes some use of moorland grasses.

Gallery Forest

Gallery forest is a band of varying thickness of frequently dense vegetation and tall trees along the banks of rivers and streams, usually characterised by species of fig tree *Ficus*, and often with true rain forest species, such as the ironwood *Cynometra alexandri*, a magnificent buttressed tree which reaches 46 m in height. This type commonly fails to receive mention in vegetation classifications because it is not very extensive, but it is important from the point of view of animal geography, for it permits the invasion of savanna areas by forest species. Thus in the Central African Republic we find the yellow-backed and the blue duiker occurring some 400 km from the forest zone, and within 150 km of the sahelian red-fronted gazelle. But it also provides an important refuge for antelopes such as the waterbuck, who use the adjacent open plains but shelter in the forest. There is, however, no species of antelope which is restricted to this type of habitat alone, which is rather limited in extent and unstable. High waters in Africa in the 1960s, for example, probably destroyed much of the riverine forest, such as along the Tsavo river in Kenya, or the Bamingui river in the Central African Republic. This process has been accelerated in recent years by over-populations of elephants, and more importantly, in many areas by cultivation.

In this forest we find, according to their geographical range, the bushbuck (probably the most common antelope in this habitat), the waterbuck, yellow-backed duiker, red-flanked duiker, red duiker, blue duiker and the common duiker. Generally these species emerge from this habitat in the evening onto the fringes of the surrounding plains, and possibly in this way it provided an important stepping-stone in the emancipation of the forest ancestor.

Freshwater or Swamp Habitat

Next to the desert, the swamps have probably been the most difficult habitat for the antelopes to conquer, pre-eminently adapted as they are to a hard terrain and relative independence from water. Yet this has been successfully accomplished by two main species.

Reduced since Pleistocene times, today there are six relatively significant swamp areas in Africa; the well-known Nile sudd, the Lake Chad region, the middle Niger, the Congo basin, Lake Bangweulu and Okavango swamps. In addition to these we have the swampy margins of many lakes, notable among which is Lake Victoria and the series of lakes in the Rift Valley. There are also the extensive riverine habitats of both major and minor river systems.

Permanent swamps are characterised by dense growths of papyrus in deeper water, while the edges are colonised by species of leguminous plants such as the ambatch or balsa wood tree *Aeschynomene elaphroxylon*, and the impenetrable thorny *Mimosa pigra*, whose sensitive leaves curl together when touched; and dense mats of reeds such as *Vossia cuspidata* may be present.

There are two main species of aquatic antelope, of which the most completely adapted to this habitat is the sitatunga; a fair swimmer, when

Figure 3.4   The colonisation of habitat types

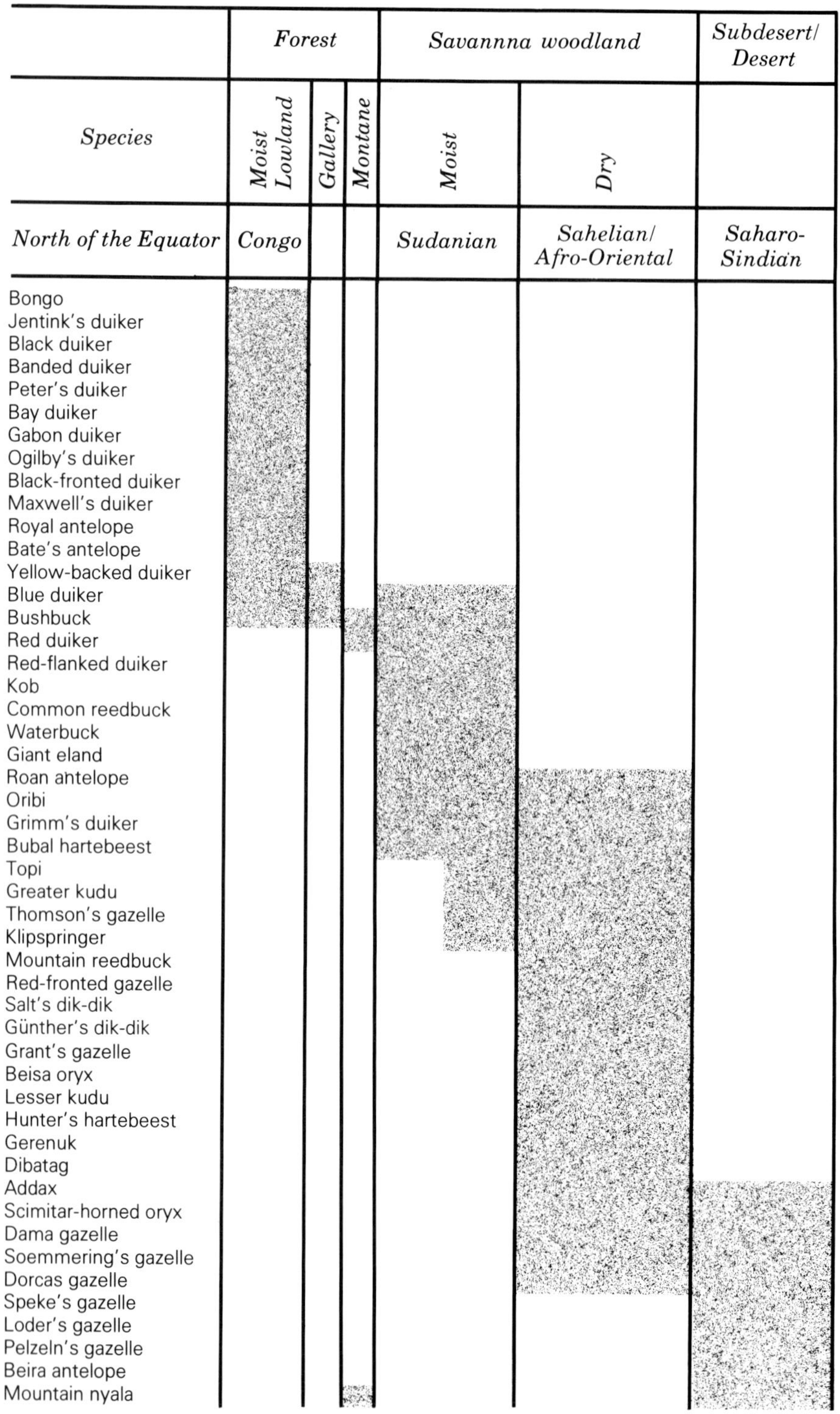

| Species | Forest | | | Savannna woodland | | Subdesert/ Desert |
| | Moist Lowland | Gallery | Montane | Moist | Dry | |
North of the Equator	Congo			Sudanian	Sahelian/ Afro-Oriental	Saharo-Sindian
Bongo						
Jentink's duiker						
Black duiker						
Banded duiker						
Peter's duiker						
Bay duiker						
Gabon duiker						
Ogilby's duiker						
Black-fronted duiker						
Maxwell's duiker						
Royal antelope						
Bate's antelope						
Yellow-backed duiker						
Blue duiker						
Bushbuck						
Red duiker						
Red-flanked duiker						
Kob						
Common reedbuck						
Waterbuck						
Giant eland						
Roan antelope						
Oribi						
Grimm's duiker						
Bubal hartebeest						
Topi						
Greater kudu						
Thomson's gazelle						
Klipspringer						
Mountain reedbuck						
Red-fronted gazelle						
Salt's dik-dik						
Günther's dik-dik						
Grant's gazelle						
Beisa oryx						
Lesser kudu						
Hunter's hartebeest						
Gerenuk						
Dibatag						
Addax						
Scimitar-horned oryx						
Dama gazelle						
Soemmering's gazelle						
Dorcas gazelle						
Speke's gazelle						
Loder's gazelle						
Pelzeln's gazelle						
Beira antelope						
Mountain nyala						

Species	Forest			Savannna woodland		Subdesert/ Desert
	Moist Lowland	Gallery	Montane	Moist	Dry	
South of the Equator	Congo			Zambesian	Afro-Oriental	Karoo-Namib
Bongo						
Peter's duiker						
Bay duiker						
Gabon duiker						
Black-fronted duiker						
Bates' antelope						
Yellow-backed duiker						
Blue duiker						
Bushbuck						
Red duiker						
Suni						
Nyala						
Sable antelope						
Puku						
Common reedbuck						
Southern reedbuck						
Cape hartebeest						
Lichtenstein's hartebeest						
Sassaby						
Bontebok						
White-tailed gnu						
Sharpe's grysbok						
Waterbuck						
Cape eland						
Roan antelope						
Oribi						
Bubal hartebeest						
Wildebeest						
Topi						
Greater kudu						
Thomson's gazelle						
Springbok						
Mountain reedbuck						
Damaraland dik-dik						
Kirk's dik-dik						
Grant's gazelle						
Impala						
Lesser kudu						
Hunter's hartebeest						
Gerenuk						
Beisa oryx/Gemsbok						
Steenbok						
Grimm's duiker						
Klipspringer						
Abbott's duiker						

alarmed it will submerge in the water with just its nostrils protruding. It can clamber over swampy vegetation by means of its specially adapted elongated hooves. Widely distributed in suitable localities, the sitatunga is found from Senegal, throughout the Congo basin, and south into the central swamps of the Okavango basin.

Next in adaptation is the lechwe, which lives in swamps and wetlands. Not secretive like the sitatunga is, lechwe are intensely gregarious animals, and under favourable conditions live in large herds, following the rise and fall of the floodwaters on seasonally inundated plains. They spend much of their time in water a few centimetres deep, but feed in depths of up to half a metre. When alarmed the lechwe splashes away clumsily, although it is a reasonable swimmer where the depth of water permits. Two main species exist, one inhabiting the Nile sudd, while the other, which has been divided into four races, is separated from it by over 3,000

Figure 3.5   A female sitatunga in her typical inaccessible marsh habitat

km, living in the central African swamps to the south of the Congo basin. Formerly the southern species was noted for its remarkable concentrations, estimated to occur in groups of over 3,000 head; but although the numbers of one race have been estimated at some 40,000, this is but a remnant of their former abundance, and other races are much less in number than this, drastic reductions having taken place in recent years.

Lechwe appear to have a similar social organisation to the kob, territorial for part of the year and using display arenas for attracting the females to breed. Little is known of the Nile lechwe, except that it occurs in large numbers; but its behaviour is probably similar to that of its southern counterpart.

The southern lechwe feeds on floodplain grasses and seems unable to survive on those of the savanna, although it apparently will do so in captivity, requiring a soft food with a high protein content. It is an interesting fact that on several occasions I saw its congener, the kob, a savanna species, standing in shallow water in the Bamingui river and feeding on what I presumed to be green algae from the stones of the river bed.

The waterbuck is so-named because it is never normally found far from water, and must drink regularly. It will enter water, but not often. Likewise the common reedbuck inhabits reedy vegetation adjacent to water, but it is not a swamp feeder, preferring relatively dry grasslands.

Island Habitats

The islands around the coast of Africa cannot be referred to one of our habitat types, although many have endemic species of plants. A surprising number of antelopes seems to have colonised them, and it is worth mentioning, as further evidence of the ability of antelopes to radiate into far-flung corners. Of 13 islands separated from the mainland by water over 100 fathoms deep, at least seven have been colonised. The Bijagos Islands off the coast of Guinea Bissau formerly had kob, bushbuck and Maxwell's duiker; and Dahlak Kebir, an island in the Red Sea, was colonised by Soemmering's gazelle. For the rest, colonisation seems to have been achieved only by the small duikers and neotragines, although it may be that we are seeing today only those species which have survived in the face of destruction by man. From the middle of the sixteenth century, when European ships began to make frequent voyages around the coasts of Africa, they often put in at islands and re-victualled with whatever food they could find, as they did regularly at the Cape. When the ships' crews had difficulty there in buying cattle and sheep from the natives, they soon found that antelopes could fill the bill, and at no cost. This soon served to diminish the numbers of antelopes in the coastal area, and on islands for all we know, several large species may have been exterminated altogether.

4 Conquering the environment

Relatively few antelopes have evolved the furthest that it is possible to go – from a humid forest home to the heat and dessication of the desert. Independence from free water, or the lack of a need to drink, represents the greatest challenge facing the evolution of mammals. Its achievement signifies the highest level of specialisation.

But specialisation is less successful than generalisation when it comes to evolution, and we have already seen how desert antelopes, which have attained this extraordinarily high degree of development, are amongst the most threatened of African species today, in spite of the vast, inhospitable refuge that is open to them. Their failure to survive has nothing to do with their remarkable physiology, except in so much as they cannot seek shelter in the woodland habitat which, with its diseases and its cover, as well as its obstruction to man's mechanised movement, still provides a refuge for those species, less advanced on the evolutionary ladder, which are nevertheless likely to persist for some time longer.

Early explorers, hunters and naturalists, made frequent reference to the fact that some species of antelope appeared to exist without drinking, especially the addax and the scimitar-horned oryx. But just as remarkable is the tolerance to heat of desert species, for in the Sahara temperatures may reach 50°C, and on sand dunes as much as 70°C. And of course nights can be bitterly cold in the desert, but paradoxically this may help the animals to survive there.

In the hot environment antelopes are faced with two apparently incompatible challenges: maintaining body temperature, and conserving water. Since water is used to cool the body to maintain its temperature, we can see the difficulty with which antelopes are faced in this environment. An object gains heat from the environment in proportion to its surface area, but as the surface area doubles in size, so the volume trebles. Thus the larger the animal, then the less the surface area; but this does not lead to large size in desert animals, because once the larger body is heated up, it then has the problem of getting rid of the heat. The happy medium seems to be achieved by gazelles in the range of 18 to 70 kg weight, although the addax can weigh up to 120 kg; while at the other extreme are the 4 kg dik-diks.

Obtaining Water

No animal can exist without taking in water, but it does not necessarily have to be free water. Antelopes of arid regions obtain their water from eating succulent plants and from eating at dawn when the vegetation is clothed with dew. The Grant's gazelle and the beisa oryx, for example, have been found to eat the leaves of a plant called *Disperma*, which is so dry and shrivelled during the daytime that it can be crumbled to dust in the fingers, its water content being only 1 per cent. But during the night it absorbs water like blotting paper, and the moisture content rises to an amazing 30 per cent. This has been shown to be ample to cover the water needs of these species of antelopes.

Water can also be obtained from the break-down, or oxidation, of food. In one study it has been found that for every gram of hay that a gazelle digested, it obtained half a gram of water. The production of water from fat deposits however, is now generally considered to be improbable as a strategy, contrary to what was once thought, for the chemical reaction involved in the breakdown demands more water than it produces.

It is reported for the addax (as it has been also for the elephant) that it possesses a compartment in the stomach containing water. This the desert hunter would himself make use of after a long thirsty hunt. Such water is of course no more than the ruminal fluid, which is indeed likely to be more watery in a concentrate feeder which takes in little bulk.

We may divide antelopes into three categories: firstly there are those that do not, and will not, drink water, even when it is available to them. This category includes such species as the addax, scimitar-horned oryx and the gerenuk. There are then those which can make do without, but will drink when water is available. Among these we can list the Cape eland, which although able to exist in fairly dry conditions, when penned and unable to wander in search of the succulents that it depends upon for its water, requires as much drinking water as cattle. Finally there are those species which cannot do without drinking water, of which one of the most extreme examples is the waterbuck.

Conserving Water

After an antelope has taken in water, whether free or in the food, then where water is limited it must try to conserve it. Water loss takes place through the urine, the faeces, respiration, and panting or sweating. The first three avenues of loss are concerned with the maintenance of essential bodily activities, the latter with maintaining the body temperature, or homeothermy. A mammal normally maintains its body temperature within fairly narrow limits, for if the temperature rises too high damage to the brain is usually the first effect, followed by a general breakdown of cell function.

To control their water losses some species use one method, some another, and yet others rely upon a combination of methods depending upon the extremes of temperature which they are adapted to withstand. We have seen how the circulation of urea through the rumen has been proposed as a possible mechanism for water conservation, as it is primarily for the removal of urea that the urine requires relatively large amounts of water; but almost all species concentrate the urine, the known exception being the waterbuck. All species also reduce the amount of water lost in the faeces. Each litre of air which is exhaled during respiration contains about one two-hundredth of a cubic centimetre of water, which does not sound much, but a litre of air is soon expelled by a large animal, and this loss totals up to about a litre of water per day per 100 kg of body weight. This can be kept down by a lowered metabolic rate, achieved by resting during the heat.

Maintaining Body Temperature

Maintaining body temperature raises greater problems; but one help is that the hotter the environment usually the cooler it is at night. An animal can thus lose heat to the environment at night in the desert, and thus, in contrast to that found in Arctic mammals which need to conserve heat, the thickness of the coat decreases with increasing body size, favouring heat loss rather than protection against heat gain. But in the humid regions for part of the year it can be just as hot at night as during the day, and this may be limiting to some species.

The effects of simulated hot desert conditions have been looked at in a range of antelopes in East Africa, namely the Grant's and Thomson's gazelles, oryx, wildebeest and eland. Evaporation, in the form of water lost by panting and sweating, accounted for from 58 to 83 per cent of the total water lost when the animals could drink freely, the rest being lost in the faeces and urine. When the animals were dehydrated, evaporation was reduced by from 12 to 51 per cent, the amounts being equal to, or greater than, the combined reduction in loss by faeces and urine. When evaporation under a heat load was compared with that of a normal temperature, 22°C, it was found that the increase in evaporative water loss was equivalent to about 2 to 3 per cent of body weight per day when water was available, and only 0.5 to 2 per cent when water was limited. It was calculated that under the latter conditions, the additional water of evaporation required for a twelve-hour day at 40°C, was reduced by 0.04 to 2.2 l per 100 kg of body weight per day. Thus the hotter and drier the animal, the less water it loses.

Large and small animals used two different methods to dissipate heat. When water was in short supply small gazelles, such as the tommy and Grant's, allowed their body temperatures to increase until they exceeded the surrounding air temperature. The smaller the animal, as we have seen, then the quicker does this take place. A large animal like the eland, by contrast, has a low body temperature in the morning and warms up slowly through the day when subjected to the same conditions as were the gazelles. The oryx uses a combination of both methods.

Once the highest temperature that the animal can withstand has been reached, then it must use evaporative cooling. So if a large animal, such as the eland, has taken until mid-day to warm up, it then only has to maintain evaporative cooling for about five hours until the air temperature drops in the evening and it can start losing heat to the environment. This is an effective way of saving water in a large animal because of its smaller surface area, relatively speaking, and its lower rate of metabolism, than that of a smaller animal. The small animal, however, may reach a high body temperature within one hour, and must then spend the rest of the day keeping it from rising higher; but by letting its temperature rise it saves on evaporative cooling.

Both the Grant's gazelle and the oryx were found to let their body temperatures rise much higher than other species which were investigated. In contrast to the gazelles and the wildebeest, which pant, the oryx sweats. But when dehydrated the oryx no longer sweated, even when the air temperature was as high as 46°C. Both the Grant's and the oryx could maintain a body temperature of 46.5°C for up to six hours with no observable ill effects, although such temperatures are lethal to most mammals. This results in large water savings, for in an air temperature of 45°C an antelope with a body temperature of 46.5°C will no longer gain heat from the environment, but *will lose heat to it*. This tolerance to such high body temperatures may be the key to the success of the desert antelopes, but how can they tolerate such temperatures when others can't?

Dr Taylor of Harvard University, who conducted most of these experiments, suggested that the arterial blood to the brain is cooled by venous blood returning from the nasal sinuses by means of the *rete mirabilia*, the 'marvellous network'. This is a small, sponge-like network of the carotid artery about the size of a large pea, situated at the base of the brain, and which lies in a venous pool of the blood returning from the nasal mucosa, the internal linings of the nose. This is the same structure that has been proposed as preventing giddiness in the giraffe, when it suddenly raises its head from ground level to nearly 5 m in height.

All of the antelopes have long noses which house large, delicate sinuses whose function may be designed to cool the blood, as well as providing them with a large sensitive area for scenting purposes. When this cooled blood comes into close contact in the *rete mirabilia* with the warm arterial blood which is on its way to the brain, an exchange of heat could take place, as has been demonstrated in the sheep. But this can only be part of the explanation, for it is inconceivable that the blood could lose 8.4°C, the difference between the normal body temperature of a Grant's gazelle, 38.1°C, and the body temperatures that it can reach of 46.5°C, in the time taken for the two cross-currents of blood to pass one another.

These experiments served to explain an apparent paradox surrounding the tommy and Grant's gazelles, for whereas the latter inhabits drier and hotter country than does the tommy, yet it needs more water. Now under a heat load, evaporation accounts for most of the water loss in both species when drinking water is freely available. This amounts to some 80 per cent, the losses from urine and faeces being relatively minor. When the temperature is 40°C, a very hot day in northern Kenya, both animals pant. Although both have functional sweat glands water loss did not increase significantly via this pathway because the animals tended to sweat in bursts. However, if water was restricted, then they both stopped panting; the loss by evaporation being reduced by 63 per cent in the tommy and 31 per cent in the Grant's. The animals then let their body temperatures rise to 41.6°C and 41.0°C in the tommy and Grant's respectively, compared with their normal temperatures of 37.8°C and 38.1°C. The paradox is that the Grant's requires more water for evaporation than the tommy because it has only reduced its evaporation by 31 per cent compared to the tommy's 63 per cent. How then can it live in hotter and drier areas?

The answer was found when both gazelles were exposed to a heat of 45°C, a temperature which the tommy would probably not normally experience. When the temperature exceeded 42°C, the tommy increased its evaporation by panting in order to maintain its body temperature well below the air temperature, so that it was only 42.5°C when the air temperature had reached 45°C. But the Grant's, on the other hand, allowed its body temperature to rise to 46°C, thus conserving water that would otherwise be lost by increased evaporation. Like other desert antelopes it would let its body cool down at night, when the ambient temperature had fallen. Thus, contrary to the tommy, it can exploit a relatively waterless environment where the temperature is likely to rise to high levels.

But Dr Taylor's detective work on this species did not stop here, because the Grant's still requires about 1 to 3 l of water a day, equivalent to some 4 per cent of its body weight of 45 to 80 kg. By watching the Grant's during a drought in an arid area of northern Kenya, Taylor found that they fed at night on *Disperma*, which we have seen was able to amply furnish the Grant's water requirements with the water that the plant absorbed from the night air.

True desert species, such as the addax and the scimitar-horned oryx, have probably developed such strategies as we find in the Grant's gazelle to an even higher degree. What is surprising about them is their tolerance to heat, and ability to remain in the open under a scorching desert sun during the hottest part of the day without apparent discomfort. But Brocklehurst, who hunted addax in the 1920s when they were more plentiful, found that they would huddle together under the sparse shade of an isolated thorn tree during the heat of the day whenever such protection was available. He also found that when the nights were cold they would lie in hollows in the sand, which they had dug out in order to get at the roots of a small shrub.

The addax changes its colour with the seasons, being pale to almost white in spring and summer, and greyish brown to brown in autumn and winter. It is instructive in this respect to see how the kongoni or Coke's hartebeest, an eastern race of the bubal hartebeest, which remains out in the sun during the hottest of days, manages to cope with its environment. It is obviously not as advanced in this respect as the now extinct northern race must have been, nor indeed the western race which extends its range up into the sahel.

Like the gazelles, the hartebeest uses panting for evaporative cooling, but the tip of each hair of the kongoni's coat is white, the stem reddish-brown. This combination produces a somewhat light-coloured coat, which reflects incoming sunlight by as much as 42 per cent, compared, say, to the Cape eland, whose reddish-coloured coat only reflects 22 per cent. Thus only slightly more than 50 per cent of the incoming heat load can be absorbed. We can now see why the addax changes its coat colour with the seasons, the desert winters being sufficiently cold to necessitate some increase in heat retention. Radiation also penetrates more deeply into loose, than into dense, flat coats, and here the hartebeest gains again. In total it loses about 25 per cent of its heat load by evaporative water loss, panting accounting for nearly twice the amount lost by sweating. Panting has been suggested as a more effective means of keeping the body temperature down, because the body surface temperature will then be higher and thus attract less inflow of heat from a hot environment.

As in desert animals, the kongoni has a considerably lower fasting metabolic rate (that is, the rate of energy turnover when it is not feeding) than have such species as the wildebeest and eland. The kongoni also requires only 72 per cent of the water that an eland does as a result of its heat-combating strategies.

The East African beisa oryx is another antelope that has been shown to require very little water, a fully-grown bull weighing 200 kg needs only slightly less than 4 l a day; almost half of that required by a wildebeest. In a hot environment this only increases to 6 l, still less than the wildebeest needs at a temperature of 22°C, a cool African day. But the wildebeest strives to keep its body temperature constant, even in temperatures of up to 50°C, panting in preference to sweating. This difference in water requirements explains the difference in distribution between the two animals, with the wildebeest limited to moist woodland, and the oryx able to inhabit semi-arid regions.

Most attention has been paid to the physiology of the eland, in view of a supposed potential for domestication. But it has been demonstrated that, where water is limited, then the oryx is far superior as a potential meat producer. Studies of the eland's physiology have been restricted to the Cape eland which, although preferring the moister woodlands, also ventures into semi-arid country, travelling long distances from water. By contrast, the giant eland favours higher rainfall areas, but its physiological demands are as yet unstudied.

The Cape eland survives in hot, arid regions, by selecting succulent food, such as the wild sisal *Sansevieria*; avoiding the mid-day sun by seeking shade, and by having a high body temperature. It also produces very dry faeces, and so can gain more water in its food by eating more, without losing the extra water in the faeces. It is estimated that it can probably obtain 4 l of water per 100 kg of body weight from its food, compared to a required 3.7 l. This means that a very large bull would need about 37 l of water per day. But the eland has a thin coat, which means that, lacking insulation yet having a high body temperature, it must increase its bodily metabolism, or burn more energy, to keep warm when the nights are cool. To produce this energy for keeping warm it must eat more, and thus it takes in more water in its food, as well as producing water from the breakdown of the sugars in its food when it is using up energy.

In most mammals, the increase in oxygen consumption which the burning up of energy to keep warm requires, involves increased pulmonary ventilation, or deeper breathing; and consequently an increased loss of water through respiratory evaporation. But in the eland this water loss did not increase with an increased rate of metabolism at low temperatures. This could be achieved in two ways; breathing out cool air, and increasing the extraction of oxygen from the air when it is breathed in.

At the low temperature, by African standards, of 14°C, it was found that eland feeding on vegetation containing an estimated 58 per cent of water, would have 35 per cent more water available to them than would be the case at a temperature of 22°C. Deeper breathing did not increase significantly with the higher consumption of oxygen at 14°C, but body temperature dropped from 38.7°C to 37.3°C. This meant that air saturated at body temperature would contain about 8 per cent less water by virtue of its lower temperature; whereas if the increase in oxygen consumption at 14°C had been accomplished solely by deeper breathing, the net gain in water would have been only 19 per cent. By having a lower body temperature the eland extracts more oxygen from the air, and loses less water through evaporation from the lungs. The increased extraction of oxygen seems to be the result of a smaller relative importance of the dead space in the lungs as the animal breathes deeper. A low body temperature at night is thus important to the eland, not only to release the heat stored during the day, but also to reduce respiratory water loss.

Studies have shown that the eland and the wildebeest derive similar amounts of metabolisable energy from similar amounts of food, the efficiency for maintenance purposes, that is, keeping the body ticking over without working hard, being more or less identical at 80 and 82 per cent respectively. But the wildebeest is notably more efficient at converting food to metabolisable energy for production, that is, storing fat; with a conversion rate of 59.3 per cent compared to the eland's 52.4 per cent. Both species require 20 to 30 per cent more metabolisable energy than do cattle, and thus they must have a greater intake of food. Being a grazer, the wildebeest's food is seasonal in abundance and quality, which probably explains the need to store energy efficiently.

To turn from the largest to the smallest, if a small body heats up more quickly than a large one, then how does a species like the diminutive dik-dik manage to avoid being roasted on a hot day in its semi-desert environment? Other scientists have looked at this species, and have found that in the Kirk's dik-dik, which inhabits the drier areas of East Africa, high heat loads are withstood by increasing the respiratory rate. Dik-dik start to pant as soon as their body temperature rises and, after eight hours at a temperature of 40°C, the normal breathing rate of 30 breaths a minute, increases to 400. The body temperature of a running dik-dik rises from its normal level of 37.8°C to about 40°C within two minutes, after which panting reaches 500 breaths a minute. Increases of body temperature up to 6°C can be withstood, but paradoxically, when this occurs energy consumption, as measured by oxygen intake, is 42 per cent lower in the panting dik-dik than when the animal is at rest. This apparent contradiction appears to be due to a halving of the flow of blood to all muscles other than to those concerned with respiration.

The Kirk's dik-dik is characterised by a unique proboscis-like snout, but it is not prehensile and not used in feeding. It is suggested that it uses it as a kind of bellows, sucking in hot, dry air over the moist surfaces of the enlarged nasal mucosa, and then pumping it out again, cooling the blood supply by evaporation. The species has often been observed to have a runny nose, and to lick up the dew-drops, swallowing them immediately.

Evaporative water loss through panting accounts for about 70 per cent of the total water loss, although it is low per kilogram of body weight. This rose by nearly 90 per cent under heat stress when water was available, but was reduced to about 60 per cent of normal when the animal was dehydrated. Only a small amount of sweating takes place, for such a small animal would lose too much water this way, and after ten hours of heat stress there was still no visible sign of sweating; only large animals can afford to sweat. If the dik-dik becomes too hot, it assists evaporative cooling by spreading saliva on its flanks.

Total water exchange in the dehydrated animal is 40 per cent of normal. Normally it takes in about 9 per cent of preformed water, or water in its food, but under heat stress food intake fell by 11 per cent, compared with 10 per cent in the eland; and when dehydrated into the bargain, its food intake fell by over 30 per cent, thus reducing faecal and urinary losses of water. Under heat stress faecal water losses were reduced to about 58 per cent of normal, and when dehydrated to 44.5 per cent; while the dik-dik can concentrate its urine more than that of any other ungulate for which data are available. Losses by this pathway may be reduced by 70 per cent, as compared to 35 per cent in the eland.

The dik-dik also has a labile body temperature which during the night may drop from a normal day-time level of 37.8°C to 36.2°C, while under heat stress it can rise to 41.9°C. Thus the animal's ability to cope with an arid environment is explained by its substantial ability to store heat and the fact that it has the lowest daily water expenditure for any ungulate so far recorded under similar conditions, because its faecal and urinary losses are so low.

Although the proboscis-like snout appears to play an important role in the Kirk's adaptation to heat, its close relative the Phillip's from the Horn of Africa, inhabits even more inhospitable areas and yet lacks a pronounced proboscis. It is thought that it probably compensates for this by being more nocturnal in habit, lying up in the shade during the heat of the day.

So far we have been looking mostly at those antelopes exposed to the more extreme environments, but let us now turn to an intermediate species, an inhabitant of the dry savanna woodland, the impala. Physiological investigations in any depth are lacking, but it has been demonstrated that the amount of water which the impala drinks is correlated with the proportion of dry matter in its food, which is predominantly grass. Indeed, it could be predicted that, when the dry matter of the forage fell below a third, then the impala stopped drinking, obtaining sufficient water for its needs from its food.

The minimum daily water requirement has been estimated at 2.5 l per 100 kg of body weight, equal to about 2 l for an adult buck. Under hot, dry conditions, this rises to as much as 4 l per 100 kg. Like other species, when water is restricted, the impala concentrates its urine and produces drier faeces, at the same time seeking the shade as much as possible. It seems to maintain as high an intake of water in its food as is possible, and although this eliminates the necessity of exposing itself at watering points, it seems unlikely that this has developed as a predator avoidance strategy, as has sometimes been suggested. It is more likely to be an adaptation to life in relatively dry conditions.

Now let us look at some of the animals of the moist savanna woodland, where temperatures can be high in the dry season and water scarce, but the nights are seldom cold; although temperatures may drop to 9°C in the Sudanian zone winter. Here, humidity at the onset of the rains, produces unpleasantly high temperatures which cannot be relieved by evaporative methods to the same extent that they can in dry areas.

One worker has compared the effects of heat stress and water deprivation on three species of the moist savanna woodland: the bushbuck, common reedbuck and the Uganda kob.

All of these species pant through the nose and require large amounts of water under heat stress at temperatures up to 40°C. This is due to an attempt to keep the body temperature normal, between 38°C and 38.5°C. The highest body temperatures reached were 38.9°C for the bushbuck, and 39.6°C for the reedbuck and kob. These fell during a night temperature of 21°C to 23°C, to 38°C, 38.1°C and 38.2°C for the bushbuck, reedbuck and kob respectively. Thus there was no heat storage during the day. Nevertheless when water was restricted all three animals made large economies in evaporative water loss, the bushbuck reducing its loss by nearly 60 per cent, and the other two by more than 40 per cent. The kob lost relatively more through evaporation than did the others, increasing its respiratory rate at temperatures under 40°C. At normal ambient temperatures of 18°C to 30°C the evaporative water loss accounted for about half of the total water losses from each. At 40°C the bushbuck increased this loss by an amount not much greater than its increase in drinking, about 29 per cent compared with a 21 per cent increase in the itake of water. The reedbuck however, lost only about 5 per cent more, compared with a 28 per cent increase in drinking. Thus the bushbuck and the kob had good evaporative heat loss responses, but that of the reedbuck was poor. Sweating was relatively insignificant as an avenue of water loss.

Overall the bushbuck had a 25 per cent greater total water exchange than did the other two, mainly due to a dilute urine. Under heat stress, at a temperature of 40°C with drinking water available, the bushbuck and the reedbuck each increased their total water exchange by about a fifth; but the kob, which almost doubled its evaporative water loss, showed an overall increase of 60 per cent above normal. When water was limited, each species reduced its overall water exchange by about 45 per cent.

Under heat stress the intake of water was similar in the bushbuck and the reedbuck, but whereas the former used it for evaporative cooling the reedbuck simply produced a more dilute urine. Normally the bushbuck loses about 39 per cent of its water via the urine, decreasing this loss to only 30 per cent when dehydrated. The reedbuck normally loses about 32 per cent this way, but under heat stress in this species the urine output *rose* to 55 per cent, and its concentration was decreased. Thus most of the extra water that the reedbuck took in was wasted as far as cooling was concerned. When water was restricted its urine output fell by 60 per cent of normal. The kob's urine loss was about half of that of the bushbuck, despite a similar intake of water, due to it having a much higher evaporative loss, doubling this loss in comparison to normal.

The bushbuck produced the wettest faeces and dried them very little, but the reedbuck under heat stress reduced its faecal water loss by about 20 per cent. When dehydrated all three species reduced it by 10 per cent, 27 per cent and 38 per cent, for the bushbuck, reedbuck and the kob respectively.

Thus we can see that none of these species is able to cope with a hot, dry environment; due both to an inability to conserve water, and to store heat in the body. The least adaptable of the three appears to be the reedbuck, since if water is available it does not use this for cooling. The bushbuck, with a very dilute urine, is able to cope if it can drink; while the kob, with a high evaporative loss but a reduction in urine, seems to be the most suited of the three to a hot environment.

The waterbuck was so named from its first contact with the Dutch settlers at the Cape because it was never found far from water. Let us now see whether it really deserves its name.

In a study of the defassa waterbuck, which may well have a different physiology to that of the common waterbuck, at a temperature of 22°C with water freely available, the waterbuck's losses were approximately equally divided between the faeces, urine and evaporation. But when water was restricted, then faecal loss was reduced from about one third to one sixth of the total water loss. Apart from producing drier faeces, almost 22 per cent less food was eaten. But what was eaten was more thoroughly digested, which could account for half of the reduction in faecal water loss. Restricting water intake had no effect upon the amount of urine which was passed, except when the animal was severely dehydrated. Under a heat load the volume increased by about 26 per cent when water was freely available.

In the laboratory the waterbuck had to be fed a high protein diet for it to survive, equivalent to about four times that fed to such species as eland, oryx and wildebeest. This high intake of protein, and the high excretion of urea which this entails, explains the high volume of urine. If the water-buck ate a low-quality hay and lost similar amounts of urea as does a Hereford steer, for example, then its daily urine volume would be reduced by about a third. Most mammals increase the concentration and reduce the volume of their urine when water is restricted as we have seen other antelopes do, but the waterbuck is an exception although having similarities with the reedbuck in this respect, in spite of the fact that its kidney has the ability to do so. So it appears that the waterbuck does not drink extra water when it has the opportunity, and always forms a nearly maximally concentrated urine; but a urine which is about only half as concentrated as that of the eland.

At normal temperatures when water was restricted, evaporation remained unchanged, about half of the loss being from respiration and the other half from the skin. When subjected to a temperature of 40°C the waterbuck's rate of evaporation approximately tripled through both pant-ing and sweating. The respiratory loss increased by 50 per cent and the cutaneous by over 76 per cent, the skin accounting for about two-thirds of the total water loss. The rate of evaporation was about 40 per cent greater than that of an eland of similar size and metabolic rate, the waterbuck not exploiting any methods of containing evaporative water loss, and losing about 12 l per 100 kg of body weight per day. Thus to maintain equilibrium under these circumstances, an adult buck would have to drink some 60 l a day.

Using panting and sweating the waterbuck's body temperature is main-tained well below the ambient temperature, even when the latter is as high as 45°C, rising only from 39.2°C to 39.8°C. But if water is restricted, then the body temperature rises steadily until the animal collapses. When dehydrated, other species that have been examined, including the camel and cattle, all reduced their rate of metabolism thus minimising water loss. This, we saw, is an important strategy in the kongoni. But the waterbuck is an exception in that its rate of metabolism remains unal-tered.

The experiments leave no doubts concerning the waterbuck's depen-dence on water. At a temperature of 22°C it requires 25 per cent more than a steer, and nearly three times more than an oryx. Only faecal loss was reduced when water was restricted, the volume of urine passed and the rate of evaporation remaining unchanged. It is thus incapable of with-standing even short periods of dehydration in a hot environment, and must always be within easy reach of water.

A further check on its distribution may be provided by low temperature. Thus the range of ambient temperature that the waterbuck can withstand, known as its thermo-neutral zone, is from about 13°C to 37°C. At Mweya in western Uganda, where I studied the waterbuck, the lowest temperature recorded in three years was 12.3°C, and the mean minimum and maximum were 17.6° and 29.7°C respectively. This must have provided an optimum temperature range for the waterbuck. By contrast, in South Africa during July the mean daily minimum temperature is 7.5°C, or less, over a great part of the country. At Skukuza, close to the Kruger National Park, the mean minimum temperature is 12.5°C. Thus if the waterbuck in this region have the same physiology as do those in western Uganda, they may experience difficulty in maintaining their body temperature during the winter. The low temperatures occurring as they do in the dry season, may explain the assertion that the waterbuck there are particularly prone to starvation at this time: a phenomenon never seen in western Uganda. This would result from the higher metabolic rate, or energy burning, needed to keep the animal warm. This entails eating more food. As we have seen, under normal circumstances the waterbuck requires a high protein diet, and this is less likely to be available in adequate quantities during the dry season.

The waterbuck's close relative, the Uganda kob, is able to withstand both heat and dehydration better than can the waterbuck itself, mainly through an ability to restrict the urinary and evaporative water losses. Its normally high evaporative water loss however, makes it also a relatively water dependent animal. Thus although we tend to find the two species in the same habitats, the waterbuck is not seen in the open as much as is the kob.

These studies on physiology, although covering only a handful of species, help to illustrate the complexities underlying antelope distribution. It is not enough to simply consider feeding habits or anatomical structures, for although each of these plays its part and influences behaviour, an animal's physiology is of greater importance. Antelopes do not exist in forests, woodlands or deserts, by chance. Each species is restricted to inhabiting an environment that its physiology is able to cope with.

5 Food, feeding and migration

Wildebeest in countless numbers shimmering in the heat haze of the Serengeti Plains for as far as the eye can see, are one of the great extravaganzas of Africa. If we were to look closely at these hordes we would see that they are all eating grass: but do they eat any sort of grass? And do they compete with the equally countless numbers of buffalo, zebra, topi and Thomson's gazelle, that also roam these plains and which are also eating grass? How can such a mixture of so many herbivores exist together in harmony? Ecological theory tells us that each species of animal has its niche; species differentiate to states in which they overlap each other as little as possible, each exploiting a resource that is different to the other's, or exploiting the same resource in a different way. Thus if two species succeed in occupying the same niche, one must greatly outnumber the other.

There is a mass of anecdotal information on the feeding habits of antelopes from the accounts of hunters since the turn of the century, and for many species even today these notes are still all that we have. But such observations are of little real value unless the species of plant which is eaten can be described in terms of its availability to the animal. If a species of plant is common but not taken, then it is avoided; conversely, if a species is uncommon but figures largely in the diet, then it must be sought after. Listing the species which an animal takes serves little value in a general account, for what is taken in one area may not be taken in another, and preferences also change with season. What is important is to what extent competition for plant species occurs.

It was not until the late 1950s that researchers into African wildlife began to try to establish the truth of the axiom of niche specificity among the herbivore fauna. The development of methods of identifying grass fragments from the arrangement of the silica particles which make up the skeleton, opened the way to studies of feeding habits by means of the examination of droppings and of rumen samples; complementing systematic direct observation which is not always very easy. It is difficult to tell what a wildebeest is selecting when its nose is immersed in a sea of grass.

The initial reaction to the results of such studies was to over-emphasise the separation of the herbivore species in their choice of plants, for the compartmentalisation of feeding habits is perhaps not always as distinct as is sometimes claimed. There is much overlap, and there is competition between species. To assume otherwise is to assume that the pinnacle of evolutionary advancement has been attained, and that no further changes could take place in the African fauna.

Studies of the Serengeti herbivores suggest nevertheless, that in some cases overlap in feeding preferences may be more apparent than real. To explain this the analogy has been proposed of looking at a grass plant as one would look at a tree. It has a stem, tough and fibrous when mature; it has a sheath branching from the stem, also fairly tough and which we could liken in our analogy to a branch; and it has leaves, the most nutritious part of all. Ah yes, and it has flowers and seeds also, but these are generally ignored by the herbivores; they are tough and prickly and stick in the teeth. So it has been found that, rather than all of the animals just eating the same species of grass, as they may frequently do, mixed herbivore populations may be selecting for different parts. Some animals favour the stem, some the sheath, and yet others prefer the leaf. The study of the proportions of these parts which are taken can be more revealing than a study of the actual species taken.

Feeding Preferences

Generally speaking, the larger the species of herbivore the more food it requires and so the less selective can it afford to be. Thus it is possessed of a wide mouth which can take in more at one bite. The smaller the species the narrower tends to be the muzzle, allowing it to select its food more precisely. An antelope's anatomy, as we have seen, is intricately bound up with its feeding habit; the angle of the jaws in relation to the brain, and the length of the neck, are just two of the factors which determine how it feeds. The sable antelope shows us how precise the limits apparently are which govern this behaviour.

A study of the sable antelope in Zimbabwe, revealed that this species is a fresh grass grazer dependent on water. Never found more than a kilometre from the latter, it drank daily; and it cropped grass, taking only leaf, at a height of 40 to 140 mm above the ground. Rarely did it feed at a height above the level of its sternum. While impala fed almost to ground level and tsessebee to 20 to 30 mm in the same swards, the sable was never observed to bite grass that was less than 40 mm tall; and it was the last species to start using the new grass which became available immediately after the late dry season when the amount of food available was critical.

When forced in a paddock to feed on tall grass, despite the fact that it was high in protein and low in fibre, and therefore highly nutritious, the sable lost condition rapidly. Rather than alter their feeding level, sable seemed to exist at below maintenance level during the dry season, when the principal food species was *Heteropogon contortus*, a relatively unpalatable grass which is avoided by many grazers. Only two browse species were recorded in the diet; one being the highly aromatic *Tarchonanthus camphoratus*, but this was in the dry season. Although this extreme specificity of habit, which is probably related to the length of the neck and the angle of the jaws, may serve to separate the sable from other grazers, it probably is also the reason for their limited success. Of restricted distribution, nowhere can it be said to be a successful species in terms of numbers.

Topi normally avoid very long *Hyparrhenia* grass, and it has been observed that when they have been panicked into running through it by lions, many often become blinded by the sharp seeds penetrating their eyes. Feeding habits in other species may well be related to a factor such as this, where spiky stems or seeds form a barrier to the animal.

But no grazing herbivore is faced with an endless grass sandwich to munch its way through. Outside of the forest, in which grass is of sparse occurrence anyway, it is seasonal; and at the height of the dry season its value as food is often below that which an animal needs for maintenance, as appears to be the case with the sable. When this occurs, the animal uses up more energy in feeding than it derives from the food. As grass matures the proportion of leaf to stem changes, at the same time the level of protein in the leaf falls, as does also the sugar and chemicals such as calcium and phosphorus.

Adopting the Malthusian view that the number of animals is ultimately limited by the food supply, the numbers of African herbivores can be said to be limited by the worst part of the year. I am reminded of the expostulations of an American tourist, visiting Kenya's Tsavo West National Park in the wet season, at the quantity of grass going to waste. Waving panoramas of green grass gave joy to the eye, but not a grazing animal was to be seen. But had the tourist in question visited the same area at the height of the dry season, then he would have realised why there were so few animals present to eat the grass in the wet season. For then the parched, dusty ground is almost bare, except for scattered sere tussocks.

But farmers in Africa have often commented with envy upon the fact that, during the dry season, the wild herbivores do not seem to suffer as much as does the domestic stock. The hartebeest remains fat, while the cow visibly starves. The difference is probably more imaginary than real during the course of a normal dry season, for whereas cattle lay down their fat reserves under the skin (an inheritance from the need to provide insulation in colder climes) the antelopes deposit theirs around various organs, the kidneys, heart, rectum and the mesenteries. When the fat is consumed the antelope's outward appearance does not change, in contrast to the cow becoming visibly thinner. But in a prolonged drought, once the fat deposits have been exhausted and the animal must start drawing upon its flesh, then the antelope can become as thin in appearance as does the cow; although it will probably well outlast the latter due to its greater adaptability to seasonal aridity and its wider range of diet.

My studies on the Grant's gazelle in northern Tanzania have indicated however that although an antelope may look in good form in the dry season, it may nevertheless be under stress. In the dry season, milk-producing Grant's gazelle mothers developed enlarged fatty livers, indicative of the rapid consumption of fat deposits because sufficient food was not available for the production of milk. Now the Grant's gazelle is primarily a browser, and browsers seem to be buffered against dry season effects because browse is generally adequate then; succulents thrive under dry conditions and it is in the dry season that many trees burst into leaf. But the Grant's gazelle mother appears to need grass for milk production, a phenomenon which may be more widespread among browsers than has hitherto been revealed.

After the dry season, the fresh flush of green growth brought on by the first rains can be a problem to ruminants on account of its richness, leading to diarrhoea and the rapid production of methane causing bloat. Many old animals succumb at this period of the year, having successfully weathered the dry season, as I found to be the case with impala in Rwanda's Akagera National Park. Following a bad drought in Kenya in 1984, waterbuck are reported to have died in the north in the first week of rain; a surprising occurrence for a species so well adapted to a rich diet and a high rate of water turnover.

A further important factor influencing the environment of the herbivore is fire. Every year south of the sahelian zone the greater part of Africa goes up in smoke, as herdsmen or hunters burn off the dry grass. This can result in a fresh flush of green grass in the absence of rain, and herbivores are attracted to it as it is short and nutritious, coming at a time of the year when food would be otherwise hard to find. In the long run however it selects for the more tough, unpalatable species; but where fire is prevented bush takes over and the plains herbivores decline. Since it is believed that fire may have been used by man in Africa as long as 180,000 years ago, perhaps antelopes have now evolved in concert with its annual occurrence.

Considerable overlap in the dietary preferences of antelope species, leading to competition for habitat, undoubtedly exists. Thus in the Queen Elizabeth Park in western Uganda I found that where the hippopotamus, a strict grazer, was plentiful, then waterbuck were low in number and vice versa. Further evidence of competition was provided when the hippopotamus, numbering some 128 animals, was removed from an area of just over 4 sq km in the Park known as the Mweya Peninsula. Following this removal the buffalo increased by 157 head, and the waterbuck by 30. What is more important is that the hippopotamus is able to modify its habitat to its own advantage, for its method of grazing, pulling up the grass with its broad, horny lips, uproots the tussock grasses which are favoured by the waterbuck, and their place is taken by creeping, mat-forming grasses which the hippopotamus prefers. Competition between species of herbivore is thus seen to be a reality, but it is usually ameliorated by ecological separation. So let us look at some of the ways in which harmony is achieved.

Ecological Harmony

The first example of a grazing succession, or interspecific facilitation as it has been termed in the jargon of the ecologist (the activities of one species helping those of another) was first proposed from observations of herbivores inhabiting the Lake Rukwa floodplain in southern Tanzania. This extensive area of open grassland surrounds a shallow, saline lake, with the grassland being bordered by *Acacia* thorn and other trees. The plains are subject to an annual cycle of flooding with a longer term of alternating flood and drought in which the grasslands contract and expand in area, with consequent changes in the sizes of the herbivore populations.

At the time of writing, a high lake level has resulted in an extremely depressed population of topi; while another characteristic inhabitant, the puku, is on the verge of extinction. In the normal seasonal cycle, the grazing and trampling of the long grass and reeds in the wake of the receding floodwaters, by such large animals as the elephant, hippopotamus and buffalo, permits use of the zone by smaller species such as the puku and reedbuck. Not only does the trampling provide access, but it also stimulates shoot growth which is fed upon by the smaller species. Similarly, great concentrations of topi, once the most abundant species in the area, accompanied by eland, zebra and buffalo, keep the grass short on the drier surrounding plains during the wet season. As the dry season advances they move onto the trampled lakeside pastures, retreating again as the water rises in the wet season.

In the Tarangire National Park of northern Tanzania, it has been shown how different species favoured different types of habitat. Here there was no annual cycle of flooding, but simply three different vegetation types: open grassland, open woodland, and dense woodland; where 'open woodland' is rather like an orchard, with the trees spaced fairly widely apart. At the one extreme the Grant's gazelle was shown to prefer open grassland, spending only a small amount of its time in the open woodland; closely followed in this preference by the wildebeest. At the other extreme was the lesser kudu, which rarely ventured out of dense woodland. In between these extremes were hartebeest, eland, impala, waterbuck and dik-dik, amongst other herbivores; all favouring the open woodland to slightly differing degrees.

Concentrations of species were found to occur at the boundaries of one vegetation type with another; particularly favoured, for example, was a drainage line flanked by *Acacia tortilis* trees within a whistling thorn tree (*Acacia drepanolobium*) zone. This attracted high numbers of impala and waterbuck. The advantages which such vegetation boundaries could offer the animals can be seen as a greater variety of food plants, and immediate access to two habitat types, one offering better protection from predation than the other, and also providing more shade.

Movements and Migrations

Among the vast herbivore host of the Serengeti plains separation into different habitat types is not evident, but we can divide the principal herbivores into two groups: those which do not migrate but inhabit the woodlands, namely the impala, topi and buffalo; and those which do migrate, the tommy, wildebeest and zebra. In order to fully appreciate the strategies that may be employed, it is necessary to include non-antelopes in our discussion.

The impala here shows clear-cut seasonal preferences for its feeding habitats. In the wet season it prefers the *Acacia senegal* woodlands and the whistling thorn savanna; while in the dry season it is found in the open grassland and along drainage lines. In the wet season grass is preferred as food, certain types being selected for, while tough, fire-induced species such as *Heteropogon contortus* and the red-oat grass *Themeda triandra* are avoided. In addition, although grass leaf was taken according to its availability, more sheath than stem was taken. In the dry season it preferred browse, forbs or weeds being an important component of the diet. The impala could benefit from the invasion of its habitat by the wildebeest hordes during their migratory passage, from the opening up of the grass layer; but the removal of forage may force them to turn to browse earlier than would otherwise be the case. The tommy's dietary preferences are similar in respect of graze and forbs, which could lead to direct competition between the two species, except that the tommy generally prefers a more open habitat.

Topi are almost exclusively grazers and display a consistent seasonal pattern of habitat use, concentrating on the higher ground in the late wet season when the grass is of short, or medium height, avoiding very short or very tall stands, or grass that is mature or flowering. Selection for species

Figure 5.1   The impala feeds to a great extent on grass. This one is undeterred by the close presence of elephants

was not found to be consistent, for what was favoured one season was rejected the next. It seems that selection is guided by the stage of growth rather than by species. In spite of the marked seasonal fluctuations in the proportions of different grass parts, the topi always selected for green leaf, avoiding stem and sheath, although elsewhere they have been recorded as taking sheath. Obviously the proportion of green leaf fell in the dry season, although as stem and sheath quality declined, the topi became more selective, trying to maintain a high protein intake. Thus they moved to keep themselves in grasslands of similar growth stages, height and proportions of leaf; in order to maintain the quality of the diet.

In the Serengeti this did not require the topi to be migratory, for it could obtain all of its wants in short, seasonal displacements which were no greater in extent than its daily movements. But formerly one of the most numerous of antelopes in western Africa, there it undertook large migrations in countries such as Chad, making use of vast floodplains in the dry season and migrating northwards with the onset of the rains.

The ranges of both impala and topi overlap extensively in the Serengeti, but nonetheless ecological separation occurs, for it appears that here the impala eats more sheath to the topi's leaf, although both eat the same species of grass. Although the two may be found feeding close together in this Jack Sprat situation, the impala generally shun the plains used by the large herds of topi. Overlap is greatest in the late dry season and least in the wet season, when each species uses different levels between higher and lower ground.

Antelopes such as the dik-dik, oribi, common duiker, bushbuck, steenbok and klipspringer, all use habitats that are not invaded by the migrants; whereas topi, hartebeest, waterbuck and reedbuck are separated partly by habitat and partly by the growth forms of the grasses that they favour. All of these species are greatly outnumbered by the migrants, of which the most numerous of all is the white-bearded gnu or blue wildebeest.

The migration of the Serengeti wildebeest is one of the best known and most studied migrations in Africa. It is probably true to say that it forms the greatest and most spectacular concentration of game animals found anywhere in the world today. This is the seasonal movement of almost one and a half million animals from their wet season range on the open plains, to their dry season refuge in the woodlands, making a round trip of about 400 km in this 25,000 sq km ecosystem. The main pattern of movement is determined by food supply, which in its turn depends upon rainfall, and which thus causes the movement to vary to some extent year by year, depending upon the vagaries of the rainfall pattern. Tommy and zebra are also involved in these migrations, with their populations numbering an additional three quarters of a million and a quarter of a million animals respectively.

Although reports from the 1930s, and earlier, referred to the vast numbers of wildebeest in this area ('Fifteen miles of game' was the caption to a photograph of wildebeest appearing in 1938) that they were migratory seems to have been taken for granted. Martin Johnson, the American wildlife photographer of the 1930s, captioned one of his photographs: 'This was a small bunch, the first of the big migration that came along a few days later when the plains were covered with millions of head of game ... yes, I mean millions. No other place on earth offers such enormous masses of wild game as these Serengetti (sic) plains.'

But it must be remembered that in those days there were no minibuses to whisk one out from Nairobi in a few hours into the midst of this spectacle; until the beginning of the 1930s visitors to the area had to go on foot. As a consequence only a small number of hunters reached there in the dry season, and they would have been unable to appreciate the seasonal displacements which the game might undertake. Following the residence of a game warden at Banagi in the western Serengeti in 1929, a better understanding of the system began to emerge. The wife of the warden wrote in 1937: 'Zebra migrate to the Plain along with the Wildebeest at the beginning of the rains.' But it is not until the mid-1950s that we find people commonly talking of a migration; after proposals were mooted in 1956 to reduce the size of the park created there in 1940 (and already reduced in size in 1951) from 11,600 to only 4,800 sq km.

By migrating to the plains, which furnish only seasonal grazing, the migratory species avoid competition with the other herbivores for a large part of the year. The itinerary varies, for the wildebeest being dependent upon water and preferring fresh green grass, tends to move through areas where it is likely to find both. The wet season and dry season ranges are approximately equal in size, and roughly equal amounts of time are spent in each. But there is a suggestion that the wildebeest leave the plains even though suitable grazing may still be available, to move to their rutting grounds; the movement serving to concentrate them into a smaller area. The timing of the movement to and from the plains is related however to rainfall, but there has been a longterm change, in that the northern part of the ecosystem, particularly the Kenya Mara region, has been used to a greater extent in recent years. Perhaps this is a necessity, dictated by the greater than five-fold increase in the numbers of wildebeest which has taken place since 1961.

Now it has been proposed that, where there is higher ground, as in the west of the area, the principal resident herbivores use this higher ground during the wet season when there is abundant, short green grass, and by their grazing they maintain it in this state. When it begins to dry out and the grass stops growing, then the grazers begin to move down to the low ground.

First in this procession come the buffalo, preceding the zebra; followed by the topi and then the wildebeest, with the tommy bringing up the rear. Buffalo appear to be as tolerant as zebra of tall, fibrous grasses, but the zebra takes a higher proportion of stem than do other species, being able to nip it off more effectively with its two sets of incisors; and also its digestion can make better use of the sugar content than can a ruminant. The topi is intermediate between the zebra and the wildebeest in selection, preferring a somewhat taller stage of growth than does the wildebeest, although taking principally leaf. The wildebeest's broader mouth is able to deal better with leaf which tends to spread horizontally rather than growing vertically. After the wildebeest has removed the rest of the top layer, the way is then left open for the tommy, which avoids long grass. This aversion may be because it cannot see predators lurking in it, but more importantly it now has access to the broad-leaved herbs or forbs of the ground layer which figure largely in its diet, and which are ignored by the other herbivores in the succession.

It is suggested that the sequence of events which has been described above, expresses itself on the plains, and leads to the seasonal migrations. The eastern plains of the Serengeti are likened to the higher levels of ground, and the western and northern parts to the lower levels. In the wet season all three migratory species are to be found on the plains; the zebra are the first to move off, opening up the tall grasses by removing the stems and exposing the leaves at the bases of the plants, allowing access by the wildebeest. Removing the majority of this tall grass the wildebeest leave a short cropped sward for the tommy, which makes use of the few scattered leaves which are left behind, but more importantly, the herbs. There is about a two-month lag between the wildebeest following the zebra; while the tommy follow the wildebeest after about three weeks, but they do not move to the north. We can understand why the zebra with their stiletto-type hooves are anxious to get off the plains as soon as they become wet and sticky.

Although this paints an elegant picture of ecological separation, it is probably only a half-truth. A moment's reflection makes one wonder how a mere quarter of a million zebra could prepare the way for six times that number of wildebeest. The wildebeest are undoubtedly able to cope without the zebra's assistance – just as they do elsewhere within their range. Although the zebra concentrates on stems in its diet, this is probably incidental to the wildebeest, which would find the leaf anyway.

The main beneficiary seems to be the tommy, for rather than competition there is a facilitation of energy flow into the gazelle population by the wildebeest; that is, the wildebeest makes easily available to the tommy what would otherwise be denied to it, through its impact on the plant community. On the western edge of the plains the wildebeest are estimated to have removed 85 per cent of the standing crop of grass, stimulating new growth which was then eaten by the tommy.

Two more Serengeti migratory species have not been considered as to date their movements still await study. These are the eland and the Robert's race of the Grant's gazelle. Predominantly browsers they do not form a part of the major cycle of events.

Of the three principal migratory species, not all of their populations participate, resident animals mingling with the migrants during their passage, but remaining where they are when the latter move on, albeit somewhat the worse off after the visitors have eaten up all of their resources. But depressed as the residents' populations may be by this sharing, or forfeiting, of their resources, they nevertheless apparently have no urge to migrate. This poses the question of why do the migrations take place at all?

Certainly any wildebeest remaining on the eastern plains during the dry season would starve, so the movement gives access to adequate food resources year-round. The wildebeest appears naturally to be a migratory, gregarious species; for its South African congener, the black wildebeest, also formerly existed in incredibly large numbers and conducted an annual migration. In the winter months it moved from the eastern Free State, over the Drakensberg into Natal, and back again at the onset of the rains. Other former large-scale migrations have also been reported, brought about by the existence of different grassland types, known in South Africa as 'sweet' and 'sour' veld. In the black wildebeest only 63 to 87 per cent of the diet consists of grass, which must be short and green; the rest is made up with browse. It tends to stay in a restricted area, keeping the grass short, and thus causes over-grazing when migration can no longer take place.

Although the two species are similar in their habits, the anomaly of the Serengeti wildebeest is that it is primarily a species of the moist woodlands of the southern savannas, and yet has attained these incredible densities at the very limit of its northerly range, under a rainfall of about 800 mm a year in the Somali-arid zone.

The Serengeti, although it is the best known, is not the only remaining example of antelope migration on the grand scale still to be found in Africa today. Another takes place in the plains at the foot of the Boma Plateau in the southern Sudan. Here, many of the species are migratory, but the most numerous among them is the white-eared kob. In 1983 its numbers were estimated at close to a million animals, thus rivalling the numbers of the Serengeti wildebeest.

Their migratory pattern is also determined by the rains. From May to August much of the grassland is flooded, at which time the kob remain on the better-drained soils to the south, moving northwards onto the open grasslands after the water subsides in late September to early October. In this way they spend a period of three to four months in each area, the remaining five months of the year being spent in covering the approximate 200 km between them.

The tall *Hyparrhenia* grasses that characterise the plains mature quickly and become useless as food, and the kob are obliged to maintain themselves on the swamp grasses along the banks of the major rivers. This forces them into dense concentrations, estimated at up to several thousand individuals per square kilometre. When the rains begin in May, they move back again in large groups to their southern feeding grounds.

Yet another species which occurs naturally in vast numbers is the lechwe, the white-eared kob's more aquatically-inclined relative found mostly in Zambia, but which extends into south-east Zaïre and Botswana. Instead of quitting the plains when they are flooded, this species exploits them. At the onset of the rains a fresh flush of growth takes place in all of the grasslands and pasturage becomes in ample supply. During the rains most valley grasslands become flooded and inaccessible to antelopes while the grasses mature. By the end of the rains the animals are either concentrated on the perimeter grasslands surrounding the floodplains, or are occupying wet season dispersal areas; but competition between the lechwe and other grazing species only occurs when prolonged high flooding forces the lechwe into other grazing areas. At other times the lechwe exploit a unique habitat that is unused by any other large mammal herbivore, namely the water meadow grasslands.

Feeding Patterns

Water meadow grasslands are a semi-floating sward of grasses and sedges which collapses when the water recedes, forming a thick cover to the ground and offering green food throughout the year. It is partially dormant during the cold season when parts of the area are deeply flooded, but lechwe will graze in water up to half a metre deep, feeding in water up to their bellies and sometimes even covering their backs. Old bucks immerse their heads and hook up submerged grass with their horns, but it is the does which spend most time in the water. Only during times of exceptional flooding is this resource denied to them, and then they are crowded into a narrow zone along the edge of the flood, often churning the ground into mud and destroying most of the grass.

Practically the whole of the seasonal grazing rotation of lechwe herds is on water meadow formations, the herds following receding floods and using the floodplain grasses as soon as they become accessible during the latter half of the dry season, then retreating before the rising waters. The lechwe require no facilitation by other, larger species, to expose their food resource for them.

Zebra, wildebeest and tsessebee all share the lechwe pastures in the dry season, but in the late dry season ample pasture is still available in the lechwe habitat, so competition is not critical. Thus the system is able to support dense concentrations of lechwe, which at one time occurred in herds of over 3,000 strong, within a total population estimated at a quarter of a million head. Even today, in one protected area, the Lochinvar Ranch, a density of over 500 per sq km has been recorded in the flood season. Deriving most of its food from the floodplain grasses, the lechwe takes more leaf than stem to satisfy a demand for a high protein diet. It seems unable to survive naturally on savanna grasslands and takes no browse to compensate for a possible deficiency of protein in the dry season, yet is said to do well in captivity in wooded enclosures without water. In nature however it is a species which is completely adapted to the floodplain cycle by virtue of its food requirements; it does not feed in permanent water because there is not the vegetation there.

A study conducted along a part of the Chobe River in Botswana, a river which meanders through an extensive floodplain, demonstrated that the lechwe, and its two close relatives, the puku and the waterbuck, all showed a preference for plants with the highest protein content; perennial grasses forming the bulk of the diet throughout the year. Although the preferred habitats of the three species overlapped to some extent, the individual choices prevented all three species from using the same food plants with the highest protein levels all at the same time.

The puku and waterbuck were obliged to make use of plants in August which were clearly inferior to those that the lechwe were enjoying on the floodplains. The sedge *Vetiveria nigritana* was used by the lechwe in December when the leaves were sprouting freshly in burnt areas, but the waterbuck used it in July and August. Again, annual grasses figured significantly in the lechwe's diet in January, while puku and waterbuck made little use of them. In March, when the lechwe left for the floodplain, the grass which they had been using in August, at a time when substantial parts of the floodplain were still submerged, was made much use of by the puku and waterbuck. This alternate switching served to lessen competition for the same resource.

Mind boggling as the numbers of wildebeest, white-eared kob, and at one time also, the lechwe, are, they pale into insignificance when compared to the incredible numbers of springbok which once inhabited South Africa. Numbers which have been described as 'literally in millions on millions'.

As for the wildebeest, there were two types of springbok: those which were resident, and those which migrated in large herds, the latter being termed 'trekbokke'. Although these treks resembled irruptions, a bursting out of excessive numbers seeking new ranges, they appear to have been more in the nature of migrations, for after rain fell the springbok returned whence they had come. Few remain today, perhaps a million, although trekking still takes place in Botswana and Namibia on a small scale; but their once staggering numbers deserve a mention.

The springbok appears to be a mixed feeder, taking up to 40 per cent of grass when there is fresh growth, but browsing almost exclusively in the dry season, taking several aromatic and even poisonous (to stock) shrubs. Normally the springbok inhabits semi-arid regions and is able to do without drinking water. According to one account they inhabited the immense tracts of desert south of the Orange River, which in normal years provided adequate water and food. But perhaps one year in four or five there was a prolonged drought. This caused them to assemble in vast herds, and to move together towards the Orange River, or south to the then Cape Colony. After rain fell they rather suddenly moved back again.

There were four 'really great' treks between 1887 and 1896, the latter year seeing the last of them. It has been suggested that the erection of fences and the slaughter apart, rinderpest may have been responsible for reducing springbok numbers after this.

Even taking into account a tendency on the part of the old Boers to exaggerate, the numbers involved appear inconceivable. There were reports of treks being so dense that they sometimes marched through the streets of small country towns, and of people seizing and slaughtering the animals by hand. One contemporary of the great treks recalled passing through a steadily moving herd for a distance of 75 km. Farmers had to move before the advance as cultivation was eaten bare, fences destroyed, and domestic stock trampled underfoot or carried along with the hordes.

In the last great trek of 1896 the animals moved well into Cape Colony, not having appeared in such numbers for the previous 30 to 40 years; calving at one point and then continuing to advance. One estimate was made of half a million head in sight of a herd which stretched, at varying densities, over an area of 5,300 sq km. As has been reported for the wildebeest in the Serengeti, when the herds reached a river, the leading animals were drowned, pushed in by the crush behind. At one time when they reached the sea, untold numbers were forced into the water and perished, likening their movements to the irruptions of lemmings.

The springbok is a unique example of antelope diversity, not solely on account of the incredible numbers which it once attained, but also by virtue of the fact that it is a mixed feeder and achieved these high densities in a semi-arid environment where resources are often at a premium. Browsers are generally small in numbers, for rich though their food may be, it is more widely scattered than is the grazer's grass layer, and so cannot be taken in as quickly.

The analysis of browse preferences is still in an early stage, the skeletal characters are still being explored and there are few studies based on this method which have been achieved to date. Attention has already been drawn to the fact that for browsers all is not what it appears to be. The endless woodlands of the Sudanian-Zambesian region provide only limited resources for exploitation by herbivores, for as the leaves of the trees and shrubs mature they accumulate poisons and are no longer edible. Thus browsers are restricted to young leaves and shoots (as well as fruits and flowers which are eaten with relish); but the young leaves are generally much richer in protein than grasses are. The range of species taken is usually wider than that of grazers, increasing with scarcity so that those animals inhabiting semi-arid to arid areas tend to have the most catholic tastes. In the dry season the choice may be somewhat narrowed due to the unavailability of many plants, particularly creepers and herbs.

A comparison of four browsers: the lesser kudu, gerenuk, giraffe and black rhinoceros, was conducted in Kenya's Tsavo East National Park, where the conditions may well have been atypical due to the destruction of the woody vegetation by elephant. All of the species studied depended heavily on woody plants and considerable overlap in feeding preferences was revealed, especially during the dry season. Gerenuk and lesser kudu overlapped by 34.5 per cent in the wet season and 38.4 per cent in the dry; which is probably not a significant seasonal difference. However the lesser kudu seeks denser vegetation than does the gerenuk which, although favouring some degree of cover, avoids the most densely wooded vegetation. The lesser kudu, on the other hand, prefers the dense evergreen riverine vegetation during the dry season, so that although the animals' preferences overlapped, there was nevertheless some difference in habitat choice. Browsing levels are also somewhat different, and the gerenuk's ability to stand erect upon its hindlegs enabling it to reach shoots up to 2 m from the ground is well-known.

Gerenuk are traditionally said to feed on 'thornbush', presumed to refer to such species as *Acacia mellifera*; but acacia species were rare in the area studied, so that the degree of preference for them could not be established. Here the gerenuk was seen to feed on leaves, shoots, flowers and a few fruits, of woody trees and shrubs. Some climbers and vines were also taken, but this was mostly in the rainy season; but no herbs or grass. This is essentially similar to the diet of the lesser kudu, except that it likes some grass, albeit an insignificant amount; but a variety of herbs is taken. No particular species was apparently preferred by the gerenuk, and at least 84 different species of woody plant were observed to be eaten; but some species were rejected entirely although known to be fed upon by other animals, including the lesser kudu. The composition of the diet varied seasonally, as well as from area to area, being dictated to a large extent by availability. Palatable items appeared to be recognised by scent, the animal sniffing a plant first before plucking it.

Figure 5.2   The gerenuk in typical feeding attitude

Another almost exclusive browser is the klipspringer, which has been studied both in South Africa's Cape Province and in Ethiopia. It was seen to be very selective of plant parts, the bulk of that eaten being growing shoots; but it fed on a wide variety of perennial shrubs, 41 species being taken in one area, and 63 in another. Although in Ethiopia up to 30 per cent of grass was reported in the diet, in the Cape Province no grass was seen to be taken, and only a small proportion of herbs. The klipspringer moves about all the time taking little bites here and there, but if flowers or fruits are present then it will spend a long time picking these; relishing fruit it will feed on favoured species until it has removed all within reach. In the spring in one area, it was observed to take up to 80 per cent of the flowers from shrubs. The dik-dik, another dainty feeder, has been seen to select a leaf and then drop it in favour of another, perhaps fresher one.

A partial browser, or mixed feeder, and the largest of antelopes, the Cape eland has been seen in South Africa to select at least 29 species of grass, and 57 species of browse plants. It browses throughout the year, but grazes fresh green grass when it is available. Studies of semi-domesticated eland and oryx in a semi-arid area of Kenya showed that, while both species grazed on the grass-herb layer early on in the season of growth, as the grass matured the eland turned its attention to browse plants, while the oryx continued to graze. When the deciduous browse plants lost their leaves, then the eland relied heavily on evergreen shrubs. Requiring a protein-rich food, the eland is unable to make use of the low levels of protein in mature grasses and is thus highly nomadic, requiring a large amount of browse to satisfy its bulk; but its search pattern is always related to a water supply.

On the other hand the oryx can do without drinking water and can feed on annual as well as drought-tolerant perennial grasses. The oryx's small mouth allows it to be selective, plucking only the protein-rich parts of the perennial grasses, while the annuals become cured on the stem, forming a highly nutritious hay. The oryx also makes use of the swollen stem storage organs of the plant *Pyrenacantha malvifolia*, and digs for underground tubers.

The giant eland seems to be wholly a browser, a fastidious feeder favouring above all the shoots of a fairly tall tree, widespread within certain limits of rainfall in the west African woodland, known as *Isoberlinia doka*. As this species is tall and with a smooth trunk, the giant eland is obviously limited to areas where young saplings are growing; but the species tends to grow in stands so that where there is one there will be another. Other favourite foods of the giant eland are the shea butter tree *Vitellaria paradoxum*, from which an oil is collected, hence its popular name; plus only two other species which are known to be taken. One is *Lonchocarpus laxiflorus*, a member of the pea family which bears masses of attractive hanging mauve blossoms; and the young shoots and heavily scented white flowers of a species of *Gardenia*. The gardenia is the only shrub that the giant eland is recorded as feeding on, and although there are three species, it is alleged that it will take only one of them. In captivity the giant eland tends to reject all else, although doubtless it has a wider range than the few species so far observed. It uses its horns to break off the branches of its favoured trees to feed on, and hunters make use of the sounds of the breaking branches to stalk them.

The smallest of antelopes, the dik-dik and suni, are concentrate feeders,

Figure 5.3   A baby suni, an inhabitant of the forest

making use of herbs and low shrubs; the dik-dik feeding extensively on litter. They have the highest metabolic rate and therefore the highest energy requirement of all the ruminants (apart from the pygmy antelopes), and meet this high energy demand, not by an exceptionally effective digestion, but by a rapid rate of fermentation in the rumen. This is achieved by using only easily fermentable foods, green and soft, high in protein and moisture content.

Summarising the feeding habits of antelopes, the species of plants which figure prominently in the diet in the wet seasons are presumably those which are most preferred, because at that time a greater choice is presented. Whereas, in the dry season an animal is obliged to take what is available. Many food preferences, which are more marked among the grasses, are consistent over large areas, particularly with regard to the more palatable species. The reason why small antelopes are selective feeders, in contrast to the large roughage grazers, is that the relatively high metabolic rate associated with small body size, requires a greater daily input of energy per unit of body weight than does a large animal.

Since rumen size is roughly proportional to body size, the best way for a small animal with its small rumen to assimilate more energy, is to select more nutritious food.

Thus the small antelopes are concentrate selectors, because they are small they need less food bulk than do large animals and so do not have to spend as much time in feeding. The klipspringer has one of the lowest recorded feeding times for any diurnal antelope.

We have already seen that these small antelopes tend to be intermittent in their feeding-ruminating, but the larger species divide up the day into an early morning period of intense feeding and an evening one. The rest of the day is then spent in rumination, digestion and other activities. Few all night studies have been conducted, but in the waterbuck I found that the buck at least, fed most intensively at this time. The intense evening feeding period continued until about eight o'clock at night, to be followed by an hour or two's rest or rumination, and then feeding would gradually increase again to a peak between midnight and two in the morning, when 50 per cent of the time was spent in grazing. Feeding activity would then decline in intensity to zero just before daylight; but although it was more intensive, in that it tended to be conducted without pausing, the periods were of comparatively short duration and long periods were spent lying ruminating. As we have seen, the night-time is important for feeding in arid zone species, which make use of the dew on the foliage.

How does an antelope know what is good to eat and what is not? A total of over 350 species of plants poisonous, or suspected of being poisonous, to man and domestic stock, have been recorded from East Africa alone. But they are not necessarily poisonous to wild herbivores, whose suscep-tibilities are little known. The most well-known example of poisoning is that of the eastern bongo. An important constituent of its diet is the setyot vine *Mimulopsis solmsii* which grows profusely among mountain bamboo. This plant flowers at irregular intervals of three to ten years, after which it dies back to produce a regrowth after two years which is highly poisonous, and large numbers of bongo apparently die from eating it.

Feeding habits in young antelopes are derived from a combination of apparently innate and learned behaviour; innate being the behaviour that they are born with and the learning coming from the older members. Observations on the calves of impala, gerenuk and lesser kudu, reared in captivity, all show that the animals will spontaneously reject some plant species and take others. A young klipspringer in the wild was seen to stand next to its mother while she fed, and appeared to investigate the plants that she took. Often moving to the same spot it would mouth and sniff at the flowers and shoots, sometimes biting off pieces for itself.

Migrations were, and in some cases still are, a means whereby a wider range of resource could be exploited than is otherwise available when it varies seasonally. It is the most spectacular expression of feeding behaviour among antelopes, and before the advent of intensive agricul-tural practices was probably much more widespread in Africa than it is today. As a consequence the numbers of many species exist at much lower levels than they would otherwise do, and have probably been obliged to modify their feeding habits accordingly.

6 Mother, offspring and growing up

The breeding seasons of animals inhabiting temperate zones are clear-cut, they follow a well-defined annual cycle of producing births in the spring so that the young can be reared on the new growth and, more importantly, the mother has ample food for the production of milk with which to feed her new-born. Among Africa's antelopes the pattern is not so well defined, for although there is a tendency to have distinctive breeding seasons to the north and to the south of the equator, as one approaches the equator itself most species are found to breed throughout the year; but nevertheless usually have two peaks in the east, related to the two rainy seasons there. Even so there are those species which adhere to a distinct annual rhythm even at the equator, notably the wildebeest.

Of wildebeest cows in the Serengeti 80 per cent produce their calves within three weeks, representing almost as tight a season as that of the blesbok in the extreme south of the continent, which produces 74 per cent of its young in just over two weeks. The topi has a season which is a little more spread out, and in some areas they apparently produce their young in waves, the result of successive movements of the cows into the bull territorial areas.

In most antelope species it appears that the male is sexually active throughout the year, although he may experience peaks and declines in the production of sperm; while the seasonally breeding impala and blesbok in South Africa become sexually active before the females come into heat. This produces the short, synchronised mating season. The black wildebeest in South Africa does not have such a synchronised calving as does its blue counterpart in East Africa, but breeding is nonetheless markedly seasonal, the calves being produced after the first rains, during the months of October–November.

Where conditions are favourable, and there is a good, year-round supply of food not unduly interrupted by seasonal changes, species outside of the equatorial belt also breed continuously; such as the nyala in South Africa.

Observations on two different populations of springbok at approximately the same latitude, showed that in one area the main rut was during the summer rainfall, with a secondary peak in the spring after most of the young were born. But farther west, the main rut was in the spring, coincident with a winter rainfall, and most young were born in the autumn. This suggested that it was the state of the vegetation which was the factor influencing calving.

Birth

Gestation periods in antelopes range from just over five and a half months in the dik-dik, which breeds twice a year, to about nine months in the eland; although for many species we still lack precise figures, and are obliged to use records going back to the beginning of the century.

Most concentrate food selectors show a double peak of births even in South Africa. Others, such as the klipspringer, Natal red duiker and the Cape blue duiker, breed throughout the year despite the southerly latitude with its cold winters. Among the neotragines in South Africa, all have a double peak except for the grazing oribi, which has only a single one. At the equator in western Uganda, I found that the waterbuck bred continuously, but had two peaks in the year. The same was true of the Grant's gazelle in northern Tanzania.

These double peaks in births are basically the result of the animals producing more than one young in the year. After the birth of a calf the female usually mates again three weeks later, when she experiences her first post-natal heat. If she is not successful in conceiving, which is not unusual among older animals or when drought conditions prevail, then she will continue to come into heat at regular intervals of about three weeks; although in the Uganda kob it is alleged to be short as one week. This means that on average slightly more than one birth per year is produced.

The production of birth peaks is complex, being partly due to the influence of nutrition, and partly to that of day length. Although the latter is almost constant at the equator throughout the year, there is still an annual cycle of change in light quality due to the movement of the earth in relation to the sun. This change may be perceived unconsciously by the animal (probably by the 'third eye' in the brain which all mammals have, otherwise known as the pineal body), to give it its cue for the timing of reproduction. The female does not think eight months or so ahead, mating in June so that she will produce her young in March, when conditions are at their best – the time of mating must be the result of a long process of evolutionary selection which has linked it to some constant cue.

What is unusual among female African antelopes, is that those which do not have a strictly annual rhythm, mate and carry the next fetus while still feeding the previous calf. Milk production ceases only about three weeks before the birth of the next.

Twins are almost unknown, but calves of many species often chum up together, leading to the supposition that they are 'twins'. There is one exceptional report of a waterbuck doe which was carrying three embryos.

Mating

In most antelopes the female comes into heat for little more than twenty-four hours. Usually when I have seen one in heat during the day, as shown by her consort of male or males, by the following morning she has returned to normal. She may give little outward sign that she is in heat, and so it is important for the male to be able to detect it since he isn't given much time. This is done by the male sampling the female's urine, for the reproductive hormones associated with heat, or ovulation, occur with increasing frequency in the urine as the period of heat approaches. I found in my waterbuck studies that whenever a doe, or a group of does, entered the territory of a buck, the buck would almost always investigate one or more of them; approaching quickly with head lowered and neck extended, in a posture usually signifying appeasement. Like all antelopes the horns are directed in the opposite direction to that which they are during threat.

Nudging the doe's hindquarters, the buck induces her to urinate, an almost reflex action on the part of the doe. Curling back his lips in a characteristic grimace, he samples the urine by letting it run over his lips and the end of his nose. Some antelopes take it into the mouth and then spit it out. Having taken his sample the buck then stands sheepishly for a few moments, grimacing and looking vacantly from side to side.

Urine sampling is a widespread phenomenon among mammals, occurring as it does in such diverse species as bats and rhinoceroses, but it is particularly characteristic of antelopes. The only exceptions are the hartebeest and topi. Each species tends to adopt a particular attitude; in the sable antelope the head is thrown right back as the bull grimaces widely, while the gazelles merely slightly open the mouth. The wildebeest, in contrast to its alcelaphine relatives, the hartebeest and topi, grimaces widely. It has been suggested that the hormonal content of the urine is detected by a pair of long, narrow sacs in the roof of the mouth, known as the vomero-nasal organ, at one time considered to be no more than a rudimentary accessory organ of smell. The strange grimaces associated with the sampling of urine appear to result from the closing of the nasal passages, in order to permit the odour to pass into this organ.

I found with the waterbuck that it did not seem to matter very much to the buck what state the doe was in, for having sampled her urine he would usually try to mount her anyway. But when a doe is coming into heat the buck may try to cajole her by rubbing his chin on her rump or flank, pushing into her udder region like a calf, or pawing her backlegs with a stiffly-extended foreleg. The latter is common among many antelopes, except for the tragelaphines. A doe in heat will stand and await the buck, making no attempt to avoid him; or she may be sufficiently excited as to try and mount the buck herself. The tragelaphines seem to have more of a courtship display than many species, the kudus and the nyala often displaying sideways on to the doe, with neck stretched in the air, then driving from behind they lay the extended neck on her back and mount in this posture.

The actual act of mating is performed by the buck rising onto his hindlegs, and is achieved with a single, quick movement, the doe usually walking forwards so that the buck is obliged to hobble after her. Due to its rapidity, true consummation is frequently difficult to detect in many antelopes, and casual observers have frequently referred to mating taking place, when it is actually no more than an exploratory attempt on the part of the buck, leading to much confusion in the literature over the time of mating seasons. In species which breed throughout the year, true mating is an uncommonly witnessed event because most does are pregnant; and when they do come into heat it is only for a very brief period.

After mating both partners may rest for up to half an hour or more before repeating the event. There is little difference between species, such differences as there are lie in the behavioural organisation of the male, or the type of territory that he holds. An exception is the Uganda kob doe which, when in heat or coming into heat, visits the buck territorial grounds for the express purpose of being mated. It is possible that the females of solitary territorial species also seek out the male when they are in heat, otherwise it is difficult to see how mating could be achieved.

Calves

When the period of heat has passed, if she has a calf then the doe returns to it. The waterbuck doe always calves in the territory of a buck, and when the territory owner discovers a doe which has just given birth, he sticks closely to her until she has her first post-birth heat. He shows no solicitous care for the calf which may be with its mother, and is indeed annoyed if it gets between him and the doe; but fortunately the calf does not accompany the mother all of the time, being what is termed a 'hider'.

Hiders are characterised by the young calf being hidden after birth for anything from two weeks, as in the eland, to four months, as has been reported for the reedbuck; and visited at intervals by the mother. The wildebeest is exceptional because the newborn calf is a 'follower', sharing this habit with only the topi, tsessebee and the bontebok. All the rest of the antelopes are 'hiders'. Predation is a matter of chance for the hider, and followers may be more at risk because they can easily become lost, as is often the case with wildebeest. Also followers tend to follow any moving object, be it motor vehicle or other animal species; even lions.

The colour of the wildebeest calf, with its black face and light sandy-coloured body, is quite unlike that of its drab grey parents, and may be

Figure 6.1 A newborn Thomson's gazelle relies on its concealing colouration for protection

designed to make it stand out among them, to minimise the chances of becoming swamped in the great imbroglio of bodies formed by the herds that this species naturally assumes. This makes the calf equally conspicuous to a predator of course, but perhaps this is the lesser evil, the chances of being lost in a herd of several thousand animals being greater than that of being picked off by a predator.

When the colours of hiders differ from those of the adult they are generally thought to resemble the ancestral pattern, and are usually cryptic. You can trip over the straw-coloured newborn tommy lying pressed flat against the ground on the open plains, before you can see it. When it is very young a hider simply has no instinct to run, pressing itself as flat as possible against the ground to eliminate any shadow, and relying on its concealing coloration to do the rest. Unfortunately this behaviour frequently leads to the finding of 'orphans', for whenever someone comes across a calf 'lying-out', as the hiding phase is termed, it seems that they simply cannot resist picking it up and carrying it off. If only such misguided persons could witness the distress of the mother when she returns to the spot looking for her offspring, perhaps they would think twice about their actions. When a leopard took a waterbuck calf that I had under observation, the mother hung about the vicinity for three days, continually going back to the spot where she had left the calf. Few hiders are probably 'orphaned'; indeed there is no such thing as an 'animal orphanage', only an animal prison.

I must confess that in my early days in Kenya I was the possessor of an 'orphan' steenbok; but had I not rescued it, it would have gone into the stew-pot of the Kikuyu women who found it while clearing land. Like so many of these animals, despite the care lavished upon it, it eventually died of an intestinal complaint; although this was three months later when it was already eating solid food. A remarkable habit of my pet was that before defaecating or urinating it would first scratch a hole just like a cat, an unusual behaviour among antelopes. It was useful for me because I was obliged to keep my pet largely indoors for fear of dogs attacking it, and whenever it began its 'rat-a-tat-tat' on the floor, or worse still started to paw the blanket on my bed, action stations were taken. The result was that I soon had it trained to a dirt-box like a cat.

We lived at the time in a rather draughty accommodation because the proprietor had knocked out all the windows in a fit of rage, and at that altitude one needed a fire in the evenings. Diddums, as my pet was named, would go to sleep by the fire in the evenings, but regularly in the morning at about three o'clock, when the fire had long gone out, he would leap onto my bed, thrust his nose into my face, and try to get under the bedclothes. Extraordinary behaviour for an antelope, that in the wild would just have to lie by itself in the cold night air and put up with it.

I have only been able to watch mother–calf behaviour in the wild with the waterbuck. In this species, about two days before she is due to give birth, the doe leaves the herd and takes herself off on her own to a suitable patch of thicket which will provide concealment for her confinement. This is an important choice for the young doe which is giving birth for the first time, as it probably determines her home range, the area in which she will live for the rest of her life. Records of does which I had captured and marked suggested that the doe always returned to the same place to give birth. One indeed returned to exactly the same spot three times in succes-

Figure 6.2   *There are no such things as 'animal orphans'. Young male and female common duiker vie for tit-bits, while a suni looks rather put out*

Figure 6.3   The pet steenbok calf which once belonged to the author

sion during the period of my study. Concealment during birth obviously has anti-predator advantages, as lions are always on the look-out for animals which behave in any way which is out of the ordinary. In the kongoni, which gives birth out in the open, it has been observed that other does will attack the doe in labour if she does not separate from the herd.

The waterbuck doe gives birth, like other antelopes, in the lying position, and rests awhile after the birth before rising and licking the fawn. This is a very critical period for both mother and calf because it is during this grooming phase that the mother–infant bond is cemented. Not only does the mother lick the calf as dry as she can, but the licking probably also stimulates the calf. The mother is induced to lick by the scent of the fluids, as a researcher working with captive eland found. When he smeared some of the birth fluid on himself, the mother would lick him as well as her calf, but became aggressive when she had licked him clean.

An equally important part of the bonding process when the calf stands, is the licking of its anal region, stimulating it to defaecate. The mother ingests the faeces so that no traces of the calf's whereabouts are left on the ground, and many species also eat the placenta. Stimulation to defaecate and ingestion of the faeces is continued at each suckling bout, and without it the calf would probably die of constipation; I suspect a frequent cause of death among captives. During the anal licking the calf holds its tail to one side and may react in some species by completely freezing. The worker referred to above, found that he could keep an eland calf completely motionless for several minutes by imitating the mother's action with his finger.

After a number of unsuccessful attempts the calf stands for the first time about 30 minutes after birth and finds the teats instinctively, its first desire being to feed. In some species it may be helped slightly in its first attempts by the mother nosing it in the general direction of her udder. Suckling takes place for the first time about 40 minutes after birth in the waterbuck, a similar length of time having been recorded for the hartebeest.

During my studies of the waterbuck I was made well aware of the strength of the mother–infant bond. I had come across a doe at nine o'clock one morning which had just given birth, and parked my Landrover a short distance away to watch and record. After an hour and fifteen minutes, when the fawn had successfully suckled on two occasions and was now resting contentedly with its mother lying by its side, I decided to move in and tag the calf as a part of the research that I was conducting. As I carefully edged the vehicle forward I expected the doe to get up and run off leaving the fawn behind, but it didn't happen that way at all. As I closed in, the doe, which had ignored me completely during all the time that I had been watching her, suddenly looked up at me in surprise. Her surprise quickly changed to alarm, and leaping to her feet she came storming towards me, halting a mere arm's length from the vehicle, where she challenged me to advance further. Snorting threateningly, standing rigidly erect with her hair on end, she looked a good foot taller than her usual height. It is hard to imagine the normally docile waterbuck doe looking aggressive, but this one had transformed herself into a sufficiently threatening-looking object as to make me change my mind and stay in the Landrover! Deeming discretion to be the better part of valour, I went in search of an assistant.

We were back within ten minutes, and when I approached this time the mother trotted off rapidly, the calf following behind. The pair had moved about 100 m away when, by driving suddenly around some bushes, I was able to separate them. Leaping from the vehicle my assistant and I seized the calf, which was standing looking momentarily bewildered by the sudden disappearance of its mother, who had continued on her way unaware that it was not following. Within seconds I had clipped a small plastic identification streamer to the calf's ear, but the brief pinch of the pliers caused it to utter a little bleat of protest. At this the mother came storming back through the bushes towards us, barely giving us time to leap ignominiously into the vehicle and drive off. But the indignant doe was not prepared to let it rest there, and promptly gave chase.

Fortunately there was no one to witness our cowardly flight from the enraged waterbuck mother. I have been charged by both elephants and rhinos, neither of which is a pleasant experience, but a waterbuck doe ... who would believe it? Nevertheless it was real enough, we found ourselves bouncing through the bush in our Landrover with the angry doe pursuing us for a good 75 m or more, persistently trying to butt the rear of the vehicle, which I just managed to keep out of her reach to avoid her hurting herself.

I am pleased to be able to record that I saw the gallant doe together with her calf shortly afterwards, although the calf did not survive for long, probably, as seemed to be the fate of so many in the area, falling prey to a hyaena. Of course, a more timid doe, less accustomed to the presence of human beings, would probably have behaved differently, keeping at a safe distance. Their usual reaction when I marked their calves was to run around me, simply snorting their disapproval, but never trying to attack.

A calf usually chooses its own place to lie out, as seems to be the case with other species; but if the doe is disturbed when with the calf, then she will lead it to a new spot. The calf does not have a regular 'form', but simply hides itself in the nearest long grass or thicket when the mother leaves it, and it finds itself alone. But unlike the kongoni calf, which leaves its mother of its own accord and goes to lie down, the waterbuck calf often does not want to leave its mother. Usually the mother makes her departure when the calf tires and lies down, or when it may simply be looking in the other direction; but at other times she may have to resort to a frantic dashing in and out of the bushes to shake it off. A behaviour which, when I first saw it, rather surprised me until I defined its purpose. But it is not all that easy, for when the calf sees its mother running away its instinct is to follow her; nevertheless she eventually outwits it, and left alone the calf's first instinct is to hide.

The mother may graze up to 1 km away, and at this time the calf is obviously very susceptible to predation if it does not remain hidden. As it gets older it tends to be attracted to other animals passing close by to its resting place, although this may be only when feeding time is approaching. On one occasion, when I saw a calf attracted from its hiding-place to a group of passing does, the rightful mother appeared shortly afterwards on the scene.

At first the calf investigated each of the strange does, trying unsuccessfully to suckle them, but unlike some species, which tend to be rather

Figure 6.4   A waterbuck mother rests with her young calf shortly after giving birth

brusque with strange calves, these does merely sniffed it gently and moved away when it tried to suckle. When its real mother appeared and saw what was happening, her first reaction was to advance cautiously, but then she seemed to identify her calf and walked straight up to it and let it suckle.

Like all newborn antelopes, the young waterbuck lacks the adult scent. The very strong odour of the waterbuck does not develop until it is about 14 weeks of age. This however seems to have little to do with protection from predation, because the newborn calf quickly has enough rubbed onto it from its mother to give it the characteristic adult smell soon after birth. I doubt whether predators try to sniff them out anyway, because the strong cloying scent of the adults must permeate the habitat everywhere. Any predator who attempted to follow up a scent would be continually following false trails.

Visits to the calf take place at about nine-thirty in the morning and last for an hour or so, getting longer as the calf gets older. Suckling takes place and the mother grooms and licks the calf each time, and removes all traces of its faeces. After the essentials are completed there is time for walking or playing with the mother. As in other species, playing consists of what are, in the adult, alarm gaits. Running madly round in circles the calf would suddenly break into a hackney gait, prancing in an erect stance as adults will do in the presence of hyaenas. Sometimes it will stott like a gazelle. In its second week the calf's play might extend to facing its mother and feinting from side to side with head lowered in threat. If the mother lowered her head in response to the 'threat', this would send the calf scampering off once more in mad circles, wild with delight. The head-down threat is an instinctive pose, present at a very early age, as I found when I presented a two-week old calf with a very small dog. The calf immediately made a head-down attack on it.

The boldness of the calf was shown to me on another occasion when a mother, running to her two-week old calf which had appeared from cover, was pursued by three curious bachelor bucks. The mother, anxious for her calf's safety, turned on the bucks and tried to drive them away, butting them forehead to forehead. The rather ungallant young bucks retaliated by fighting back, and seeing this attack on its mother the tiny calf ran up and unhesitatingly challenged the biggest of the bucks, which answered the calf's head-down challenge with a blow which sent it running back to its mother. Undaunted by this experience the calf then proceeded to take on one of the others, but the louts decided to leave the couple in peace and departed.

The duration of the initial phase of reciprocal stimulation, which takes place immediately after the birth of the calf, varies among species; 24 hours has been reported for the greater kudu, and 40 minutes for the Grant's gazelle. In the waterbuck it is probably of the order of two or three hours. From then on, among the hiders the calf will only be visited for relatively short periods, and as we saw these periods in the waterbuck tend to have to be terminated by the mother. My guess is that, for those species which give birth out in the open grassland, such as the kongoni or tommy, it is necessary that the calf has the desire to act independently of the mother, as she would find it difficult, if not impossible, to throw off the calf out in the open in full view.

The kongoni is unique among the acelaphine antelopes in having a calf which is a hider, with the possible exception of the bontebok which seems to occupy a rather intermediate position. The calf of the bontebok is said to hide in tall grass while its mother grazes, but if the calf is approached then the mother runs up snorting and the calf runs off with her, suggesting that it is kept under close observation by the mother. Although the topi calf is not as precocious as that of the wildebeest, it does follow its mother within a few hours.

In my observations on waterbuck I found that during the calf's play with its mother, the mother usually spending the time grazing, the couple may move some short distance away from where the calf was hiding. When the mother's departure takes place the calf does not go back to, nor does it try to find, the original spot, but simply enters the nearest piece of suitable cover; be it long grass, or more commonly, a thicket.

It is alleged that the mothers of most species will not approach and make contact with their infant actually at its hiding place, but wait some distance away for it to appear. This may be 20 to 40 m in the Uganda kob, to 10 m in the dik-dik. But if my experience with the waterbuck is anything to go by, then the mothers probably do not know the exact spot where their calves are lying; although the gerenuk is credited with recalling the spot very accurately. In the waterbuck I imagine that it is the mother's walking about in the general vicinity which attracts the calf from its hiding place, but it could be by calling to it.

The kudu mother calls her calf with a soft, smacking sound, and when the waterbuck calf is older it is certainly called by its mother. Sufficiently detailed observations have yet to be published on other species before one can determine how widespread this is among antelopes. Generally it is thought not to occur although it has been reported for the Uganda kob, and eland are very vocal. Eland mothers moo, while the calf replies with a whimper. The sable antelope grunts at its calf, but it is not clear in this species if the calling is used to attract the calf from its hiding-place. I discovered that it occurred in the waterbuck, a species which was credited with being mute.

One day in my vehicle I was following a waterbuck doe when I became aware that the low, intermittent squeaky noise in the background, which I had put down to being made by the swifts flying over the bushes, was actually being made by the animal which I was following. Sure enough, she soon met up with her calf. Once I knew what to listen for, I could stand outside of my house in the morning at about eight o'clock, and actually hear the chorus of mothers' bleats in the distance as they called to their young. I have watched a mother call her six-month old calf out of a group to suckle with bleats audible from 100 m away. The calf may answer with a more high-pitched call, which sounds rather like a squeaky penny tin trumpet. Sometimes the wrong calf answered, but after mutual sniffing no further interest was shown by either party.

My observations suggested that a combination of sound, scent and sight might be used for recognition in the waterbuck. Sound, as we have seen, because the mother calls her young; and scent, because this is followed by sniffing before acceptance. On one occasion I watched a four-month old calf stand and stare before running to its solitary mother. The wind was blowing from the calf to its mother so that it could not have scented her. This suggests that visual recognition may also play a part. Other evidence for visual recognition was provided on two separate occasions by calves which were lying apart from their mothers, although no longer lying-out in the strict sense of the term. These ran to a termite mound when they were disturbed, and climbed it to look for their mothers. In one of the cases, the calf, disturbed by me, ran to a mound, climbed it, saw its mother, and apparently recognising her by sight, ran to her. In the other case, the calf was disturbed by a herd of buffalo, and climbing a termite mound to scan the horizon, was rewarded by the sight of its mother about 500 m away. She was coming to look for the calf, perhaps because she had seen the buffalo in the vicinity. The calf ran to her, and rubbed its face eagerly on her forequarters before suckling.

Sometimes, when they have reached the following-at-heel stage, two waterbuck calves may team up together and follow one doe, but I was never able to determine whether they were both allowed to suckle her. Where waterbuck densities were high, 'nurseries' of young animals were found, as many as six calves resting together some distance from the grazing adults. But these groups are not nurseries in the strict sense of the term, for they appeared to be associations of choice on the part of the calves, and were quite unguarded. There were no 'aunties' to watch out for them for predators.

Such groups are also reported for impala, topi, tsessebee and sable antelope. In the latter species, if danger threatens the older animals run one way and the calves, when in a group, another. They then hide, sometimes altogether, as many as eleven having been seen to do this. In the tsessebee, calves of only a few hours old tend to associate in groups of two to five, often resting together while the mothers graze nearby. In the topi and tsessebee this may be related to a relatively precocious existence in the open, though the calves not being quite as advanced in this respect as the wildebeest, are unable to keep up with their mothers all of the time. Its only defensive object must be as for the grouping of adults in gregarious species, the hope that the other fellow may be the one to get it if a predator comes along. But it seems to be more of a question of young animals simply preferring to associate with others of similar size, rather than having any survival value.

Perhaps on account of its lying-out period when newborn, the waterbuck calf is an independent creature. Often it does not stick close to its mother when it is in the at-heel stage, but if the mother knows that danger is present then she will try to lead the calf away from it; just as she was seen to do in the lying-out stage. One day I came across a three-month old calf standing quite motionless near to the path which two lionesses had taken about three hours beforehand. The calf, which must have smelt their passage, literally looked too terrified to move, standing as if transfixed to the spot. It was not long before the mother appeared, and note that in all of these accounts the mother always seemed to arrive on the scene just at the right time. She stalked warily towards the calf, frequently standing motionless and staring intently for long periods at a nearby bush. I knew that the lionesses had left the area, but she did not; indeed, did she even know that they had been present or was it the calf's attitude which warned of predators? The calf continued to stand as if mesmerised until its mother reached it. She licked it once, lightly on the forehead, an unusual gesture of affection among the normally undemonstrative waterbuck, and then turned and walked slowly away with the calf following.

On yet another occasion I was witness to a hyaena running near a group of does, which scattered at the hyaena's sudden appearance. The latter was intent upon some strange business of its own and kept on running without so much as a sideways glance. But one of the does trotted after it, to be followed by another, and although the hyaena soon disappeared into the distance, the does continued to watch intently in the direction in which it had gone. Driving around, I found a calf lying immobile in the grass, which the hyaena had passed within a few metres of.

I calculated that just over 50 per cent of the waterbuck calves in my study area never reached weaning age, most of them dying in the first two weeks of life; that is, during the lying-out period. Why then do so many antelopes use this method in which the survival of the calf depends simply upon chance, the chance that a predator will not stumble upon it? Perhaps there is no alternative. Unlike the precocious young of the wildebeest, most other antelopes are too weak to keep up with their mothers for long after birth. The mothers of most species have no offensive weapons with which to defend the calf. They are not very good at biting, and though a kick might be nasty for a man it would have no effect upon the thick hide of a carnivore. Butting with the head of the hornless female antelope is more of a gesture than anything else, and is certainly no deterrent to a carnivore.

For species which give birth in the dry season, such as the kongoni, the lying-out calves would seem to be particularly vulnerable to being burnt to death in grass fires. Nevertheless I do not know of any cases of this happening, and although I have found the remains of an adult reedbuck immolated in its form, I have never found remains of calves.

One day in the Bamingui-Bangoran Park, in the Central African Republic, I was parked on a freshly-burnt area in the wake of a grass fire, when a very young common duiker calf came along calling for its mother, confused and frightened by the fire but nevertheless unhurt. It came and lay down in the shade of the Landrover and was sufficiently young to be easily caught by hand. I offered it some water from my bottle but it wasn't interested, so I released it knowing full well that its mother would soon come looking for it.

Maturation

Should a calf survive the rigours of early life in the bush, it is not weaned until the mother's milk dries up in preparation for the production of colostrum for the next birth. At the equator antelopes do not have a prolonged dry period and a continuous breeder like the waterbuck may only be dry for three or four weeks. Calves may be weaned at nine months of age in the waterbuck, a similar period being reported for several other antelopes of similar size; but by the time that it is seven months old the calf will be spending just as much time in grazing as does the adult. Calves commence to graze at a very early age, so that if they lose their mothers at as early as three weeks, as in one recorded case, they can still survive. When she is dry the waterbuck mother turns on her offspring and tries to drive it away; but this is of a relatively gentle nature, for waterbuck does are never violent. A harmless butting of the calf when it approaches is usually sufficient.

Weaning and separation are two different things, and the young doe keeps up her relationship with her mother for some time after weaning has taken place, but does not accompany the mother when she goes off to calve. The young buck, on the other hand, may be separated from his mother at an earlier stage by territorial bucks, who show antagonism to other bucks accompanying a doe too closely. But this is not until the youngster's horns have made their appearance at about nine months of age, just about the time that a full weaning period would finish.

The Buck

In following the career of an antelope from calfhood to adulthood, I will continue to take as my central theme the waterbuck, a species which I have studied in some detail. Waterbuck are territorial, a subject to which we will return later, but before becoming territorial the buck must pass a period of about five years between the time that it leaves its mother and the age at which it can normally become territorial and participate in breeding.

During this period of waiting and maturation, it is known as a bachelor buck, and has a gregarious instinct, associating with other young bucks of up to territorial age in bachelor herds. Such herds are common to many gregarious species of antelope, and were noted by hunter-naturalists long ago. But the latter usually stressed the fact that they were made up of old bulls, those which could no longer compete for females. In the waterbuck I found no evidence of this, the herds were always made up of young bucks which had not yet obtained a territory; and old bucks would rather live on their own somewhere in a peripheral habitat, than join a bachelor group. This is not the case with all species, and among the kob, impala and wildebeest, there is a movement back and forth into and out of bachelor herds. But this cannot be so with the waterbuck, because the bachelor herd uses the territories of the adult bucks, who would not tolerate old bucks in them.

The role of the bachelor herd is to provide a measure of safety for the buck from the time that it is separated from its mother, until it can stand on its own feet as a territorial buck. So we do not find such herds among the eland, which is not territorial, the bulls in this species forming part of a mixed herd of males and females; although we do find that the most dominant associate together, or perhaps are kept together by the leading bull.

Once the young buck's horns make their appearance, at about eight to nine months of age, it is no longer tolerated keeping close to the does by adult territorial bucks. But even without horns the young male calf can be recognised for what it is by the adult buck, and I have witnessed a six-month old calf chased away from its mother by a bellicose buck. When the buck gave up the chase the calf returned to its mother, who gave it a reassuring lick on the flank. Had it been three months older I have no doubt that she would have repulsed it.

The rate of horn growth in the waterbuck is rather slow compared with that of many other species. The fastest known is that of the oryx, in which the calves are actually born with short stumps; while in the wildebeest and the hartebeest the horns first make their appearance at about one month. It may be significant that in these three species both sexes are horned, so that their appearance does not distinguish them sexually. In the impala they first appear in the second month, but this species matures much more quickly than does the waterbuck, the male becoming territorial at two and a half to three years of age.

In contrast to the gentle butting of the doe, these initial harassments by

Figure 6.5   Horn growth in the defassa waterbuck. The age is given in years, adult horn length is reached at six years old

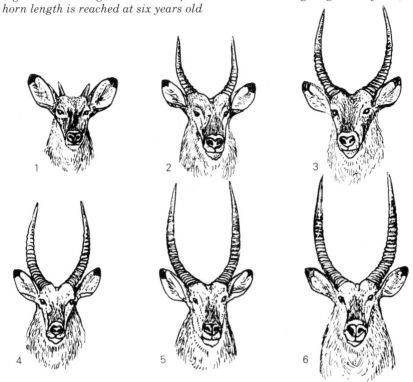

Figure 6.6   Horn growth in the Grant's gazelle, in which adult horn length is reached in three years

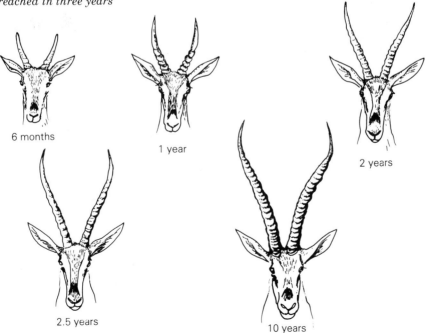

the bucks consisted of short, aggressive vigorous chases over a distance of about 30 m; the buck soon giving up the chase and the youngster wandering back to the doe group keeping a careful eye on the bully. Such repeated antagonism quickly has the desired effect of making the youngster seek more congenial company, and if there happens to be a bachelor herd in the area, then he joins it.

But separation from the mother may not be abrupt; some juveniles are reluctant to break the maternal bond, and although they may join a bachelor group, they rejoin their mothers again a few days later. When this happens the mother is also unwelcoming, so that sooner or later they get the message and stay away. Wildebeest calves join a bachelor group as yearlings, when their horns are quite long spikes and when the mother has her next calf at heel. They are thought to encourage harassment by the territorial bulls from their habit of trying to come between the calf and the mother, which attracts the bull's attention to them.

If there is no bachelor herd in the vicinity, a waterbuck youngster that has been chivvied from its mother's side, may be obliged to take up a virtually solitary existence; in which case it may attach itself at a respectable distance to a territorial buck. One such of my acquaintance lived for ten months like this. Although it associated with the bachelor group which lived in the area and passed by from time to time, it never joined them. Generally it appeared to be tolerated by the adult buck, but every so often bursts of rage were vented upon it, and the unfortunate youngster pursued vigorously with murderous intent, a chase once lasting a full five minutes before the adult was exhausted. Undoubtedly the youngster only escaped being horned to death by its greater fleetness of foot; running round and round in large circles, it uttered plaintive, protesting bleats, until the adult buck finally gave up. So fixed was this young buck either on the spot, or on the adult, that it never ran out of the territory into another one, but simply went round in circles.

Eventually it did join the bachelor herd, but in areas of high lion predation such solitary young bucks probably do not survive for long. Most joined up with the nearest bachelor group quickly, and remained firmly integrated into its company. The youngest buck that I recorded doing so was one of about eight months of age, while most had achieved membership by the age of one year, staying in the herd until they were about six.

This relatively long period of bachelorhood is related to the slow maturing process. Among the small forest antelopes the youngster seems to be driven out at an early age, but then the whole life process is accelerated. A dik-dik for example becomes sexually mature at six months of age. These small species have no bachelor groups, and the ousted youngsters must learn to live an independent existence from scratch. The oribi seems to differ, for it lives mostly in couples and the young male is permitted to stay with his mother for the first year, while daughters may stay for longer than this.

The waterbuck system is typical of that of many antelopes. In the smaller, but gregarious, impala, the territorial bucks also harass the young weaned bucks which they find accompanying their mothers. The mothers show no aggression towards them at this stage when they are about five months old, and the length of their horns is more or less equal to that of their ears. As in the waterbuck, they are not chased out of the territory by the adult buck, only out of the female groups. They are likewise obliged to find refuge in a bachelor herd, but seem to spend much more time lingering on the edge of the maternal herd before doing so; and even then rejoining it after an initial absence, full integration with the bachelor herd taking them from three, to as much as eight, months.

In the bontebok, both sexes start to leave their mothers during the height of the calving season, when they are about a year old. At this time groups of yearlings can be seen together; or some might be solitary, and some seem to return to their mothers after the latter have calved, as in the wildebeest. Others remain with the parent well into their second year, especially if she has not given birth, but the majority separates within three months of the calving. Unlike most other species, they seem to do this of their own accord, there being little evidence of harassment by territorial bulls. The bontebok differs also in that yearling females may associate with the bachelor herds until well into their second year.

Among the kongoni in Kenya, the young remain with their mothers also until almost two years of age. Up to the age of about ten months the young males simply follow their mothers without any change in behaviour when in the presence of the territorial bulls. But from that age onwards, whenever they meet such a bull they exhibit a type of deferential behaviour which consists of retracting the neck and making a quacking sound. Territorial bulls sometimes toss their heads in answer to this, but do not usually chase the young males. If they are chased, their mothers often follow them. In the population studied, the age of separation was not definite and ranged from as little as 10 months to 30 months of age, often coinciding with the birth of a new calf. Once the youngsters were leading separate lives the territorial bull would no longer tolerate them, and always chased them out of his territory.

After this the young kongoni male would try to join a bachelor group, which in this species occupied areas separate from the territorial network. Sometimes they were repulsed in this and were then forced to live in marginal scrub habitat not favoured by other kongoni, or they joined with others who had been similarly rejected by other bachelor herds, thus forming groups of their own of similar age. By the age of two years however, most had become accepted into bachelor herds, which comprised anything from two to 100 animals; although they continually broke up and reformed again. Grooming between the members of such groups takes place, and also much sparring. Pushing forehead to forehead, they tangle the horns and sometimes clash them together by leaping forward onto their 'knees'. These contacts serve to produce a linear hierarchy, sorting out who is tougher than whom, as they do in other gregarious species.

Maximum size is reached by the kongoni in two and a half to three years, half the time that it takes a waterbuck. At about four years of age dominant bachelor bulls leave the group and live on their own, challenging territorial bulls. If they do not succeed in soon winning a territory for themselves, then they return to the bachelor herd for a while, before leaving it once more to try their hand. A similar behaviour has been reported for the Lichtenstein's hartebeest in Zambia.

Sable antelope operate an intermediate system, the young bulls not being chased out of the female herds until they are over three years old. It is interesting to note that in this species the young bulls look like the cows: both sexes are horned, and they both have the same roan-coloured livery when young. An adult bull might therefore find it difficult to identify young males, and so the system operates to prevent undue harassment of the cow herds, the young males not being chased out until their coat colour begins to darken. As in the waterbuck, sable bulls do not become territorial until they are six years old.

In the bachelor herd the young buck, of whatever the species, enters a linear hierarchy, up which he progresses as he grows. When the herd size is small this is fairly straightforward in the waterbuck, for it simply means that each animal dominates the ones that are younger to it. Where births are spaced out, as they are in seasonal breeders, this dominance is achieved almost entirely from weight, the heavier animal demonstrating his weight during sparring contests. But if the herd is large, then complicated hierarchies develop at different levels when there are several males of similar age and weight. Dominance may then be established by skill and aggression.

Among the waterbuck, sparring bouts, in which usually all members of the bachelor group take part just as if they were programmed work-outs, usually take place in the early morning, especially after light rain. The head to head sparring which this entails is of a relatively inoffensive nature, and if two participants get too vigorous an older one comes up and separates them, taking on the most aggressive one himself. This is not, as one might be tempted to think, to maintain law and order, but for the older one to assert his dominance; just showing the other that he must not get too cheeky. It has the incidental advantage of saving the weaker members from harassment by those members of the group which are too truculent.

The programmed nature of these bouts means that all the rest of the group's activities of feeding, ruminating and resting, are conducted in a harmonious manner without strife. Some species however, such as the Grant's gazelle, are credited with being somewhat belligerent; the young bucks being notably active and aggressive. Impala, on the other hand, are more like the waterbuck, but even more amicable towards one another, to the extent of indulging in mutual grooming.

Waterbuck bachelor groups may range in size from two to 60 members, even more, but the average I found to be about five. Although they may be reported in the same areas for many years, such groups are by no means permanent, and in large regions develop and die out in different parts of the range. If two or more young bucks leave their mothers in an area where no bachelor group already exists, then they may form the nucleus of a new one, eventually perhaps being joined by other, younger recruits. One herd of twelve that I had under observation, had a rather crowded second-year age group with five members. One day three of them emigrated, swimming across a channel of deep water, and I later found that one of them had joined up with another bachelor group. Perhaps they had been stampeded by lions, although I could find no evidence of this.

It was my experience that bachelor herds tended to operate a 'closed shop', being joined only by young bucks who left their mothers in the area in which the herd lived. Several attempts were made by older outsiders of two to three years of age to join the group that I had under observation, but none succeeded. They were simply harassed by the older members until they left; which was usually after two or three days. No actual fighting was seen to take place, the oldest member of the bachelor group would simply keep following the newcomer around with his nose against the latter's tail, or indulge in pushing with the forehead, but the horns were never used.

The size of bachelor groups does not seem to be related to density, except in an indirect manner. Obviously the more waterbuck there are in an area, then the bigger will be the bachelor groups. But my analyses suggested that grouping was related more to circumstances than intent. Thus in a small, relatively confined area, such as a lake peninsula, herds were rather consistent in size because the animals would, by chance, keep on running into one another. In large areas, by contrast, groups might break up and come together again less often. With impala, the much larger bachelor groups continually split up and reform, and in the dry season some tend to become nomadic, moving up to 10 km away, but returning again to their original range when the rains break. It seemed to me that fundamentally the tendencies creating grouping in bucks and does were the same; chance encounters in a restricted area, more than a conscious wish to associate together.

Like doe groups, bachelors occupy a home range; an area which covers the territories of several adult bucks which tolerate the bachelors' presence. My studies suggested that the territories of some bucks were more favoured than those of others, some were avoided entirely. But this may have been due to the food or habitat type, rather than tolerance or intolerance on the part of a territory owner. Over a period of time these home ranges changed in position, and their sizes varied according to the suitability of the habitat and its resources of food and proximity to water.

In one area eight bachelors occupied a range of 100 ha while in another four occupied 340 ha. But this is small compared to that observed for impala in the Serengeti, where bachelor herds had a range of 600 ha.

Where I studied my waterbuck, breeding was continuous throughout the year, so the situation was not the same as in those areas farther from the equator, where breeding is of a seasonal nature. Thus in Zambia it was found that the bachelors were excluded from the territories of the bucks during the mating season. Some workers assert that sub-adult males are only found in peripheral habitats, habitats that are too poor to support females or adult breeding males. But this was not my finding; in one case the bachelors shared 75 per cent of the range occupied by the does. Where a species has a quick turnover, such as among the smaller mammals which have multiple births, young males can be relegated to areas where their chances of survival are impaired. But in slowly maturing species it is clearly necessary that adequate numbers of young males survive to maturity to fill the gaps in the adult ranks, and their chances of achieving this would be considerably lessened if they were unable to share the same resources.

Although they become sexually mature at three years of age, waterbuck males have little chance of mating for another three years, when they can hold down a territory for themselves. Being sexually active probably provides the drive for territorial possession, and during their life in the bachelor group they will have learnt how to fight and what confers dominance. Similar motivation probably exists among other species, but very dense species have a more rapid turnover. Bachelors become territorial at an earlier age and only hold their territories for a short while before rejoining the bachelor herd, allowing others to take their place. This is the situation found in the wildebeest, where the bachelor herds consist of hundreds of animals. Impala join a bachelor herd at six months of age, and remain with it until they are about two and a half years old, rejoining again after abandoning or losing their territories. Lechwe mature in their third year, and kob in their fourth, exhibiting a similar type of behaviour.

The Doe

In contrast to the male, the female waterbuck 'grows up' very quickly. She passes straight from juvenile status to breeding female, but sometimes life is made just as hard for a young doe as it is for a young buck. After weaning, antagonism is shown towards young does by their mothers just as much as it is towards a young buck, and those getting too close to their elders, or getting in the way, find themselves butted firmly and vigorously. The reaction of the young doe however is just to move aside and continue with whatever she was doing. But the antagonism has its effect, for a number become separated from the maternal group.

When this happens the young doe may lead a bewildered, solitary existence for some months on the outskirts of the group. But most of them team up together, possibly forming spinster groups, and these can display antagonism among themselves just like the bachelors. They even butt one another head to head, perhaps to establish a hierarchy, but such behaviour is not common and was rarely witnessed.

The members of these groups ranged in age from 18 months to three or four years; the older ones perhaps being infertile does which had persistently failed to conceive.

It was clear that some young does were allowed to remain with the maternal group, while others were not. What guided this choice I was unable to determine, and as far as I know it has not been reported in other species, more through want of study than the probability that it does not take place; but it was interesting to note that some form of control of numbers was obviously practised by the female sector of the population.

Those which are ousted from their mother's range probably emigrate. I had evidence of only one actually doing so, but waterbuck does are difficult animals to keep track of, because they usually lack distinguishing features with which one can easily recognise them. Four others emigrated after capture and release; the longest distance that one of these travelled being 32 km, where she was found killed by a lion some months later.

Once they have given birth in a particular area, does seem to be accepted by others as being a member of their home range, and no longer find themselves objected to by the others.

7 Life's game of chance

During its lifetime an antelope will be exposed to many risks of death from accidents or fights, but above all from three major factors: disease, predation and drought. Only one of these threats can it consciously take action to minimise, and that is predation.

In the months of January and February the wildebeest of the Serengeti plains produce their young, and in the space of three weeks perhaps 400,000 calves appear. Wildebeest are remarkable animals, for apart from having one of the most synchronised calving periods known to exist among the antelopes, they are also distinguished by giving birth to the most precocial young known in all of the mammalian kingdom.

Calving takes place out in the open, on the plains. Not that this can be any defence against lurking predators, for as soon as the calving starts there is no hiding the fact, and the predators are alerted for miles around. But the advantage is seen in the predators being overwhelmed with prey: they cannot kill all of the calves when so many are produced at once. Such synchronised calving, which implies of course an equally synchronised system of mating, for which the trigger as yet remains a mystery, is considered to be related to grouping. The greater the tendency to group, the more synchronised the calving.

The first one or two calves to appear is an event which causes the other wildebeest cows to crowd round, excitedly trying to examine and sniff them. But soon almost all of the cows are engaged in the same thing, and among the indescribable uproar of half a million honking wildebeest, accompanied by the rush and snap of hyaenas, it must be a bewildering world indeed for the calf to be born into.

But if danger threatens, the mother can urge her newborn calf to its feet in minutes, the calf running away in an average of seven minutes from the time that it was first expulsed from its mother. Times even as short as four minutes have been recorded. No other terrestrial mammal is endowed with such precocity. The calf may even 'wake up' before it is fully born, shaking its head, struggling, and bleating while still held by the mother. Within three minutes most are struggling to rise from the ground, and the majority is able to stay on its feet within another three. Although the calf may remain unsteady on its feet for the first few hours, some start to gallop around their mothers before their coats are even dry. They are able to run quite fast from birth because they are born with disproportionately long legs, which provide them with a wide gait.

This outstanding precocity has intrigued me, and I have conducted some research into trying to determine its causes. The big question is: where does this remarkable newborn calf get its energy from? During the last few days before birth fetuses lay down large stores of sugars, in the form of fructose and glucose, which are passed to them through their mother's bloodstream. These sugars are stored particularly in the liver, but also in the heart and other muscles. The phenomenon has been well-studied in sheep, and at one time it was thought that this store of sugars was to provide energy to burn to keep the newborn lamb warm. Subsequent studies have shown that the amount is too small to be significant in this respect; it would be used up within a matter of minutes, or at least hours. It is now believed that its purpose is to provide the newborn with sufficient energy to allow it to suckle its first meal. Thus the same high levels are found in the livers of baby rats, which are born blind and helpless; as well as in human babies and monkeys. I have found that they are also present in the newborn of the Grant's gazelle and wildebeest; but although the levels are high, it has not been possible to tell whether they are higher than those reached in other less precocious animals which have been investigated.

Protection against cold does not seem to be a problem among the newborn of African antelopes, although we need to know more about the breeding seasons in western and southern Africa, as well as at higher altitudes, before we can be sure about this. The bulk of our studies stems from East Africa, where the climate is relatively benign. The wildebeest of the Serengeti, for example, does not experience winter snowfall, as the black wildebeest does in parts of its range in South Africa.

My field observations suggest that most antelopes give birth in the early morning, so that the wet coat of the newborn will be warmed by the rising sun; and not, as is popularly supposed, at night to avoid being spotted by predators. Death from hypothermia resulting from being born when the temperature may be low at night, would be a much more *certain* event than is the chance of being taken by a predator when birth takes place during the day. In the wildebeest most births are between six in the morning and noon; but kongoni, which also give birth out in the open, seem to peak in the afternoon.

Although it may not need to burn sugars to keep warm, the newborn wildebeest must get energy from somewhere, otherwise it would be obliged to lie helpless for the first few hours like a newborn lamb: and this energy must come from sugars, as fat deposits could not be converted to energy quickly enough. Or is it that, if it is obliged to run for its life to escape a predator before it has had time to suckle, as is frequently the case, it dies afterwards? The expenditure of energy that such running demands, could leave its muscles charged with lactic acid (caused by the breakdown of the sugars when they release energy), and with no energy left to take that first, vital meal. This is a question which still awaits an answer.

One worker has suggested that the time of the wildebeest calving on the Serengeti, in January and February, coincides with the period of the year when grass growth is at its best, forming abundant nutrition for the mother to produce milk. But the kongoni in Kenya, although it gives birth throughout the year, has two peaks; one in each of the dry seasons when grass is poor. Yet in spite of this the kongoni mothers somehow normally manage to produce all the milk that is needed.

Suggestions have been made from time to time that antelopes can prolong their gestation, calving when the conditions are just right and waiting perhaps up to two weeks for rain to produce a fresh growth of grass. There is no evidence to show that this is other than an association of ideas in people's minds; there is no known physiological mechanism by which gestation can be prolonged. During the drought in Kenya in 1960–1, all of the wildebeest calves in the Nairobi Park died shortly after birth, the mothers being unable to provide milk for them.

We have to face the fact that, under normal circumstances, very few young antelopes actually survive. In most cases I would put the loss at least as high as 50 per cent in the first year, and sometimes it can be as high as 80 per cent, as has been recorded for waterbuck in South Africa. The stock farmer may well be envious of the hartebeest's sleek appearance in the dry season, but what farmer would tolerate such losses as these among his calves? In the wild this is normal, a high rate of mortality among the young indicates a healthy adult population. If this were not so we would soon be over-run with antelopes, and of course, every other living creature. It was Charles Darwin who calculated that if a pair of elephants brought forth six young in every 60 years, then in 750 years there would be 19 million elephants alive, all descended from the first pair. This is a total which the Serengeti wildebeest could theoretically achieve in about thirty years.

The case of the Serengeti wildebeest is a special one to which I shall have to return again; but normally the young can only fill gaps which are left in the ranks by the death of adults. In the healthy, balanced population, a good proportion of the adults will survive well into old age, making use of all the available habitat and its food resources. African antelopes always breed at the maximum rate, we do not find females absorbing their fetuses in times of poor nutrition, as is the case with some North American ungulates. Thus if gaps in the population appear, they can be filled immediately. But there is no altruism, or regard for the future wellbeing of the young; the young are the expendable part of the population. It is this fact which explains the remarkable resilience of antelope populations, which recover their numbers after droughts or other catastrophes with astonishing rapidity.

Disease

But why has the Serengeti wildebeest continued to increase from an estimated quarter of a million animals in 1961, to a prodigious 1.4 million in 1980? The answer lies in disease. From about 1889 to 1896, a terrible malady struck the ungulate populations of Africa, both wild and domestic alike. Not only were antelopes affected, but buffalo, giraffe and warthog as well. This was the great rinderpest plague; a virus disease which swept the length and breadth of Africa, causing an estimated 90 to 95 per cent of deaths in all of the populations which it struck.

Believed to originate in the steppes of Russia, this dreadful disease was nothing new to Europe, where it had repeatedly struck the cattle causing a similar rate of mortality. Jack Hawley, a Doncaster farmer who died in 1875, insisted on being buried in the grave of his cattle which had died in the major epidemic which took place in Britain in 1870. Almost a hundred years before, in 1746, an epidemic had lasted for ten years in Europe and

'Swept away nearly the whole race of horned cattle throughout Europe.' The horrors of rinderpest were thus nothing new, and it is unwise to suggest, as is often done, that because of its deadliness among the African fauna, that this disease was new to Africa. There had been many catastrophes among the cattle of Africa before the 1890s, and who is to say that these were not caused by rinderpest? Between 1845 and 1850 near Colesberg in South Africa, Cumming reported: 'Thousands of skulls of springbok and wildebeest were strewed around wherever the hunter turned his eye' ... 'I was astonished at the numbers of skeletons and well-bleached skulls with which the plains were covered.' Drought? Rinderpest? We shall never know.

Whatever its history, the disease seems to have become fixed in the cattle in the region of the Serengeti; as doubtless it did elsewhere in Africa. The result of this was that every year a large percentage of the wildebeest calves died from what was termed 'yearling disease', identified as early as 1933 as being rinderpest. The calves died after they had lost the immunity acquired through their mothers' colostrum; the result was that the population was kept far below the potential that the habitat could carry.

From about 1952 a vigorous anti-rinderpest campaign was pursued, inoculating the cattle around the Serengeti – and the virus disappeared in the wildlife. Freed of this insidious infection, the wildebeest (and buffalo) calves no longer died in their thousands each year, and the population has since continued to grow and grow. Unfortunately the monitoring studies, regular sample counts carried out using light aircraft which were introduced in the 1960s and 1970s, have now been discontinued. So we do not know whether the population is levelling off, as it must do when the food supply becomes insufficient to maintain them all, or whether it still continues to grow. Great alarm was expressed in 1982 when a number of buffalo died from rinderpest in the area, but the strain does not seem to have had the catastrophic effect that was feared.

Will we therefore see the wildebeest of the Serengeti irrupting into the surrounding farmland like the springbok hordes used to do in South Africa? During a recent drought in Botswana, wildebeest were driven in desperation to eating the thatch from the roofs of native huts, and they only numbered about 30,000 head.

This story underlines the fact that what we see among the antelopes are the *survivors*. Antelopes are popularly credited with being immune to many of the diseases which afflict domestic stock in Africa. Particularly is this true of cattle sleeping-sickness, the deadly disease transmitted by the tsetse fly, of which a strain is also fatal to man. But the likelihood is that many of them *do* succumb to such diseases when they are young, contributing to the high rate of calf mortality that takes place.

Wildlife has always been blamed as the source of infection for both human and cattle sleeping-sickness. After the great rinderpest plague had eradicated much of the ungulate wild life, tsetse flies also died out in some areas, or at least were greatly reduced in number. Hence the idea was born, destroy the wildlife and you will do away with the tsetse which denies to cattle some 37 per cent of the total land area of Africa. But paradoxically, some years after the rinderpest plague had terminated, serious outbreaks of both human and animal sleeping-sickness began to manifest themselves; and tsetse flies began to spread into many areas from which they had formerly been absent, or apparently so. Several theories have been propounded to explain the spread of the tsetse, but it seems likely that the increase of bush after the disappearance of cattle and wildlife, coupled with favourable climatic conditions and the usual response of an organism to a reduction in numbers (that is, a vigorous increase), seem to have been the most likely causes.

Whatever the reason for the spread of the tsetse fly, a policy of wildlife destruction was initiated in Southern Rhodesia in 1919, and actively pursued at least into the 1960s, particularly in Zimbabwe (formerly Southern Rhodesia) and Uganda. Some three quarters of a million head of game were shot in Zimbabwe, among which were over 88,000 greater kudu and 37,000 sable antelope. Nevertheless studies have shown that tsetse flies have definite likes and dislikes in regard to which species of animal they feed upon, just as antelopes have for the plants which they eat; so that the blanket destruction of wildlife was quite unjustified. Furthermore, following the disappearance of their wild hosts, some tsetse flies have taken to living around human habitations and feeding solely on man and domestic animals.

The controversy over whether wildlife should be shot to control tsetse, an argument which raged for over 40 years, has now been replaced by that of the use of insecticides to control the tsetse. The end result for Africa's antelopes is the same, because the biggest populations of wildlife exist in areas which are presently denied to domestic stock by the presence of the tsetse fly. Once the fly is eradicated the areas will be open to exploitation by cattle, and the wildlife will disappear.

Early European hunters in Africa often expressed astonishment at the numbers of parasites which they found in the animals which they had shot. But they were neither farmers nor slaughterers, otherwise they would have been familiar with them in domestic animals. Most antelopes have a goodly supply of worms in the rumen – whipworms, barber's pole worms, tapeworms and the like; while the long-nosed species such as the wildebeest and hartebeest have to put up with ugly, fat, inch-long fly maggots living in their nasal sinuses, which they sneeze out onto the ground when ripe for pupation. Warbles, a similar maggot, but one which lives under the skin and is also common in domestic animals, is relatively rare in antelopes. As far as is known it occurs in only a few species such as the Grant's gazelle, reedbuck and lechwe. The adult fly, called the oestrid or gad fly, is known for its habit of driving cattle frantic in the spring when it tries to lay its eggs on them.

Old hunters seem to have been responsible for developing the tale that wild animals use salt-licks to purge themselves of their intestinal parasites. Attractive as this theory of animal pharmacies sounds, the most probable reason for visiting salt-licks is for salt – ordinary sodium chloride. How important such sources of salt are to animals depends upon the amount that occurs naturally in the diet, some regions of Africa being more deficient than others. Salt-licks are generally uncommon in East African national parks, although present in the Aberdares and other mountain areas; but in the impoverished, mineral-deficient soils of countries like the Central African Republic, they are a common sight in the savanna woodland or the tropical rain forest. Some, dug out of the sides of river banks by elephant and rhino, are of spectacular appearance. I have often found hartebeest in the vicinity of such licks during my wanderings in the woodland, and a herd of over 30 giant eland made regular morning visits to one, enabling me to get my first and only pictures of this impressive creature.

Mud baths and dust baths, the former much favoured by buffalo, are rarely indulged in by antelopes, so that their stated purpose of being to remove ticks seems again to be an unlikely explanation. The tick is one of the most common external parasites and, as usual, wildlife has been blamed for harbouring species harmful to cattle. But again, although some ticks have catholic tastes, many are confined to specific hosts. All antelopes have them, usually in the groin and on other parts of the body which are not easily reached in grooming, and normally they do not cause much inconvenience to their hosts. One sometimes hears of antelopes supposedly dying from an infestation of ticks, but usually when an animal dies the ticks take their blood meal quickly, all swelling up together because the animal's resistance has gone, and thus giving the impression that the animal has been walking about covered with bloated ticks. Ticks do however transmit several diseases and may in this way be instrumental in causing death.

Healthy animals are able to support their parasites, although this may not be without suffering. The waterbuck is afflicted by a particularly strange parasite, an ear mite, species of which have only been found elsewhere in the kob, the cow and the Australian wombat! In Uganda I have seen an old waterbuck doe with half her face rubbed bare from scratching in a vain attempt to relieve the irritation from this parasite; but in other areas of Africa it does not seem to cause much distress and waterbuck show little signs of scratching their ears.

Predation

Whereas there is little that an antelope can do about parasites, predation has undoubtedly influenced antelope behaviour. It has been said that the difference between a parasite and a predator is that whereas the former lives on income, the latter lives on capital. It is suggested that the grouping of antelopes, the size of herds which they adopt, has a relation to the type of predators which they have to contend with; animals of the open plains, subject to attack by lions, cheetah and hunting dogs, grouping together in the hope that it will be the other fellow which will get it, rather than an instinctive belief in safety in numbers.

When we think of the predators to which a newborn antelope is exposed, it is small wonder that such a high rate of mortality takes place; the wonder is perhaps that any manage to survive at all. Since the time of Malthus, the vicar who in 1798 first enunciated the theory that the numbers of animals and human beings were controlled by their food supply, scientists have pondered upon the question of the regulation of animal numbers. In many cases, animals in the wild do not seem to be limited by their food supply, and attention has frequently been turned to the role of predation. I think that we have already seen part of the answer to the question of food supply, and that is that one must look at the worst time of the year to find the controlling factor. When we look at predation among the vast herds of African antelopes, it also does not seem to be of consequence; the numbers of carnivores are always well below what we might expect. In fact, predation does not seem to be important on the adults, of which only a small proportion fall prey to carnivores, but on the very young. If predation does exert a controlling effect, then it is at this stage;

and it is due more often to the spotted hyaena than it is to the more glamorous carnivores, the big cats.

In wildlife studies it is very difficult to determine exactly what very young antelopes die of, for they tend to just disappear. If they have been taken by a lion or a hyaena, then they will be gobbled up without trace; bones, hooves and all. Rarely does one witness the seizure of a young calf, unless it is in such a place as the Serengeti or Ngorongoro Crater, when the wildebeest and tommy are calving in large numbers. Then the snatching of young by hyaenas and jackals, or even lion and cheetah, is a common sight.

Birds of Prey. When a bird of prey is the culprit it is somewhat easier, because the bones and other indigestible debris are regurgitated in a pellet, which can be found at the foot of the nest during the breeding season. There are few studies of predation on the smaller antelopes, but one conducted in Tsavo East Park revealed that dik-diks were the main item of prey of the tawny, bateleur, martial and African hawk eagles. In 110 sq km of study area these eagles are estimated to have killed between 1,000 and 1,500 dik-dik each year; equivalent to 36 to 56 per cent of all the dik-diks in the area.

I studied some of the jaws which were recovered from below nesting sites, assigning them to age groups from the appearance of the teeth; the stage of eruption of the permanent teeth, the amount of wear, etc. This did not reveal that there was any selection for juveniles, except in the case of the hawk eagle which seemed to take only this category. It was not surprising that they did not normally take juveniles, because after birth the newborn dik-dik is kept well hidden, so that it is only when it starts to venture from its hiding place that it is likely to be taken. Why the hawk eagle should be successful in finding them is not known. As the dik-dik breeds twice a year, it is well able to sustain this high rate of mortality; but where the species was less common in the park, the eagles turned their attention to other prey. In this area the martial eagle was observed to also take young gerenuk; and in the Kruger Park it is recorded as taking the young of impala, bushbuck, and klipspringer, as well as adult steenbok and grysbok.

The larger the antelope, the less the number of predator species it has to fear once it has survived the juvenile stage; but the spectrum of predators depends also upon the antelope's choice of habitat and its social organisation. Forest species, the young of all of which remain hidden for some time after birth, have only the python (in wet places), the leopard, and perhaps the golden cat to contend with. Rarely do they have to fear jackals, hyaena, hunting dog or lion which generally avoid the dense forest. In contrast the inhabitants of woodland and open grassland must face all of these, as well as birds of prey. In the more open country we can add cheetah also, which once extended into the desert regions, along with the lion.

Lion. Lion will kill literally anything that moves, having a diet which ranges from tortoises to young elephants; but they normally content themselves with the prey which is the most abundant. This is usually a species of antelope, but it may be buffalo or zebra. There is some indication that they have preferences, but this is difficult to establish, and may be due more to a learning process than to actual preference; as for example when they turn to man-eating.

In the Kruger Park it is the waterbuck which figures most consistently in the lion's diet, and has done so since the park's records began in 1926; to the extent that it is thought to be a factor regulating, or depressing, the waterbuck's population level. This is because the waterbuck is a relatively sedentary species; always found near to permanent water, it does not disperse in the rains as other species do. But I found in my studies in Uganda that, although lions were the adult waterbuck's main predators, the number that they actually took was very few. Here, with water everywhere within easy reach, the populations were well spread out. On the Mweya Peninsula in the Queen Elizabeth Park, lions made only an occasional visit, and no animals were molested there during my studies. So tranquil was the area that one aged doe was able to die quietly of old age, while another with a broken leg was able to survive until the fracture had healed. But after I left, such is the contrary nature of these beasts, a pride of lions installed themselves there for several weeks, and drove all of the waterbuck away.

Animals which were the most frequently killed by lions in the Kruger Park were wildebeest, impala, zebra, kudu and waterbuck; in that order. The impala, the most numerous antelope in the area, figured low in preference; that is, the number taken was low in relation to the number available, perhaps due to a greater alertness and agility. In the Serengeti, wildebeest, zebra, buffalo and topi comprised three quarters of all the species taken by lions; while in Zambia's Kafue Park the rating was buffalo, hartebeest, zebra and warthog. In Kenya's Nairobi Park it was wildebeest, zebra and hartebeest.

The food habits of lions can be considered as influenced by four main factors. Firstly, the size of the prey. They do not waste too much time on small prey, but whereas a single lion normally takes on prey only up to its own size, a group of lions will tackle even a rhinoceros, but more commonly the buffalo. Secondly, availability. Usually lions take what is available, and where populations are dense then obviously more kills can be made. Some lion prides and nomadic lions prey on wildebeest in the Serengeti for over four months of the year when the migrations are passing; but yet others live away from the migration routes and seldom see a wildebeest. For the former the wildebeest comprise about 25 per cent of the diet in one year, amounting probably to only some 0.5 to 1 per cent of the total population of wildebeest. At the last count there was no evidence to suggest that the lions were increasing with the increase in wildebeest, but in theory this is what should eventually happen. However, since the lions do not follow the wildebeest in the migration, they can only take advantage of this food resource for a limited part of the year.

Thirdly, there is the density of the prey to consider. When the density of a preferred species, such as the wildebeest, declines due to some factor such as drought, lions will still continue to prey heavily on the species which they are accustomed to take, and predation may then become a limiting factor on the prey population. But in the Nairobi Park, where the wildebeest numbers were reduced by drought in 1961, the lions at first continued to take a disproportionately large number; four times more than expected, considering the number that was available. However, in 1967 when the population got low, the lions turned their attention to other, more numerous prey, such as the eland, at one time rare in the park. In the densely populated central district of the Kruger Park, 394 lions killed

1. A herd of giant eland at a salt-lick in the Central African Republic stare curiously at the photographer

2. A large bull Cape eland in the Ngorongoro Crater, Tanzania

3. Klipspringer, the ballerina of the bush, stands tip-toe on its specially adapted hooves

4. A herd of sable antelope, the bull with his roan-coloured cows and young bulls. Shimba Hills, Kenya

5. A pair of gerenuk

6. A blue wildebeest cow rests with her fawn-coloured calf

7. Wildebeest watch curiously as a lion stalks across the plain in the Ngorongoro Crater

8. A roan antelope drinking at a woodland pool, Central African Republic

9. A common duiker

10. A pair of bohor reedbuck in typical habitat

11. A kongoni bull standing on a termite mound, Nairobi Park, Kenya

12. The migration of the blue wildebeest in the Serengeti, Tanzania

13. The Buffon's kob

14. A herd of Buffon's kob females in their flood plain habitat in the north of the Central African Republic

15. A herd of giant kudu, Mikumi
Reserve, Tanzania

16. The eastern bongo.
(Photograph: Alan Root)

17. A group of lesser kudu in the Tsavo East National Park, Kenya

18. A herd of defassa female waterbuck, western Uganda

19. A territorial male impala with his herd, Tanzania

20. A subordinate male impala displays his lavatory-brush tail as a dominant
    male approaches right

21. Topi in the Akagera Park, Rwanda

twice as much prey as did 506 lions in the more sparsely populated northern part, during a twelve-year study period.

Finally there is scavenging. The lion will not bother to kill if it can find
enough carrion, as may be the case during a drought or an epidemic.

Contrary to the herbivores, lions find the wet season to be their leanest
time, because then the antelopes are dispersed and are not obliged to come
to a central point to drink; or even, as in the case of the impala, do not need
to drink at all. Long grass and thick bush also may make it more easy for
the lion to hide, but so is it for the prey.

Leopard. Our second largest carnivore, the leopard, has a wider range of
diet than the lion; taking smaller prey ranging from freshwater crabs and
giant land snails up to medium-sized antelopes, but yet is powerful and
ferocious enough to kill adult doe waterbuck and greater kudu. It rarely
hunts the open plains, but makes good use of the watercourses with their
tangle of riverine vegetation.

A high proportion of the leopard's diet seems to be provided by the
bushbuck; which is not all that surprising since they both prefer the same
habitat. You may not infrequently come across the carcase of a bushbuck,
or other small antelope, hauled up into a tree, the 'leopard's larder'; its
characteristic method of storing prey out of reach of other predators and
scavengers. I have surprised leopard at night hunting yearling waterbuck
in Uganda, but in the Serengeti the tommy is its favourite food. In the
Kruger Park it is considered to be the most important predator on the
impala, more of which are taken than any other species in the area;
namely, bushbuck, waterbuck, reedbuck, nyala, duiker, steenbok, grysbok
and klipspringer. All of which find their way into its larder. Leopards
however have never been known to be so numerous as to have a limiting
effect on a population.

Hyaena. Driving one evening in the Nairobi Park in the 1950s, I came
across a group of hyaena attacking a wildebeest. They had already torn its
shoulder and had it standing at bay, but were reluctant to give it the *coup
de grace* and it was time for me to leave before the park gates closed, so I did
not witness the inevitable end to this tragedy. Although the role of predator, rather than scavenger, on the part of the hyaena was well-known
from observations made in South Africa, where waterbuck and kudu are
its main prey, it was not until the late 1960s that a study conducted in the
Ngorongoro Crater revealed just how widespread this behaviour is among
hyaenas. Indeed it was found that it was often the lion which drove the
hyaena from its kill, rather than the hyaena trailing after the lion's
leftovers. But this is probably related to hyaena density, and in areas
where they roam singly, it is unlikely that they do other than mostly
scavenge.

On a dark and stormy night on the Serengeti's Mukoma Plain, hyaenas
once created havoc among the tommy, wantonly slaughtering over a
hundred of them confused in the wind and rain. It is unusual for hyaenas to
have the chance to destroy so wastefully, even though they are often
luridly described as becoming glutted on the abundance of wildebeest
calves. In the Ngorongoro Crater, where they are the most numerous
predator, there is no evidence for this. Studies have shown that they take
an average of only 0.12 wildebeest calves each, the intake during the

calving season being scarcely higher than normal. But in 1967 it was estimated that, out of a total of 4,300 calves, only 940 survived. Many hyaenas were reported as looking bloated, while some carcasses were only partly eaten. This wastefulness was not observed in other years, and was attributed to the delayed effects of a drought which had taken place the year before. It is thought that, when the grazing conditions deteriorated, the mothers were unable to feed their calves adequately, so many became weakened and fell easy prey, while others died of malnutrition.

Except during the peak of the calving which only lasts for three weeks, in the Ngorongoro Crater it is the adult wildebeest which are preferred as prey, because the hyaena does not like a hard chase for a small reward. When the calves become nearly as hard to catch as the adults, which happens very quickly, then the game is no longer worth the candle.

Hunting Dog. Another major carnivore which has often been described in lurid terms is the hunting dog. For well over a century the only person who had had a good word to say for it was Cumming, who likened them to his own 'noble deer hounds' with which he had hunted in Scotland. But we have come to learn in recent years that hunting dogs are by no means as wantonly destructive as they are often portrayed, nor disruptive to the prey community. There is no evidence that antelopes quit the area once hunting dogs appear on the scene, as asserted in earlier writings. Hunting dogs specialise in the most abundant, small and medium-sized antelopes and are highly efficient hunters, a success rate of over 85 per cent has been reported in the Ngorongoro Crater. Fortunately their numbers always remain curiously low due to disease, otherwise such efficiency might well have a depressing effect on prey numbers.

In the Serengeti the hunting dog favour tommy, in the Kruger Park it is impala; but they will take any antelope that is not too big, including kudu and waterbuck, and down to such small species as duiker and steenbok. In Ngorongoro Crater the proportions of prey observed to be taken were: tommy 54 per cent, newborn and juvenile wildebeest 36 per cent, Grant's gazelle 8 per cent and kongoni 2 per cent. In contrast to lions and leopards, they prey more heavily on pregnant females during the calving seasons; but in the dry season they take a comparatively large number of territorial males, or males from herds.

Cheetah. Few people have a bad word to say for the cheetah, even though it is also fond of killing newborn calves. These it is known to take from wildebeest, waterbuck, kudu, tsessebee and sable; although all age classes of tommy and impala are killed. The full-grown larger antelopes are not usually hunted, but there are occasional records of this happening; there is even one report of an adult roan bull being killed in East Africa. In the Kruger Park, reedbuck had a high preference rating, but they were not as important in the Kafue Park, where puku was the favoured prey.

Other Predators

Other predators on antelopes are the brown hyaena, which in the Kruger Park hunts in packs, killing mostly kudu, followed by waterbuck and impala. The side-striped jackal and the golden jackal both kill the smaller antelopes, plus the young of even roan and wildebeest; while the caracal will take impala calves, adult steenbok, grysbok and klipspringer. The serval cat is also known to kill impala calves, but this is rare. Let's not forget the baboon from this criminal array, big males of which will kill impala calves, and those of duiker, bushbuck, nyala and reedbuck; or in fact any species that it comes across and which is small enough for it to tackle.

Any antelope drinking from a river or lake where crocodiles exist may be taken, but the waterbuck figures largest in their diet. The python takes bushbuck, reedbuck does and the calves of wildebeest, kudu, waterbuck and impala. I once found a dead python in Rwanda's Akagera Park, with a male bushbuck inside which had horns of about 20 cm in length. It was not clear what the snake had died of, but it looked as if it had been attacked by a lion or other carnivore while lying bloated with its prey.

Predatory Selection

In the Kruger Park the detailed recording of carcasses and incidents involving predators has been maintained for many years, and this has revealed a marked seasonal variation in predation pressure. This is influenced by the degree of concentration or dispersal of the prey, habitat conditions, long grass or bushes in full leaf making capture more difficult, while the animals do not need to concentrate near to waterholes in the wet season; and the breeding seasons of the major prey species. The new calves provide an abundance of relatively easily captured prey, although there is no evidence from lion kills for selective predation on young animals. Although they do choose animals in poor condition, the majority of the prey consists of victims in good condition, in prime to old age. But deductions from skulls found in the field, rather than actually observed kills, are likely to be biased on account of the lack of durability of young skulls, and also that of female as compared to male skulls. The latter are frequently much tougher, with a reinforcement at the base of the horns; while the horns themselves make the skulls too cumbersome for scavengers to drag far away.

During my study of waterbuck in Uganda, I collected three times more buck than doe skulls. I found none of either sex that were under one year old, and few under three years old; and there were more old bucks than young ones. In the Akagera Park I collected only one and a half times more buck than doe skulls. But in a sample of 450 impala skulls from the same area, there were also three times as many bucks as does, and nearly six and a half times more animals older than three years than there were younger than this; in contrast to approximately equal numbers of each age group in the counts that I made of live animals. In a collection of eland skulls there were only slightly more bulls than cows; and for zebra the numbers were approximately equal.

The significance of this is that mare and stallion zebra skulls are almost indistinguishable, except that the latter possess prominent canine teeth; so we would expect that if the skulls were destroyed, or carried away by hyaenas, then they would be so in equal numbers. We would also expect to find this happening in species with very large skulls, such as the eland; and indeed this was more or less the case. Of course these skulls resulted from all forms of mortality, but they would have been exposed to the same degree of scavenging whatever the cause of death. From observation I recorded only twelve known deaths of waterbuck from lion in the Queen Elizabeth Park in almost three years: one calf, one young doe, one doe of unknown age, and nine bucks; with no apparent selection for either territorial or old bucks. Two were old, two were aged two and a half years, and the rest were middle-aged.

In the Serengeti the tommy is preyed upon by more predators than any other antelope there: lion, leopard, cheetah, hyaena, hunting dog, black-backed and golden jackals, baboon, martial eagle and two species of vulture. One might think that as a result of this ravenous army lying in wait the tommy must live in a state of perpetual terror; but its fleeing response is in the order, hunting dog, cheetah, lion, hyaena and jackal; being thus most afraid of the hunting dog and least of the jackal. But it increases for hyaena if there are more than one. It also depends upon whether the predator is hunting, for if so the tommy will flee at distances of up to 2 km away from hunting dogs; but it will let them approach to within 50 m if the dogs are just walking along minding their own business. Resting lions are usually ignored, and a territorial tommy will stay in his territory when a lion decides to rest in it, sometimes remaining as close to the lion as 25 m. But moving lions elicit snorts of warning from the tommy, no matter whether the lion is gorged or lean.

Defence Tactics

It is one of those seeming anomalies of nature that, although the ancestral tommy doe was well horned, just as is the living Grant's gazelle doe, today's tommy doe has only skimpy, rudimentary horns; so fragile that they have been known to break off when the animal is knocked over. Perhaps it is a question that the doe is too small and relatively weak to be effective against its main predators anyway, and those smaller ones, like jackals, are not important enough to operate a selective effect. When hyaenas chase tommy fawns the mother does not show any aggression, but tries to distract the hyaenas' attention. As with other small creatures, the tommy compensates for the increased hazards of life that its small size imposes by an increased fecundity, for there is evidence to suggest that it gives birth twice a year.

If cheetah are strolling over the plains tommy and some other species of antelope display a curious behaviour which has been termed 'fascination behaviour'. Running from several hundred metres away, they all come to stare at the cheetah from distances of as little as 50 to 80 m, to follow along behind it at about 100 m, occasionally venting snorts of alarm or derision, like jeering urchins following a dandy down the street. They do it also with leopard and a single hunting dog, but not with a pack of the latter; while it is less striking with lions, and only rarely shown with hyaenas and jackals. Cheetah have been known to get sufficiently close to tommy, and the calves of wildebeest, when they are playing this game, that they have been able to rush forward and seize one. The causes of such behaviour are obscure; perhaps it is just to learn and gain experience of the predator, or it may be to alert other animals to the predator's presence. Wildebeest will follow behind lions and hunting dogs at a distance of 100 m or more, but keep twice this distance behind the dogs if they have been hunting.

There is a report of a young male waterbuck in the Queen Elizabeth Park, which appeared to be so mesmerised by a lion that it allowed the lion to walk up to it and seize it by the nose! On one occasion in the same area, I was witness to a territorial buck which suddenly found itself face to face with a crouching lion at a distance of no more than 20 m. The buck's immediate reaction was not to flee, instead it carefully confronted the lion and stood motionless watching it. A full two minutes passed in this manner, then suddenly the waterbuck leapt at least 15 m to one side, and turned to study the lion's reactions ... The lion merely crouched a little lower and, like Brer Fox, 'he lay low'. The buck then began to give warning snorts at ten to twenty-five second intervals, but still the impassive lion continued with his imitation of Brer Fox. The waterbuck then deliberately turned on its back and walked away slowly for a short distance, turned round once more to look, and then quite unhurriedly walked off altogether. Not until the waterbuck was out of sight did the lion relax its crouching attitude. Perhaps it was just as surprised as I by this waterbuck's aplomb.

The more usual reaction of a waterbuck was to snort and indicate the position of the predator, and if a lion that was being watched disappeared from view, then the buck instantly ran off to a safe distance, stopped, and tried to spot it again. Some does will snort and point just as vigorously as a buck, but the doe's main advantage seems to lie in its habit of moving in herds and of copying one another's actions.

As the herd grazes, from time to time one will look up and glance around. If she notices anything unusual then she stares fixedly at it to see if it will move. As soon as others in the group notice her staring, then they copy her, until the whole herd may be watching and several pairs of eyes are focused on the object from many different directions. This enables a perception and recognition of form which cannot be met by one pair of eyes alone, so solitary territorial bucks should, in principle, be taken by lions more frequently than does. Certainly one old territorial buck, who took up residence in a long grass area seldom frequented by other waterbuck, was taken within a few days when a roaming pride of lions paid a visit to the area.

Waterbuck does show fear of hyaenas, snorting and running away in a 'hackney gait', with the neck held stiffly erect, bringing the legs sharply up and down, flexing the joint as they trot. They are also capable of 'stotting', although I have only seen this in play; but gazelles, especially the tommy, often react by stotting, bouncing up and down on stiff legs like a rubber ball. This odd gait seems to be brought on by a high state of excitement, so that they will sometimes break into it when they have been pursued and have been running for some time. Its purpose is obscure because it is slower than running. It differs from 'pronking', which is a similar gait used only by the springbok, for in pronking the back is arched, displaying the springbok's unique dorsal ruff.

When attacked, gazelles and impala tend to scatter in all directions, while the wildebeest tends to bunch. The adult wildebeest has two strategies for eluding capture by predators; one is to avoid being singled out by keeping at a distance or staying in a group; and the other is to outrun its pursuers if it should be singled out. A wildebeest can run at about 80 km an hour, similar to the hartebeest, tommy and Grant's gazelle. The eland and topi have only been timed at speeds up to 70 km an hour, but can probably go just as fast as the others. The lion lacks speed, and once it has lost the advantage of surprise in its initial rush, most antelopes can outrun it. But even they cannot keep up these high speeds for long, as has been shown from animal capture operations. Most antelopes, if pursued for longer than two minutes at full speed, and some for only one and a half minutes, will die afterwards of a literally burst heart, caused by

Figure 7.1 '*Stotting' in a young tommy (After Walther, 1969). Compare this with 'pronking' (Figure 8.5)*

rupturing of the heart's finer blood vessels; and from acid blood resulting from the over-production of lactic acid in the muscles.

A wildebeest cow with calf has both an increased flight distance and is more alert to predators. Although the calf can hide in the herd, the youngest newborn get left behind if the herd is pursued at speed, so this is not a very successful method of protection. More important against predators other than the lion, is defence by the mother, which has been observed to save the lives of calves in almost 30 per cent of cases. If the calf is overtaken by hyaenas the mother will turn back and charge them, often bowling them over and horning them. But this is of little use if there is more than one attacker, whether a pack of hyaena or wild dogs, because while the mother turns to deal with one of them, another takes the calf.

In spite of the fact that the wildebeest is the single most important item in the diet of hyaenas in the Serengeti region, it has a small reaction distance to them. Perhaps because they are the most common carnivore there and are often to be seen slinking about in their cur-like manner without any intention to hunt. When hyaenas do hunt they do not simply throw themselves onto the nearest animal, but first select their victim, often after much preliminary running in and out of the herds.

In contrast to the mother's spirited defence of her calf, if a wildebeest is brought to bay it does absolutely nothing to defend itself against its tormentors, and will simply let itself be eaten alive by hyaenas or hunting dogs, doing little more than emit the odd groan as it is disembowelled. David Livingstone was the first to suggest that the attack of a carnivore might produce a state of stupefaction in its victim so that it does not feel pain, after his personal experience with a lion. He wrote in 1857: 'Growling horribly close to my ear, he shook me as a terrier-dog does a rat. The shock produced a stupor, similar to that which seems to be felt by a mouse after the first shake of the cat. It caused a sort of drowsiness in which there was no sense of pain nor feeling of terror, though quite conscious of all that was happening. It was like what patients partially under the influence of chloroform describe, who see all the operation, but feel not the knife ... This peculiar state is probably produced in all animals killed by the carnivora ...'

Sable, roan and kudu, are all reported as having gored lions, while no lion will face a male waterbuck's horns. The wildebeest's fatalistic attitude is surprising when we consider that its horns are pretty dangerous too. One acquaintance of mine was badly gored in the thigh when he turned his back for a moment on a penned wildebeest; while there is a report of one causing death in the same circumstances.

The horns of male antelopes, dangerous and effective weapons as they are, seem to be designed solely for the purposes of intra-specific behaviour; that is, for fighting and establishing dominance among the species of antelope themselves. On this basis, antelopes do not seem to have evolved any significant protection against carnivores. The alternative view is to suppose that horns evolved as a defence against predators, but with the increasing evolution of social behaviour this function was largely discarded. This would more readily explain their absence in females, indicating that they are largely unnecessary, or ineffectual in the long run, to combat predators.

Both horns and colour play little, if any role in the protection of antelopes from their hereditary enemies, the whole tendency in evolution seeming to be towards a higher development of social organisation. Co-operation, the herding of animals as a protection, even if it is individually guided by selfish motives, and agility, are the main weapons with which predation is combated. The gentle herbivore has learnt to live with its aggressive enemies without fear; in stark contrast to its behaviour towards man in areas where it is hunted.

From the earliest days of the science of ecology, there has been speculation, and indeed controversy, as to whether predation plays an important role in the regulation of animal numbers. In the Kruger Park, almost from the day of the park's inception, a policy of carnivore control was pursued in the belief that this would permit the herbivore population to increase. The policy was discontinued in 1961, and in 1967 was followed by the culling of excess numbers of impala and wildebeest. By the following year the park was considered to hold more game than it had done in all of its known history. So there was no evidence to suggest that predators exerted any controlling effect, in fact, quite the opposite. Some species however, namely waterbuck, roan and sable, have declined in numbers since earlier times; but this may be due more to habitat changes, and the bad droughts which periodically strike the area affecting particularly sable and waterbuck.

In Ngorongoro Crater, it has been estimated that 75 per cent of cow wildebeest recruits produce their first calf in their second year, indicating that the population is vigorous and healthy. But hyaenas, and to a lesser extent lions, prey so heavily on the population that mortality is equal to recruitment, preventing the population from increasing. In the Serengeti, by contrast, only 35 per cent of females produced a calf in their second year, this percentage apparently falling to only 4 per cent when the population increased. Thus in the Ngorongoro Crater the heavy predation was compensated for by an increased fecundity of the females, but in the Serengeti predation had little effect. If the females were not producing a calf in their second year, then this meant that they were not sufficiently well nourished, because there were too many of them.

Drought

If antelopes can survive all of these pitfalls to existence, in many cases they still have the spectre of drought to face. During a bad drought in the Serengeti in 1966, only 21 per cent of the wildbeest calf crop is estimated to have survived. This compared with 72 per cent in 1963, which was a normal year. There have been over five bad droughts in the Kruger Park since the 1920s, each taking a heavy toll of wildlife. During one in Nairobi Park in 1973–4, a total of over 1,600, or 27 per cent, of the kongoni population died; and over 760, or 10 per cent of the population of wildebeest. Many of the kongoni and wildebeest had moved in from the area to the south to be near to permanent water; so that in the region to the south of the park the losses were estimated at only 7 per cent of the kongoni, and 3 per cent of the wildebeest. Other losses were estimated at 4 per cent of the tommy, 3 per cent of the Grant's gazelle, 3 per cent of the eland, and 2 per cent of the impala; but these species were little affected in the park. The grazing, nomadic species, were the worst hit. Those species like the waterbuck and impala, existing at a much lower density on a more dependable food supply, were much less affected. Many species died once again in Kenya in the 1984 drought; and this widespread drought is believed to have sounded the death-knell for the scimitar-horned oryx in Niger, as well as large numbers of dorcas and dama gazelles. These sub-desert inhabitants were forced south into the inhabited areas, where they fell ready prey to poaching.

During a drought, herbivores generally die of a lack of food rather than from a lack of water. Congregating as they do near permanent water supplies the food in the vicinity quickly becomes eaten out, and if they range too far away searching for it, then of course they will die of thirst. The desert species in Niger did not move south looking for water, but for food.

These constant checks to survival; disease, predation and drought, serve to keep most animal populations in check. With the greater part of Africa prone to periodic drought, this factor alone is probably the most widespread and the most important factor limiting the numbers of herbivores today. Its effects are now becoming aggravated by the restriction of animals to areas from which they would normally migrate in search of new pastures at such times; as did the springbok and the wildebeest in South Africa's recent past.

8 Antelope communication – scent, colour, display and fighting

If the antelope is successful in surviving the numerous hazards to juvenile life imposed by its hostile surroundings, the male of the species is then faced with the task of contending with the impediments to survival imposed upon him by his own kind. While the doe is occupied with the business of rearing young, the buck, if he is to survive, must establish himself in antelope society. What this entails, the behaviour of antelopes in relation to their social organisation, is by far the most interesting aspect of antelope study. Not least because the most common expression of this is that of territorial behaviour; the defence of a piece of property, usually by one adult buck against other adult bucks. The gaining and defence of this piece of property brings into play all the array of antelope communication; scent, colour, display, and the last resort, fighting.

The antelope grows up in a world of scent and sight rather than of vocal communication, although its large ears testify to the importance of sound in its environment. To us the world of antelope communication is still largely a closed book; the tilt of the head, the flicker of an eye, the swish of a tail, all have meanings beyond our interpretation. Paramount among these mysteries is the use of scent, which appears to be the most primitive form of mammalian communication, but is widely used among antelopes in spite of their having evolved visual methods.

Scent

In its crudest form, communication by scent may be by means of dung or urine, or both, and some species adopt highly ritualised postures when indulging in urination or defaecation. Particularly is this true of the dik-dik, Grant's and Thomson's gazelles, impala, and occasionally the oryx. The smaller antelopes, especially the neotragines and the duikers, deposit dung piles around the borders of their territories apparently as signposts to their property, rather than simply a preference for doing it 'on their neighbour's doorstep'.

With the dik-dik, whose dung piles can be nearly 2 m across and 10 cm high, when a female is present with a male, using the family latrine takes on the form of a ritual. The female first lightly scrapes the pile, then hunches over the spot that she has scraped, urinating on it and then defaecating. After she moves away the male takes his turn. First he sniffs the spot most carefully, then scrapes it vigorously with both forefeet, using first one leg and then the other. He then likewise hunches over the spot, urinates and then defaecates. The contortions which these animals undergo are of course necessary if they wish to deposit both urine and faeces on the same spot; for the female would otherwise urinate to the rear, and the male in front, of the dropping.

Dung piles are also a characteristic feature of hartebeest territories, being particularly frequent along the borders. They are deposited in the centre of a roughly circular patch of bare earth and scraped over with the forefeet. It has been suggested that these may be territorial signposts, but this has not been convincingly demonstrated.

Figure 8.1   The defaecation posture of the male Kirk's dik-dik

Most antelopes, if not all, are possessed of some sort of concentrated scent glands; possible exceptions to this are the waterbuck, bongo and sitatunga, which instead possess diffuse glands spread over most of the body. Pride of place for smelliness goes to the oribi, which has no less than six specialised scent glands. Such proliferation probably relates to this small antelope's adoption of the rather ephemeral grassland habitat, even more of a jungle down amongst its close-knit stems when the grass is high, than is the forest floor.

The oribi's battery of scent glands consists of one beneath each ear, visible as a round bare patch of black skin, one on the face in front of each eye, sac-like pouches in the groin, glands between the toes of each foot, a gland on the 'knees', and another between the false hooves of the hindlegs. All of these glands occur in different combinations in other species; while the steenbok has a gland under the chin, the impala has a cyclops-like one in the centre of the forehead, and the grysboks have a preputial gland in addition to their eye and face glands.

Although some analyses of the extremely complex chemicals produced by these glands have been carried out, and some imitations have even been synthesised, we can still only guess at their uses. It seems very likely that facial glands, more highly developed in the oribi, suni and dik-dik, than in any other antelope in relation to the animal's size, are used for marking out territory. This is extended to the marking of females during courtship,

Figure 8.2   The scent glands of an oribi

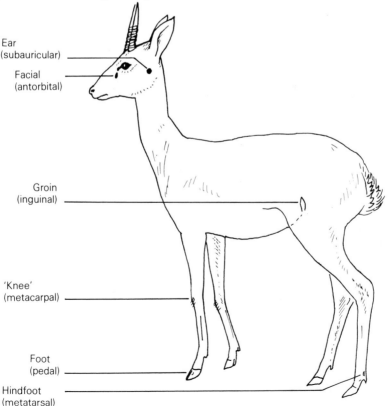

Ear
(subauricular)

Facial
(antorbital)

Groin
(inguinal)

'Knee'
(metacarpal)

Foot
(pedal)

Hindfoot
(metatarsal)

or even, in the case of the blue duiker, marking rivals during fighting. Some species, such as the topi and hartebeest, even appear to mark themselves more than anything else, rubbing the gland on their own forequarters with a sideways swing of the head, creating a prominent dark patch on the coat. I say that they *appear* to mark themselves, because it is questionable whether this is a deliberate marking action, or whether they are just wiping the gland to relieve irritation, just as we would wipe our nose.

When the oribi marks with its facial gland there is no mistaking its intention to mark. Before depositing its scent marker, the male oribi first

Figure 8.3 Portrait of an oribi, showing the ear gland, and the facial gland just in front of the eye

bites off a grass stem at the required height and then pushes his sac-like gland over it, covering the tip of the stem with a sticky, black exudate. He re-marks the same stem at regular intervals, first nipping off the old, stale piece, and then anointing the tip afresh. Although this is mostly executed along the boundaries of a territory, it is apparently also done at random throughout the area; during feeding, after mating, or during or after conflict situations. The grysbok male also licks, or bites off the tip of a stem, in the same way.

Glands below the ear, found only in the oribi and reedbuck, seem to be for the purpose of producing an aura of scent around the animal, the odour apparently evaporating on the surface of the bare skin. In the reedbuck doe they are said to exude when she is on heat, which would be a very limited occurrence in the naturally-breeding animal, taking place for only a few hours once or twice in the year.

The pocket-like glands in the groin occur in several species, and have been variously suggested as having some relevance to mating activity, or possibly, in the case of the female, producing a scent for the calf to identify with its mother. But perhaps their function is to produce 'fear' or 'alarm' scent, for there is a report of a common duiker killed by hunting dogs, whose groin glands were found to be 'actually dripping'. Reedbuck indeed produce a popping noise with these glands when they leap away in fright; which may be incidental or it may result from a deliberate contraction of the gland to puff out an alarm smell.

Figure 8.4   Portrait of a Kirk's dik-dik, showing the facial gland in front of the eye

'Fear' or 'alarm' smells are real enough and widespread among mammals, and are even present in man. We have all heard of the term 'the smell of fear', and it is particularly noticeable in some races. A dog or other animal can scent it easily. Many antelopes stamp on the ground when they make an alarm call or warning snort, such as in the presence of a lion, and it is possible that this action is designed to release a 'fear' or warning scent from the glands that may be present on the legs. It has been suggested that this may explain the impala's magnificent leaps into the air when it is alarmed, the object being to distribute the scent from its conspicuously marked glands sited between the false hooves of the hind feet. Leaping into the air would distribute it so that other members of the herd can follow the scent without putting their noses down to sniff a trail. When a herd of impala explodes into leaping, jinking, confusion, it is not a wild panic reaction but certain action patterns are repeated each time. Thus each leap appears to be oriented towards other members of the group; magnificent leaps of 3 m in height and over 11 m in length, often passing over the back of another. These high-jumps are followed by a last high kick with the hindlegs as the forelegs touch the ground; so high indeed are they that the animal nearly somersaults.

Casting left and right brings the animals together, and the leaps quickly establish the direction of flight, especially if the herd split up initially. Contact is re-established without a sound, and often in fairly thick bush, the animals following the scent trails spread by the high kicks.

Another antelope which is believed to distribute a warning smell by leaping into the air is the springbok. When alarmed it leaps into the air, indulging in a characteristic pronking display; curving the back to display its white dorsal ruff which surrounds a scent gland. There is no better description of pronking than that of Cumming written in 1850: '... away start the herd, with a succession of strange perpendicular bounds, rising with curved loins high into the air, and at the same time elevating the snowy folds of long white hair on their haunches and along their back, which imparts to them a peculiar fairy-like appearance, different from any other animal. They bound to the height of ten or twelve feet, with the elasticity of an india-rubber ball, clearing at each spring from twelve to fifteen feet of ground, without apparently the slightest exertion. In performing this spring they appear for an instant as if suspended in the air, when down come all four feet again together and, striking the plain, away they soar again, as if about to take flight. The herd only adopt this motion for a few hundred yards, when they subside into a light elastic trot, arching their graceful necks and lowering their noses to the ground ...'

The exudate of the dorsal gland has been analysed and shows no difference in the chemicals produced between male, female and juvenile, supporting the idea that it is an alarm scent, spread to all members of the herd by these remarkable leaps into the air.

Pedal or foot glands, which are sited between the toes of some species, would seem to have the obvious function of leaving a scent trail behind the animal. Studies in South Africa showed that the foot gland of the bontebok was much more productive than were the facial glands of duiker and grysbok, but this may of course be dependent upon the physiological state of the animal. A synthesised imitation of the scent caused great interest in two captive males, one of which was regarded as normally v approachable, so that the gland would appear to have some real communicatory

Figure 8.5   Springbok 'pronking'. After Millais, J.G. 1895. A Breath from the Veldt. Henry Sotheran, London

function. However, if antelopes go about leaving a scent trail wherever they walk, then it would seem to be an easy matter for carnivores to track them down. But carnivores do not seem to do this, probably because the confusion of scents is too great. But if this is so, why aren't other members of the same species equally confused? One can only conclude that such scents are general and not directional, or that they are used only in certain situations.

Glands on the 'knees' which occur in some species would seem to serve the purpose of marking the spot where the animal lies down. Again, for an animal which does not lie in a form, the object of such marking is obscure.

The big question is, how does a waterbuck mark its territory? The boundaries are, at least in many cases, fairly precise, yet the waterbuck has no concentrated scent glands. Instead much of its body is covered with relatively large sebaceous glands, common to both buck and doe, which produce a dark-coloured, water-soluble grease, with a characteristic sweet musky smell. So powerful is it that I have often smelt the presence of waterbuck at a considerable distance while driving through the bush. At one time I found myself becoming addicted to the smell, wanting to keep on sniffing a particularly odorous cloth that I used for blindfolding captured animals. The fact that both sexes possess the glands in equal numbers and size suggests that they are not used in territorial marking; but if individual scents can be recognised then possibly the marking is passive, achieved simply by the buck's smelly perambulations through his territory.

I devised a simple experiment to try and determine whether the scent of a strange territorial buck was offensive to another territory owner. Capturing a territorial buck I sponged him vigorously with a clean, washed sponge. Then I hurried with the sponge to another area where I drove across the path of another buck who knew me well and took not the slightest notice of my presence in the vehicle. Quickly I dropped the sponge in front of his path via the offside door. Coming up to it, he sniffed it gingerly and then shied away with a snort, but then continued on his way as if nothing at all had happened! My experiment was rather inconclusive, yet there is no doubt that one waterbuck could recognise the scent of another.

As it is often alleged that territories are marked with dung, I next repeated the experiment with droppings in place of the sponge. It is an easy matter to obtain fresh droppings from an antelope, because if you drive up to one suddenly, when it is not expecting it, such as after you have been watching for a while from a short distance, its reaction is to run away a few metres and, if it is not very wary of human beings, turn to stare at you and defaecate; an involuntary nervous reaction. Inducing a prime territorial buck to do this, I rushed forward and scooped up the droppings with a small shovel, and then drove helter-skelter to the buck that I had previously used in the sponge experiment. This time I tipped the still-warm droppings into his path. The result was even more disappointing than on the previous occasion – he simply walked straight past and did not even deign to sniff at them. This, and the fact that droppings were distributed at random within the territory and no interest was ever shown in them, suggests that they play no part in the demarcation of waterbuck territory.

Although the clearest use of scent seems to be shown by those antelopes which actively mark their territories, this idea has been criticised on the grounds that there is no evidence that others take note of the marks, or even avoid an area on account of them. But one view is that the odour marks the environment of an animal, letting it know when it is 'at home'. By marking the animal indicates that the area is safe, it provides the owner with something that is familiar and puts others ill at ease, even if it does not prevent them from entering the marked area altogether. So it is only necessary that a territorial owner marks what it considers to be its own; whether or not this is observed by others is another matter, for the owner succeeds in making himself feel at home.

But not only do antelopes mark their environment with their own odours, they also try to mask strange ones. Thus explaining the apparent anomaly of a territory owner adding to another's dung pile, or covering another's scent marks with his own. In cases where marking is not possible, as for example with a large dung pile or a smelly dead animal, an animal may attempt to become a part of the new smell by rolling in it. Additionally to the 'pipe and slippers' concept of the territorial male making himself feel at home, the female, in the case of species like the oribi and reedbuck where couples share territories, is provided with a sort of perfumed garden to prevent her straying away.

Colour and Display

Colour and pattern play an important part in the social behaviour of all antelopes, and in many visual communication has replaced some of the roles of scent. Much attention was paid at the beginning of the century to the idea of cryptic, or concealing, colouration: a major body of opinion claimed that almost all animal colouration was protective by either being concealing or warning.

One Victorian naturalist even went so far as to paint a picture of pink flamingoes in a red sunset to show how concealing their colouration was. The American sportsman-president Theodore Roosevelt retorted that the raven's colour was concealing if one put the raven in a coal scuttle, '... and if chalk is added to the contents of the coal scuttle, then a magpie's colouration might also become concealing under the same circumstances.'

Antelopes are among the most colourful of mammals. Using only combinations of white, brown and black, they display a whole range of permutations from the painted clown colours of the bontebok (whose name is afrikaans for 'pied buck'), the magnificence of the bull sable in his white tie and tails, through a galaxy of fawns, reds and greys to the blue-fox fur colour of the little blue duiker.

Ancestrally, before ways and means of eluding predators by cunning were evolved, colouration probably was principally concealing; but as more complex social behaviour developed the antelopes became emancipated from relying on simple camouflage, enhancing their conspicuousness. Being colour-blind in the sense that we perceive colours, having sacrificed this ability for night vision, they had no need to develop colours of the spectrum in their attire, relying only on contrast to achieve effect.

Contrast was increased along the margins of countershading, around the genitals, and along the underside; while the ears, face and hocks were elaborated to produce an increase in complexity of pattern from the small vulnerable, and less social species, to the larger, less vulnerable and more

Figure 8.6   The Thomson's gazelle, with its contrasting black lateral line, the most prominent among the gazelles

social species; focusing attention on the head, flanks and rump. Of course some, indeed a great deal, of antelope colouration is concealing, particularly in calves. But this is not the case, for example, with the wildebeest, whose adult coat is more conspicuous as far as a predator is concerned; nor is it the case with such colourful antelopes as the sable bull or the bontebok. Some patterns may be merely decorative, perhaps for use in individual recognition; for in the tommy, the white patch on the forehead and the black patch above the nose, vary considerably in shape and appearance, and one or the other may be absent altogether.

The coat pattern of the adult tommy, with its sharp black line along the flank and its bright white belly, has been postulated as being 'obliterative', the dark lateral line serving to divide the animal into two distinct halves thus distracting attention from the whole. If that is the case, then it is a puzzle as to why the Grant's gazelle doe possesses such a band along her flank which is very variable in both occurrence and intensity, and may be absent altogether; as it always is in the buck.

In fact it is now generally thought that colouration is probably more important in social communication and recognition, allied with physiology. Thus we saw how the hartebeest's pale coat deflects heat away from the body; just as is true of the gazelle's white belly, once considered as an example of countershading, to lessen the dark shadow created by an overhead sun. White bellies are most conspicuous in arid-zone species, which need them to deflect away the high temperatures which are radiated upwards from the surface of the ground.

A prerequisite of mammalian camouflage is immobility; movement gives the game away, so concealing colouration can be identified by the behaviour of the animal. Those which keep still until the very last moment are undoubtedly relying on their colour to protect them from being seen. Against a predator it may provide that split-second advantage which is so necessary to survival, for the feline predators spend a great deal of their time just watching for movement. But I have sat among some rocks, clutching my camera and watching for a klipspringer to come within range, when a large she-leopard has walked right past me, coming up from my rear. She had fortunately passed me before she could detect the large quantities of 'fear smell' that I no doubt produced! Keeping still avoids detection, but antelopes cannot spend all of their time keeping still.

The conspicuous flared white bunny-rabbit tail of the fleeing bushbuck is the most that one sees of this species in some parts of its range, as it makes a hasty dive for cover in a thicket, where it abruptly switches off the white signal and creeps away. It is one of the most vividly coloured antelopes with its rich red coat, overlain with a contrasting pattern of white dots and stripes. The pattern of stripes is most accentuated in species from the forest block and western Africa, giving it its name of 'harnessed antelope', and is weakest in those from southern and eastern Africa. Nevertheless a complete range of colour and pattern from the harness to no markings at all in the buck can be found in East Africa, because it is the main area of overlap between the harnessed and the woodland types. But many bucks get darker as they age, and old, light-coloured bucks have been found, suggesting that the dark colour is controlled by male hormone levels. Thus variation in coat colour and pattern in this species is both geographic, sexual and individual; which makes one wonder what possible significance it could have.

Figure 8.7   The bohor reedbuck stays put until the very last moment, hoping to escape detection

All types and both sexes do however have geometrically-shaped white flashes on most mobile parts of the body; on the ears, chin, tail, legs and neck; whiter and clearer in the buck than in the doe. Their effect is to increase the conspicuousness of the slightest movement, and emphasise the posture which the buck adopts in his displays. When two rivals meet, they circle each other in a tense, high-stepping gait, and, as excitement mounts, they leap into the air with backs arched, flaring a white dorsal crest and their large white bushy tail. As antagonism mounts, they may change to high-speed chasing, interspersed with sudden horn clashes. If they fight, it is vigorous and deadly, with few of the niceties of ritual.

The habit of the lesser kudu, the bushbuck's slender and graceful relative, is to stand ruminating and resting, perfectly immobile, in the dappled shade of a thorn tree with its tail to the trunk. The pale grey coat of the buck, with its thin vertical white stripes, provides a perfect camouflage in the dry season, especially amongst the grey trunk and branches of the commiphora bush. Less so can this be said of the doe, whose background colour is a light fawn. Like the bushbuck, when it flees the lesser kudu flashes a conspicuous large white bushy tail. When confronting a rival it is possible that the buck communicates by means of the three traffic-signal white patches on his throat, neck and chest. When he lifts his chin, he reveals a fourth. But this seems to signify 'go' to a doe during courting, rather than 'stop' to a rival.

The bongo is a strikingly coloured antelope, with its rich, chestnut-red background, laced with ten to 16 vertical white stripes; and black and white markings on the extremities, the head, legs and hindquarters. The contrast which its pattern affords is probably related to its poorly lighted habitat and possibly nocturnal habits, designed to make the animal stand out in a characteristic way when it wants to; as in displays between rival males. These are conducted according to the usual tragelaphine pattern, with the rivals presenting lateral displays. The conspicuous mane which runs the length of the backbone is erected, while the neck is bulged and the eyes rolled, showing their white borders, as the contestants circle each other. The rich red colour on the forequarters and limbs darkens and turns black with age in the bull, distinguishing it from the cow who maintains her bright red and white colours.

The signalling flashes on the face and throat of the tragelaphines are outdone by the gaudy painted black-and-white minstrel faces of the hippotragines. Both oryx and roan have a black line running from the base of the horn, passing over the eye, bordered on either side by white; a pattern which is also present to a lesser extent in the sable. It is most accentuated in the oryx, clearly outlining the head; but is present equally in both sexes, making them difficult to distinguish apart except that the female has more slender horns. But all three species, oryx, roan and sable, are possessed of dangerous horns in both sexes; and black and white are warning colours among mammals wherever warning has to be signalled. The apache-striped face of the oryx reminds me of the warning colouration of the skunk; and I wonder therefore if the faces of the oryx and roan are not designed as a warning display, drawing attention to the lethal horns. Disguising the eye in this pattern may prevent it from becoming a target. Such a pattern is not universal, for although the eye is well-disguised in

Figure 8.8   A herd of roan antelope, with their conspicuous faces

the wildebeest, a species which not uncommonly loses an eye in fighting, in the reduncines it is outlined by a pale surround.

But whereas the sandy-coloured coat of the roan could be seen as providing the animal with a camouflage in its woodland habitat, the gaudy black and white pattern of the oryx, its painted face, piebald forelegs, black lateral line and coloured hindquarters with their black tail, seem designed to make it stand out and ensure that its postures can be easily interpreted by others. One suggestion is that its pattern may have evolved in close connection with its peculiar 'tournaments'.

These tournaments most commonly take place in the early morning or at the start of a rainstorm, just as sparring often does in many other species. They consist of one or more animals running around a herd in broad circles, a galloping spurt changing to a hackney gait, the animal hunching its neck back and throwing up its chin, swinging the head from side to side in rhythm with its motion, so that the black and white of the apache-painted face flashes in unison with the coloured knees. Only the war-whoops are missing from this extraordinary display, as the young bulls circle, feinting towards individuals in the centre which may meet the feint with a clash, even with juveniles, the oryx using its horns like staves to strike or fend off blows. Excitement may spread, until many of the herd are running around in the circle with spurts of galloping and hackney gait pacing, interspersed with brief clashes with the horns. Those challenged may fend off with their horns, avoid the challenge or actively respond; the whole seeming to function as a ritual device for testing rank order. Such a ritual minimises the risk that fighting entails with such dangerously-

Figure 8.9   A herd of fringe-eared oryx at a waterhole, with a female getting a better view from a termite mound

armed animals, and at the same time allows a wide range of ages to participate, as well as both sexes.

The magnificent adult bull sable in his jet-black cowl, leaving only his black and white face poking out, seems to separate the face from the forequarters, which, with their erect mane and huge curving horns, accentuate the power of the animal; an impression which it puts to good use in its lateral displays. In open country the bull's colour is highly conspicuous, but its preferred habitat is woodland where the dappling by sunlight and the obstruction to vision, render it less so. The chestnut-coloured sub-adult bulls mimic the no-less handsomely coloured cows; and it is probably in connection with this similarity that the adult bull's distinctive finery has evolved. The cows themselves show a darkening of the cheeks, neck and mane with age, which may help to signify their status in their hierarchically organised female society, their colour grading them by age.

Visual emphasis of the horns and shoulder mass is common to bulls of several species of antelope; the greater kudu has both mane and beard, and the eland has a great dewlap to magnify the effect; the impression of size reinforcing male dominance. But the other end of antelopes is usually just as gaily attired as is the front, snow-white buttocks outlined by black stripes and colourful black or white tails cannot fail to draw attention.

In the female it is very easy to visualise this patterning as having significance, both for the attraction of the male and for the imprinting of the juvenile on the mother. In the Grant's gazelle for example, there is a vertical stripe of black perineal skin between brilliant white buttocks, while black skin surrounds the teats, contrasting with the white hair of the udder. It is reasonable to suppose that this provides a visual focus for the fawn as has been suggested, the attention then being transferred to the vertical black stripe on each side of the buttocks, which mimics the perineal area, imprinting the juvenile's attention on the rump so that it follows its mother. An imprinting which later transfers to adult society an important social bonding. Such outlining of the buttocks is conspicuous in other gazelles, and also in the impala where it undoubtedly plays a role in herding.

Rump patterns of one sort or another are usually common to both sexes but seem unlikely, in my opinion, to act as sexual releasers, or 'guides' for the males. Both sexes in the defassa waterbuck for example, have a distinctive white blaze on the rump; replaced in the common waterbuck by a thin white ring, described as looking as if the animal had just sat on a newly-painted lavatory seat. Its retention in this reduced form, or alternatively its enlargement in the defassa, suggests that the white pattern has some significance to the species; but I once witnessed an inexperienced adult male repeatedly trying to mount a rather bewildered-looking female from the side, so that it was obviously not reacting to any stimulus provided by the rump. The significance probably lies in herding and following responses, but it may play a part in appeasing dominant males, providing them, we might say, with thoughts of following their mother in infancy.

In the kongoni the hindquarters are very pale, forming a contrast with the armed forequarters with their conspicuous horns raised up on their bony pedicel – perhaps this is the significance, the hindquarters are signalled as non-aggressive. When hartebeest or topi territorial bulls meet, they tend to approach one another with nods or sideways shaking of the head, drawing attention to the horns. In contrast the wildebeest shows little

Figure 8.10   A young male sable bows his head and tucks in his tail in deference to the bull on the left, resplendent in his black and white livery

Figure 8.11   A female Grant's gazelle with her calf, showing the contrasting rump pattern. Note the well-developed horns in this species

horn silhouette from the side view, so meets another with jerky tosses of the head in order to draw attention to the horns.

Some displays are obvious, like the white dorsal ruff of the springbok, which is only erected when alarmed. Such a distinctive signal doubtless has some connection with the dense numbers that this species adopted in the past. Other, less numerous small antelopes, have much less-developed signals; like the tommy which can flare only its rump. Other species which also flare the rump are the dik-dik and the oribi.

Predators watch and wait. They take the animal which makes a mistake, they take the sick and the injured. They take animals which have concealing colouration, and those that do not. It all depends largely on chance, so antelopes have been able to turn their outward appearance to other uses. But the reader must be aware that the remarks concerning the use of colour and pattern in communication are only speculative; we have no experiments to confirm the reality of this. Suitable experiments are not beyond the wit of man: one zoologist studying red deer tied a pair of antlers to his head and painted the seat of his trousers white, to see how the stags would communicate with him. As far as I recall they fled in terror! But I would not recommend anyone to try such methods with the larger antelopes, they might find that it is they who are put to flight, and not the experimental subject.

Fighting

Fighting is the last resort among male rivals and is generally avoided by innate or ritual displays comprising threat, intimidation and bluff. Sequences of actions designed to impress the other with the strength and power of his potential adversary, in which colour and pattern probably all come into play. Rivals signal to each other with perhaps a lick of the lips, a flick of the ears or tail, movements of the eyes, as well as the much more obvious postures relating to the carriage of the head and body. And when one of the rivals fails to be intimidated, perhaps by not turning away and presenting the appeasing view of his buttocks, then they fight.

Rushing violently together in a flurry of dust, two waterbuck males lock their horns with a loud crash, each belligerent thrusting with over 250 kg of weight behind their needle-sharp points. The two contestants are fast and they are adept, with a lightning-like rapidity of thrust and parry of moves quicker than the eye can follow. Licking their lips vigorously and violently wagging their tails, penises erect in their excitement, now falling to their knees in a desperate attempt to maintain position, laboured bleats and grunts mingle with the clash of horns and the thud of their dancing hooves; as they wrestle to and fro, each seeking to stab the other in the side, and at the same time avoid being stabbed himself.

Such is the fight of the waterbuck, sharp and ferocious in its intent. If a mortal blow cannot be dealt the fight comes to an end when both combatants are exhausted, and each turns and slowly walks away with laboured breaths and as much dignity as he can muster. There is no ritual thrust and parry; each makes his thrusts and parries like a fencer, trying to get in his horn points before the other can stop him, while the horn's elegant chippendale ridges act as a brake, so that when opposing horns clash they do not slide easily down on each other to crack the animal on the head.

The horns are the waterbuck's sword or rapier, and the 2 cm thick skin of the neck, once prized by the Boers for making boots or *veldschoen* because

Figure 8.12   The furious fight of territorial male waterbuck

of its toughness, is his shield. It is on this shield that he receives his opponent's rapier-like thrusts if he is not quick enough to parry them. To deal a mortal blow the waterbuck must get past this defence and stab his opponent in the side by managing to push the head to one side, disengaging, and thrusting all at the same time before the opponent can recover himself. From time to time an animal is successful in doing this, but the reason that fatalities are relatively rare is because if one of the contestants is younger or weaker, he will turn and run as soon as he feels that he is outmatched. Thus the most serious fights are those between equally matched pairs, where a fatal blow can only be dealt if one of the pair happens to make a slip. Large animals generally try to avoid the potentially more dangerous conflict by their displays of bluff, than do small ones. The grysbok, for example, shows little evidence of ritual displays or posture, and wades straight into the attack, dropping to its knees and stabbing with its short spikes.

In the Queen Elizabeth Park I recorded three deaths of waterbuck caused by fighting, the result of horn wounds in the abdomen where the victor had managed to penetrate his rival's guard and get in a side thrust. This can be a relatively slow and evidently painful way to die for the wounded animal often goes and lies in water. I saw one do this in Uganda, and another in the Saint Floris Park of the Central African Republic. In the latter case, after lying for a day or so in the water, the unfortunate animal evidently committed suicide by thrusting its head under the surface and keeping it there.

Other cases of waterbuck being killed are reported from both South Africa and from Kenya; but the most famous instance of all occurred at Kenya's Treetops Hotel. Here, a buck was pursued by another into the water. Stumbling against a sunken log, the buck was horned in its side by its pursuer who left it lying there, colouring the water crimson with its blood. Not the least remarkable thing about this incident is that it was filmed by Her Royal Highness Princess Elizabeth, who the next morning descended from Treetops as Queen of England; His Majesty King George the Sixth having died during the night.

In mediaeval times animals were endowed with virtues representative of God's meaning, and there seems to be but little difference between this fantasising and the school of thought which developed, particularly in the 1960s, contrasting man's violence with the peaceful nature of animals. Animals were alleged to rarely maim or wound one another in combat, let alone murder each other. Horns were for decoration, to impress rivals with, not to use on them. One well-known authority went so far as to say that animals which had dangerous weapons seldom used them against others of their own kind, but this is of course exactly what they are both designed and used for. If they were for the purpose of protecting the bearer from predators, then surely both male and female would require horns of equal capability. Yet the female's horns, when present, and this is not often the case, are always much more slender than are those of the male.

Fights are frequent on the territorial grounds of the Uganda kob, the opponents running into one another with great determination. I never witnessed any deaths myself, although I know of one certain occurrence, simply because I was unable to devote the time to watching them. But large numbers of skulls near the arenas probably testify to death from this cause, and are not those of lion kills as has been suggested. Indeed the kob abandon their activities when lions are present.

The most pugnacious fighters, whatever the species, are easily identified by their worn down and battered horns. There is no doubt in my mind from my observations in the wild, that among those species which use their horns primarily for fighting, large size is not intimidatory. Those record trophies so beloved of sportsmen denote, as often as not, weak males; those which avoid using their horns in combat. I analysed horn length in relation to the age of the buck in both waterbuck and impala, and found that although in rare cases very long horns are possessed by an old buck, they are found most frequently in the young adults which have not yet had a chance to wear them down.

By making measurements on live animals which were captured and recaptured, I found that the waterbuck actively wears down the length of his horns, seemingly by goring the earth to keep the tips sharp. But I recall in my study seeing one magnificent buck which carried the biggest horns that I had ever seen; however his appearance belied his nature, for he was no monarch of the glen but a timid and cowardly animal, always deferring to those others less well-endowed than he, and keeping well out of my way also. It may be true, when we come to the ornate structures of the kudu, for example, that the horns have evolved more for intimidatory display than as effective weapons of aggression; but this does not seem to be so among the strictly territorial species.

The primitive horn was probably a short, smooth straight spike, sticking up at right angles to the skull. This is similar to that found in the modern rhebuck, a species reported to kill its rivals frequently during the rut. The shape of the horns determines how the animal uses them; the departure from a short stabbing spike (dangerous for the wielder as well as for the receiver, for the former may dislocate his own neck if he cannot withdraw his horns quickly enough) demanding a variety of different techniques. The waterbuck with its slightly forward-curving horns lunges; the sable with its backward-curving arcs hooks at his opponent, sinking on his knees to do so. The greater kudu wrestles with his horns, locking them together with those of its opponent, and trying to throw him off balance; while the wildebeest, for his part, deals vicious, sideways hooks.

Figure 8.13   The powerful horns of the male waterbuck, showing their elegant Chippendale ridges

When wildebeest fight in earnest, they go down on their knees and press their foreheads flat against the ground, countering boss to boss, while each tries to disengage and launch a swipe at the other's throat, which is protected by its thick skin and mane of hair. All of the alcelaphine antelopes fight like this, and the aim seems to be, as it is in the waterbuck, to gore the opponent's side. Scrabbling on their knees the wildebeest pivot quickly in a flurry of dust, racing sideways like crabs. They often break a horn in such violent tussles, many lose an eye, but mortal injury is relatively rare for the same reason as in other species – that only well-matched individuals reach the stage of such aggressive encounters.

It is considered that the objective in antelope fighting is not to kill off the opponent, but merely to drive him away. The function of the contest is to decide who is the stronger, not to kill the weaker. This is a matter of conjecture, for there is no inhibition to killing once combat is engaged. If one of the combatants makes a slip he is attacked mercilessly, as we saw in the case of the waterbuck at Treetops; although only one thrust is given, and I know of no case where a victor has repeatedly horned the vanquished. But there is always considerable danger involved in serious fighting, as even wounding may be a death warrant if predators are numerous in the area. Even so, antelopes do not normally just rush straight at one another and fight, unless a female on heat is involved. More usually, if a mature territorial waterbuck, for example, sees another trespassing in his territory, his reaction as often as not is to gallop at the intruder. If the latter quails before the charge and turns and runs, then the chase is on, and woe betide the trespasser if the pursuer catches up with him. But if the intruder has the nerve to stand his ground when the owner comes galloping at him, then the latter will slow up, stop, and take his opponent's measure. There then follows a ritualised performance which has basic moves common to most ungulates, parts of which we have already touched upon in the discussion of colour and pattern.

Four movements can be identified which serve to avoid direct combat. They are:

The rush-threat. The galloping at another, such as that just described. If the one on the receiving end is unsure of himself he flees, and contact is avoided.

The weapon-threat. Having rushed at another who stands his ground, or simply having walked up to him, or when being approached by another, the horns are inclined towards the other; usually in a slow, stiff-necked manner.

Displaying. This has been given such names as 'proud posture' or 'present threat'. In this move the intimidating male adopts a characteristic posture, usually broadside on, to show off his power; for example, his thick neck or large body size.

Scar-threat. Usually executed by the less confident of the two and consists of fighting bushes or horning the earth, to show how brave and ferocious he is.

Ritual

Let's see how this happens in practice when two waterbuck of unequal status meet. This is common enough, for whenever the older members of a bachelor group, who are beginning to become aware of their maturity, see a territorial buck nearby, it seems that they simply cannot resist approaching him and testing his reactions. To begin with their approach is by no means bold, and indeed may only be tried on with the younger territorial bucks that the bachelors do not regard as aggressive.

A young buck would approach cautiously, at first standing and sniffing from a distance; perhaps with the object of identifying the territorial buck from his scent, or to determine what social odours he was emanating. Encouraged, he would then advance with neck held low and outstretched in the submissive posture, champing his jaws in the same manner that a submissive doe will do. This posture is rather like that of the dog, neck stretched out and head held low; but in this way the horns are directed maximally away from the other, in the same posture that the buck adopts when courting a doe.

Accosted in this manner the territorial buck adopts his display stance, sticking his tail out behind him and showing his penis (not all species do this), he holds his head with his neck stiffly curved rather like the attitude of a Viennese Lipizzaner horse. Sable and greater kudu tend to exaggerate this stance even more, so that the head is bent lower. This shows off the buck's fighting potential, his size, the thickness of his neck (his shield), and the readiness of his horns. With a young buck approaching this is usually as far as it goes for the dominant buck, who holds the stance while the other approaches and sniffs him gingerly on the nose and neck. He then some-

Figure 8.14   A territorial male waterbuck displays himself, in the broadside position with arched neck, to an approaching young bachelor male

times engages horns, leaping away as soon as any pressure is felt from the adult. If there is any sudden movement of the adult's horns, even if it is only a twitching caused by flies, the younger buck will instantly leap out of range. If the bucks are equally matched, then the engagement of the horns would be the signal for a struggle to start in earnest.

One day I was watching such an interaction which involved a fairly new territorial buck, perhaps not yet quite sure of himself and not entirely respected by the bachelors, who having adopted his intimidatory stance seemed to be at a loss as to what to do next. This encouraged the bachelor buck who had approached him, to start horning him in the rump, and, becoming bolder at the lack of response, in the side. The territorial buck, for his part, did not seem to know what to do, seemingly inhibited against turning on the impertinent younger buck, until a particularly painful prod in the belly caused him to jump, and the younger animal immediately ran off like a teasing child. I never saw such a display take place with the older bucks, which would presumably have just threatened the younger buck if he tried to take such liberties. The explanation on the part of the younger buck can be explained in terms of 'dominance testing', more or less a routine checking to confirm whether the older buck is superior in status or not; whether in fact he really *is* a territorial male. The latter's actions seemed to suggest that there is a certain amount of learning involved which he had not yet fully apprehended.

When interactions between adult males are much more frequent, as they are among the sedentary wildebeest during the territorial season, there is much more ritual involved. In the Ngorongoro Crater territorial bulls are estimated to have at least seven encounters with their neighbours each day, and yet more are known to take place at night. Obviously few of these lead to fights, a mutual display of intolerance satisfying the animals' ego.

No two sequences are ever the same in the ritual of the wildebeest, which has a repertoire of some 30 actions which he may use; but some actions stand out. A typical challenge ritual has been described as one in which a bull invades the territory of another with his head down in the grazing attitude, apparently feeding. At the approach of this intruder, the owner presents his broadside view in challenge, head held up but not exaggeratedly so. The would-be challenger then walks close by in the opposite direction and rubs his head on the other's rump. At this the latter urinates, the challenger sniffing the urine and curling back his lips in the characteristic lip-curling display usually reserved for testing whether cows are on heat, while the former inclines his horns. The two may then circle one another, usually, but not always, grazing or pretending to do so, until one or the other makes a feint, and both drop to their knees confronting each other, horning or plucking grass. They then both get up and perform what has been termed the 'alarm display', each looking at an imaginary source of alarm, heads up, alert, snorting and stamping. After this elaborate ritual the invader may return to his own territory in the grazing attitude, or take up the fighting stance on his knees once more. But these actions may come in any sequence. Sometimes the challenged bull will simply lie down in the middle of it all, refusing to play and causing the other to copy him; or one of the pair may indulge in rolling on the ground as the bull often does when he is on his own.

At high intensity displays, pawing the ground, head shaking, and cavorting take place. Cavorting early on earned the wildebeest the name of 'clown of the plains', and consists of prancing, bucking, twisting the head and lashing the long, conspicuous tail. At its highest level of intensity the hindlegs are kicked up in the air (perhaps distributing scent), tail flying, as if the animal were being ridden in a Wild-West rodeo; and it is most spectacular when two bulls race alongside their common boundary blowing metaphorical raspberries at one another. A person walking through a territorial network particularly provokes this display, as individuals are forced to run out of their territories to those of others; which is why attention was drawn to this behaviour at a very early date.

The black wildebeest has almost identical rituals, while many of the same elements are found in a wide range of species. Head shaking, in which the animal twists its head from side to side on its axis, as opposed to nodding, I have seen only among young waterbuck sparring, never during fighting among adults, but as we have seen there is not much ritual about the waterbuck's interactions. Exclusive to the wildebeest appears to be the rubbing of the head on the other's rump (perhaps a form of scent-marking with the facial gland), the urine sniffing accompanied by lip-curling, and rolling. Rubbing the head on the rump, if it is not a scent-marking gesture, would seem to be more in the nature of a friendly appeasement gesture than an aggressive one; while the significance of urine sniffing between males is unknown.

During these challenge rituals the bulls, normally very vocal grunting warnings at others approaching their territories, do not grunt. This is taken to underline the fact that these ritual encounters are for the purpose of confirming the status of the owners, not to take possession. When possession of another's territory is the object fighting takes the place of ritual, in the manner already described. Serious fights last for up to 20 minutes' duration; while bulls competing for cows during the rut usually run at each other without any preliminaries, bang heads together and then run back again to their cows immediately afterwards.

Displays by impala are usually between territorial bucks, and the broadside presentation differs from that of the waterbuck, for example, in that the head tends to be held up, the upright position of the neck showing off its thickness. The horns are initially directed backwards rather than forwards, while the tail is tucked in. Accentuating the stance, the buck inclines his horns like a waterbuck. At the approach of a challenger the tail is half lifted and the white hairs expanded. A sub-dominant buck initiating this reaction then usually cautiously smells the tail region. The two may then promenade in a circle in a stiff-legged deliberate gait, while the dominant buck may incline his horns as the other approaches and sniffs his forehead gland. The two may then stand and each turn his head away from the other, while the dominant buck may yawn in an exaggerated manner or rapidly flick the tongue in and out.

If such displays do not solve the dispute, the next stage is more threatening demonstrations, which are characterised by much more rapid movements. One buck may 'push' another back into his own territory without touching him, simply advancing with horns lowered while the other retreats before him. But the farther that one is pushed back into his own territory, the more confident does he become, until the point is reached where the roles are reversed. In this way two bucks may oscillate back and forth over a territorial boundary for 10 to 15 minutes. Rarely, such encounters lead to actual fighting. This is most commonly only a brief clash of horns, sometimes resulting in one of the bucks immediately giving up and turning away, at which the other gives chase.

Impala often feint without touching the horns, but when engaged and fighting with force, they pivot round in a circle with great rapidity. In the Serengeti one was recorded as breaking a front leg and yet another dislocated one, since during scrabbling with the front legs in an attempt to prevent themselves being pushed backwards, they often get their legs mixed up with their horns. There is one report of a contestant which looked away for a moment, and paid for the error with his life.

Fighting among kob has many similarities to that in impala, particularly feinting without engaging the horns, the contestants spreading their legs before them and facing each other like playful dogs; or standing erect with each buck facing away from the other. The Grant's gazelle adopts a similar stance but it differs in that the gazelles face in opposite directions instead of towards each other, but turn their heads and tilt them back. The two bucks approach each other with their heads slightly tilted away, and when about to pass they both stop, whipping their heads round to face one another and throwing them back and up so that the neck bulges prominently. Returning their heads to the normal position they then flick them back again, repeating the action or moving around one another in a circle. If one of them neglects to present a side view of its body, or if the horn tips touch, this triggers a clash. If neither gives way then they confront each other, and after a few preliminary feints, clash horns. Pushing with their noses almost flat on the ground like the wildebeest, each attempts to twist or throw the other off balance so that it can stab at its opponent's side.

The gerenuk with their long necks are clearly not built for fighting by ramming at one another in this manner, and so have developed a unique form of fighting by clashing the horns together with violent nods of the head.

During these encounters, whether simple challenges or fights in deadly earnest, most species show irrelevant behaviour or 'displacement activity' as it is called; licking, scratching or feeding during pauses in the conflict.

The life of an antelope buck is not an easy one, for belying the grazing herd's placid appearance, his survival is based not only on an ability to avoid the dangers of predation, but also his ability to secure a position of power for himself by his skill in lethal battle. His success in this determines his reproductive success, for unless he can hold a territory, or a position of dominance in a rank hierarchy, then he cannot reproduce. Whether we like to admit it or not, sex and violence are inextricably linked in his life.

9 Territoriality – the basis of antelope social organisation

Display, fighting, and the assertion of superiority, are designed, in the vast majority of cases, with the object of gaining and maintenance of a territory. Antelopes may lead solitary lives and be territorial; they may be solitary and not territorial, in which case they live in what we call a 'home range'; they may be gregarious and territorial; or, the least common, they may be gregarious and non-territorial.

The wide occurrence of territorial behaviour in the animal kingdom has considerably intrigued zoologists, wildlife naturalists, and even an American playwright, the late Robert Ardrey who popularised the concept in his book *The Territorial Imperative*; and it has led to much speculation as to its advantages over other possible types of less competitive behaviour. It is in the expression of territorial behaviour that we see the horns of the buck coming into play in all their variety of shape and grandeur, and we are led to ponder whether the development of horns and other male accoutrements are designed to this end – the maintenance of territorial supremacy.

But rather than enter into the polemics of territorial behaviour and its functions, let us content ourselves with simply looking at some of the better-known examples of territorial behaviour among the antelopes, illustrating the several ways in which the buck may find his place in society. To do this we must first look at what we mean by the terms 'territory' and 'home range'.

Definitions

Territory was first identified in birds, the earliest reference being attributed to the ancient Greek Zenodotus who, in the third century BC, quoted the proverb that one bush did not shelter two robins. But lamentably enough it was a remarkable description of the family life of a now extinct species of dodo *Pezophaps solitarius*, published in 1707, which set naturalists thinking; and led to a detailed account of territory in bird life appearing just after the middle of last century.

Some little time before this, in 1824, the first description of territorial behaviour in an African antelope was unwittingly made by the explorer-naturalist William Burchell in South Africa, who described the solitary habit of the black wildebeest and its territorial advertising. Later, in 1850, the hunter Cumming described in the same species a 'cunning old bull wildebeest' which kept others out of its valley. But Cumming supposed that the animal was warning others away from him, and not from itself. Neither of these writers was aware of the significance of what they saw, and the great numbers of hunters and naturalists who were to follow after them in Africa, all seemed to be totally blind to the idea of animals 'behaving'.

Famous writers like Selous, Stigand, Roosevelt and Heller, or Percival, make no mention of what was enacted before their eyes. Solitary bulls were always regarded as old animals that had been ousted from the herd, or they were 'sentinels'. We had to wait for almost a century from the time that the phenomenon was described in birds, for territorial behaviour to be related to a social context in a large mammal, when in 1937 Fraser Darling described rutting in the Scottish red deer; although the red deer is not territorial in the sense that we understand the definition today.

By the late 1950s territorial behaviour had come to be recognised in a wide range of mammals; but interest in this aspect of behaviour in African antelopes seems to have been awakened by the discovery in 1957 of a 'lek-type' of territoriality in the Uganda kob. This was first noticed by the wife of an American researcher who was studying elephants; a casual percipience that led to the unfolding of a remarkable story. What the elephant researcher's wife noticed was that on the Semliki plains, where the population of kob was estimated at some 12,000 head, numbers of bucks were concentrated on small 'stamping grounds'.

These stamping grounds were patches of ground worn almost bare by the bucks' circumambulations, where they displayed to does in a characteristic manner, in between fighting and displaying among themselves to retain their pitch. It was in fact the most extreme type of territorial behaviour to be revealed as existing among African antelopes; and indeed for any mammal.

Any definition of territoriality is likely to be fraught with qualification, since there are so many variations for the semantic purists to squabble over; but the defence by the male of a piece of ground against competing males, a concept which can be extended to the female, is sufficient for our purposes. This immediately reveals an important principle, that the male does not defend the female – the idea of the 'bull with his harem' as was so often thought to be the case in the past, following Darwin's views on sexual selection – but a piece of ground. Even in the moving, migratory wildebeest, the bull is seen as defending an area around himself, and not the cows which are in the area.

There is a clear distinction between territoriality and the concept of the 'home range', for in this latter there is no defence of property, each tolerates the other's presence and no specific claim is laid to the land. We saw in the waterbuck that the bachelor herd may operate a 'closed shop' on their home range; but this consisted of preventing others from joining the group, not chasing them off the property over which the group roamed. There was thus no defence of property, and indeed one could say that the 'property' did not belong to the bachelors, but to the territorial males. Among those species which live in a home range, rather than a territory, the males establish a hierarchy among themselves to determine their mating rights. All of the African antelopes adopt one or the other of these two categories of social organisation, the vast majority being territorial.

Types of Territoriality

The most basic form of territoriality is that shown by the small forest antelopes, and it is possible that this approaches the ancestral type of organisation. Territories are owned by individuals, and this type seems to occur among the suni, and probably most of the forest duikers. We know little about them because of the difficulty of observing these wary and secretive creatures, although some studies have been carried out on the blue duiker in the Gabon forests with the aid of radio-transmitters attached to the animals. This species apparently lives in pairs, and both male and female will live amicably together in captivity; but I have rarely, if ever, flushed two blue duikers together in the west African savannas. Many of the small species are noted for their antagonism towards one another, suggesting that they only come together to breed; the doe then separating to rear the young on her own.

In the naïve belief that each would enjoy some company, I once placed a young pet common duiker in a pen with a forest duiker. As soon as the two saw one another their hackles rose, and the common duiker very warily and slowly lay down in the opposite corner of the pen as far away from the other as possible. There they lay, staring with hostility at each other until I finally removed the intruder.

A farmer acquaintance of mine in Tanzania was very successful in the difficult task of rearing small antelopes, several of which were brought to him by his workers. Among his collection he had a small suni which lived in a paddock, with a heap of brushwood in the centre which it used as a hideaway. I well remember my first meeting with this little creature. When I entered the paddock the suni came bounding out of the pile of brushwood towards me. How sweet! Or so I thought as I bent to reciprocate his eager welcome with a pat on the head. But no such friendly thoughts were in the suni's mind, for when he was within striking range he launched himself at me with all of his might, and I yelped in pain as his tiny, needle-pointed horns jabbed into my outstretched arm. Undaunted, he repeatedly hurled himself in a fury against my ankles until I beat a hasty retreat! Despite its diminutive size, and a weight of no more than 8 kg, the suni is a very pugnacious animal indeed; and I was dealt the same harsh treatment as would be dealt to any other suni that might have the audacity to venture into his territory. Nevertheless, as many as four males and three females are reported as having been reared together in captivity, so their aggressive instinct can be suppressed.

These small forest species probably occupy their territories year-round, since there is little seasonal change in the rain forest. They do not use vocal or visual displays to advertise either their presence or their territories as far as is known, methods which would be of limited use in the forest. Instead they live in a world of smells, marking their territories by means of their prominent scent glands, and possibly dung piles. Although duiker are said not to be vocal, it is well-known in certain quarters in Africa that they can be attracted by a nasal call. In the dense tropical forest in the Central African Republic I was once exploring with some pygmy guides and asked one to give me a demonstration of calling up a duiker; which he did thinking that I wanted to shoot it. We sat down in the gloom of the forest floor and he proceeded to make an intermittent bleating sound, holding his nose between the thumb and forefinger. In a few minutes it seemed, suddenly there was a red duiker (I never identified which species) tentatively stepping towards us, already but a few metres away. My companion made a movement with his camera and it was gone. Whether the sound resembles that of another male, or that of a female, has yet to be determined.

Scent marking has been studied in captive Maxwell's blue duiker. These mark by means of a gland just below and in front of the eye, which they press against the object to be marked. When released into an enclosure a male's first reaction is to go around the perimeter marking the trunks or stems of trees and saplings, two or three times in succession. After pressing the gland hard against a stem the duiker would then often thrash the stem with his horns, and paw the ground around it. Thrashing and pawing are identical behaviours to that shown by such a widely-separated species as the North American white-tailed deer; and it is also shown, for example, by the impala.

It has been suggested that the function of tree-thrashing and ground pawing is to provide a visual signal as well as a scent one; a sort of 'trespassers will be prosecuted' sign. More frequent marking was observed after another male had been present, but not if a female had been present beforehand. In this species the females also marked, and also did so more frequently after the presence of another female but not after that of a male.

Before two blue duiker males fight, they anoint each other's faces with their glands in the manner of two people touching cheeks in greeting, repeating this gesture during pauses between combat. Males and females also marked one another's faces, as did two females; so it is hard to determine the reason for this behaviour when in the one case it appears to be used in a pair-bonding situation, and in the other in a conflict one.

The common duiker, whose habitat is woodland and bush rather than forest, is the possessor of a similar face gland, opening by a series of pores along a slit-like mark; and marks its territory in the same way. This species is often found singly, but seemingly just as often in pairs. Captive males placed together will always fight violently, while females are belligerent to newcomers of their own sex, but do not fight those that they are brought up together with.

Fire must be a rather traumatic experience for the common duiker, removing without trace all of the familiar smells of its environment in a matter of minutes, as well as its territorial markers. A pet, reared in captivity in the Akagera Park, showed me just how much one could be affected by this experience. At about six month's of age it was released into the wild, and although I expected to see it often about my house, I was disappointed to find that it disappeared completely. Some two months later there was one of the usual annual grass fires, and soon after it had passed I was called outside by the cook. There was the duiker standing in the open in the centre of the back yard, hunched up and with head hanging down, the very picture of defeat and dejection!

'Now that his house has been burnt down, he's come back to ours', was the cook's apt interpretation. The duiker had returned to what were the only familiar surroundings remaining in a charred and blackened wilderness. I approached the dejected fellow, stroked him and offered him a tit-bit; after which, somewhat consoled, he made his departure. But thereafter he was often seen in the vicinity of the house, and if I went out to him he would run up to greet me and stand to be stroked. The fire, and perhaps more so the subsequent openness of his surroundings, had completely altered his nature. He was now back in balance with his artificial upbringing.

From the fundamental type of territoriality which seems to be shown by the duikers, we progress to that in which both male and female live together in the territory and join in its defence; male to male and female to female. Here we find the romantic situation so beloved of the earlier naturalists where, in species such as the dik-dik, couples apparently stay together for life; an otherwise rare situation in the polygamous world of the antelopes.

This type of territory seems to be mostly confined to the neotragines, small to very small antelopes such as dik-dik, klipspringer, possibly the steenbok, oribi, and also possibly the southern reedbuck. Female neotragines, with the exception of the East African race of the klipspringer, are hornless, and so cannot contribute to real territorial defence except in female to female situations. All of the species listed, with the exception of the reedbuck, have the prominent pouch-like gland below the eye, filled with a sticky black exudate.

Dik-dik pairs occupy a territory of from 2 to 10 ha in area in the Serengeti, where both male and female live together. They are usually accompanied by their current offspring, which remains with them in the territory until it is mature, or until the next birth. With probably one of the shortest gestation periods known among the antelopes, the dik-dik gives birth twice in the year and so the turnover is quick. At high densities there may be more than one female sharing the territory, but when they live in couples, if one of the pair dies or disappears, then the bereaved survivor remains alone for a long time, making no attempt to seek another partner. Dik-dik do not have a reputation for aggression, and vigorous fighting has not been observed. Disagreeing males rush together with heads lowered, but normally do not make contact, contenting themselves with threatening one another and erecting the crest on the forehead.

Territories are marked by means of the facial gland secretion which is placed on twigs and stems by the male, the female's glands being undeveloped. Instead of pressing or rubbing against an object, the gland is placed over the tip of a stem, as in the oribi; but unlike the latter the dik-dik does not clean up the old exudate first but simply adds to it so that accumulations can become as big as a pea. Reference has already been made to the species' habit of making dung piles, but to what extent these mark the territory is not clear.

Probably all of the neotragines have a similar system of pairing and territorial occupation. Klipspringers are usually seen in pairs, but in Ethiopia a fifth of the groups comprised one male and two females, while up to eight animals have been reported together. In this species the male spends less time feeding than the female, thus possibly allowing her to feed more efficiently, while he spends more time looking out for predators. Both sexes defend the territory, but only in the East African race is the female horned. The size of the territory varies greatly according to the habitat, from about 8 ha in Ethiopia to 15 to 49 ha in the Cape. The prominent facial gland is used by the male to mark the territory in the same manner as the dik-dik.

Among the neotragines most is known about territoriality in the oribi; the only one to inhabit grasslands. About a third of the territories in this species have been observed to hold pairs, while others have a solitary buck, or a buck with a doe and her offspring; but sometimes there is more than one doe, and up to five members have been recorded in a territory. But despite an early report, oribi have never been seen to be gregarious; never concentrating together for example on a post burn flush of new grass. Usually a neutral area containing water or a salt-lick was visited by different groups, but these groups never mingled, and threatened too close an approach by one another. The territories are permanently maintained, and seem to be about 25 ha in extent in the Akagera Park, quite large enough for such a small species; but the density in this area was sufficiently low that all territories were not necessarily adjacent to one another.

The beira antelope, although classed as being related to the neotragines, lacks a facial gland in both sexes. Nothing is known of this now rare species, although at the turn of the century a hunter reported seeing as many as six together, but less than this was more common.

An apparently intermediate type of territorial organisation is shown by the reedbucks, which seems to be similar in all three species. The southern reedbuck is said to occupy a home range, within which is a defended territory. In the Kruger Park this averaged about 35 to 60 ha in extent. Inhabiting long grass and avoiding bushed or wooded areas, the reedbuck lives in pairs or small family groups of buck, doe, and current offspring. Notoriously pugnacious in captivity, I knew of one in Uganda which would chase the native servants, knock them to the ground and pin them there! The owner finally removed its horns for fear of it inflicting serious injury.

Figure 9.1   Oribi pairs defend a territory together, even though the female is hornless

Fittingly enough this pugnacious animal has his own 'growlery', a core area where he spends most of his time, characterised by good food and cover, but the site is not necessarily permanent. The reedbuck male does not always move about with the doe, but the doe is attached to the same territory so he does not have to try and keep her in it; and the does have been recorded as assisting in its defence. The boundaries do not seem to be precise, and fluctuate in position, while adjacent boundaries often overlap and a neighbour may enter deep into another's territory. This apparent laxity conforms to the method delimiting the territory, which seems to be by the buck whistling to advertise his presence, and displaying in a sort of stotting motion. Whistling is the characteristic method of advertising as used by its cousin the kob, and results, as in the kob, in a chorus of replies from other bucks in the vicinity. I suspect that this is the principal method by which the territory is announced and accounts for the somewhat imprecise boundaries. Dung piles are deposited at random, and so would seem to be unlikely to serve as markers.

During the dry season reedbuck may concentrate on areas of good pasture, like those provided by a post burn flush, in temporary aggregations of up to a dozen animals in the southern reedbuck. Up to 50 have been recorded for the mountain reedbuck, but small groups of three are more common, as they are for the other species. They are thus able to suppress the territorial antagonism which they show towards one another for the greater part of the year, although during the dry season those which have their territories near to permanent water are often obliged to retract their boundaries as others press in on them from farther inland. But those which lack water in their own territories, are permitted to pass through the territories of others in order to drink; just as we shall see is the case in the waterbuck.

An average density of reedbuck seems to be about one to the square kilometre, but in some areas they are much more numerous than this. The biggest concentration that I have seen was in the Saint Floris Park. The highest density known for the bohor reedbuck is in the Dinder National Park of the Sudan, where some 225 to the square kilometre have been recorded. Up to 400 were counted in one place although large groups were the exception, most of the animals being in groups of five or less. But when they were alarmed they fled as a herd, contrary to the dispersion in all directions that we would expect to find to a truly independent species, and indicative of their apparently being on the borderline between herding and non-herding antelopes.

Other antelopes which tend to hide as the reedbuck does, do not adopt the same temporary herding habits. The reedbuck's cousin, the waterbuck, is a herding animal, with the exception of the adult buck; while its other close relative, the kob, carries this to its most extreme form, the bucks being territorially gregarious at high densities.

The waterbuck male operates what might be regarded as a standard type of territorial society, with the year-round defence of an area which supplies all of his needs in the form of food and cover, but not necessarily water. The latter point is rather surprising, considering the animal's absolute dependence on water; but as we saw in the reedbuck, no matter how aggressively a territory is defended, the owner never denies another the right to drink. Through this territory the does wander more or less at will, covering the properties of several bucks in their home range.

Bucks leave the relative security of the bachelor group at from five to six years of age to try and take over a territory for themselves. At least this is so in areas of high waterbuck density where the territorial potential is saturated and they cannot simply walk into a vacant place. They make this attempt at independence at the time at which body weight, testes weight and horn length, have all reached mature size; and the normally-growing buck has no possibility of accelerating this process. If he tried to obtain a territory by fighting at an earlier age, then he would be easily beaten by the older animals by virtue of their heavier weight alone. But probably before the testes have attained full weight the buck will not be sufficiently motivated to fight desperately, lacking a high enough level of male hormone to trigger the required aggressiveness; even although bucks show an interest in the does from about four years of age.

But the age at which a territory is successfully held will depend upon the degree of competition for territorial space; and to obtain a space the buck must fight for it, either killing, wounding or frightening another into giving up ownership. But bucks over nine years of age are already heading for retirement, so that even if all available territories in the area are occupied when a bachelor buck makes his first debut from the herd, at least by the end of his seventh year he will normally have managed to obtain a territory by ousting an older inhabitant. Indeed a vigorous enough six-year old might achieve this with a senior of ten or eleven years, although what the older ones lacks in youthful vigour they make up for in determination and the experience of many previous tough encounters.

My studies revealed how, in the absence of a suitably ageing owner who might be usurped, a young buck could obtain a territory. One approach was to move into an already occupied territory and to simply share it against the other's will, by restricting himself to a part near the boundary and trying to behave as unobtrusively as possible, by not competing for the territory itself. In this situation the rightful owner seemed to tolerate the intrusion at first, but eventually attacked and drove the would-be usurper out; or forced him to restrict himself to a very small part of the area. Here he would remain until he could either successfully challenge the owner, or give up and try again elsewhere. But most likely he would return to the bachelor herd to wait awhile before trying again. In one case history that I followed, the buck returned to the bachelor herd, left it again after six months to take up residence in a fringe area, and then returned once more to the original buck that he had challenged, 19 months after his first encounter with him. This time his perseverance was rewarded by his winning a third of the territory for himself.

Another method which I observed was for one to take up a position at the border between two or three territories, so that if threatened by one territory owner, the tyro could nip over the boundary into another territory where he would not be followed. If this was at the junction of three territories, then it was most unlikely that all three territory owners would be there at the same time.

Once a territory was won, I never saw any attempts to try and enlarge it. Although my studies showed that the bucks in the prime of life, that is at about nine years of age, possessed the biggest territories, this was because they graduated from smaller to larger ones. Finally, in old age, conquered in their turn, they were forced to retire to a small area again. Even when a neighbour was killed, either in battle or from other causes, there was no attempt to take over his territory. It was simply left vacant until taken up by another. Boundaries could thus be said to be 'inherited', although they do change over a period of time.

Among populations bordering rivers, territorial boundaries are apparently related to water frontage; but in areas surrounding lakes, access to water is not always the most important factor in deciding territory siting. Thus in one area of high density that I studied, all of the bucks had their territories inland, while the lakeside area, highly attractive with its water and lush green pastures, was used communally. When he wished to drink, which was a daily occurrence, a buck with a territory inland had to pass through the territories of others. He was permitted to do this provided that he adopted a submissive attitude, showing the necessary degree of deference to the territory owners. Thus the waterbuck system shows an intelligent flexibility of organisation, where rigid protocols are not insisted upon when necessity deems otherwise. Of course an animal which tried to defend a territory at the lakeside would be so continually harassed by animals which wanted to drink, that it would soon learn the futility of such an attempt.

Another example of the flexibility of the system may be seen at very high densities. The highest density recorded for waterbuck was in the Lake Nakuru National Park in Kenya, a density largely artificially induced by the protection given to remnant animal populations in the area, and a former absence of predators. Here a density of 72 to 106 to the square kilometre was estimated in one region; up to almost six times higher than the highest density that I found in Uganda, and from eight to more than eleven times the normal density that I was dealing with. But in spite of these very high densities, there was no evidence of the lek-type of territoriality developing as found in the kob at considerably lower numbers. It did seem, however, that young adult bucks, probably in the five to six years age range, were tolerated in territories. They apparently shared in the defence and even had opportunities to mate, whereas the bachelor groups as a whole were excluded.

At such high densities no doubt territorial owners had to compromise, total defence becoming impossible, with the younger bachelors being easier to keep out than the older ones. Such situations are not representative of the social structure as a whole, but do illustrate how it can adapt to different circumstances.

Boundaries were rigidly observed in the area of moderately high density that I studied. They were probably based upon topographical features which were apparent to the animals but not always to me, although in some cases they seemed to follow a natural feature such as a ridge of high ground. But even when they ran across open grassland their position was clear enough to their owners. Whenever one buck overstepped the limits into another's territory he was instantly challenged if the owner saw him, and displays would then take place resulting in the chasing of the intruder back across the boundary. If it was a weaker buck, sometimes he was just pushed back firmly forehead to forehead. When neighbours were each on their own side of the invisible boundary, although they might not be standing far apart, no crossing over would take place, although one might approach to the boundary and display. Only when a doe was on heat did neighbouring bucks sometimes disregard boundary etiquette, seeming to do so only when bucks from the bachelor group were involved.

One day I was watching a territorial buck placidly grazing with a group of does when he suddenly stopped and stared into the distance. Picking up my binoculars and following the direction of his gaze I could see a strange buck watching him from a good half a kilometre away. The territorial buck had not needed binoculars to tell him that it was a stranger, and the next moment he began to walk quickly and purposefully towards the trespasser. As soon as the latter saw his studied approach he took fright and ran off out of sight, long before the two were within any distance of each other. Without checking his pace the territorial buck continued straight to the spot where the visitor had last been standing and sniffed around. Clearly picking up the scent, he proceeded to follow it like a bloodhound. His nose held half a metre or so above the ground, he tracked it to his boundary where he abruptly lost interest and ambled back the way he had come.

Shortly afterwards the intruder ventured out of hiding, a lightly built young buck with slender horns rather close together, and made his way back sniffing in turn the places where the territorial buck had passed. There was no doubt in this, and in subsequent encounters, that bucks were identifying each other by the scent which they left in passing.

After the long wait through adolescence to achieve it, territorial mastership is relatively brief; for having passed their ninth year bucks are already in decline, and after ten years have little chance of holding their position against younger bucks. When vanquished they are driven to inhabiting marginal areas and do not go back to the bachelor herd, for as we have seen, the territorial owners would not tolerate them. So in this species at least, it is the old bucks which are forced to live in marginal or unfavourable habitat, and not the young. The most logical arrangement, since the old bucks have become the expendable part of the population.

The unfavourable habitats are either very small in size, sparse in vegetation, or have a vegetation cover not favoured by waterbuck, such as large tussock grasses or the coarse Indian sword grass; or they are far from water. In my study area I found their size to be just under 18 ha, which is probably inadequate to supply a waterbuck's nutritional needs year-round. Old bucks relegated to such areas do not survive many dry seasons.

I found no evidence to suggest that such old bucks ever lost their territorial urge. When ousted from their territory they often tried to return to it. One of my acquaintance, driven out in his tenth to eleventh year and forced to occupy a small area on eroded ground near to the lakeshore, returned to his former abode at least three times, each time to be chased away by its new owner. I remember how one day I was following the new owner when he entered a thicket. Great was my surprise when suddenly the old buck burst out of the other side and went streaking away, fleeing for all he was worth with the other in hot pursuit to the limit of the territory.

Unlike the reedbuck the waterbuck has no preferred spot in his territory, but ranges over the greater part of it fairly frequently, choosing any spot to rest. This is most often in the open, so that early hunters were wont to refer to 'solitary' bull waterbuck probably more than any other species of antelope.

The size of territories ranged from as little as 4 to as much as 146 ha in one of my study areas, and from 54 to 226 ha in another. It seemed that bucks could only defend a territory of a certain size, for whereas in the second area they had more than twice the area of land available to them than they did in the first, the territories of the prime bucks were only just over one and a half times larger. This suggested that the maximum defendable territory size was about 200 ha, compared to the 290 ha that I would have expected them to occupy. This means that the younger and older bucks can occupy larger territories in the less popular areas.

Figure 9.2   Bland-Sutton's interpretation (1911) of a kongoni bull advertising himself on a termite mound. From Man and Beast in Eastern Ethiopia, *Macmillan & Co*

An analysis of the visits made by does to a territory suggested that this might be the factor influencing territory size, for the bigger the area, concomitant with habitat desirability, then the greater would be the number of random doe visits. That is to say, the bigger the area then the more chance there was of does wandering into it. Or the wider the territorial buck casts his net, the more chance of success does he have. Thus it seems it is not the buck himself which the does are attracted to, unlike in the kob or the lechwe's lek-type of territorial system.

A kongoni bull, advertising his territory by standing on the top of a termite mound, is one of the few expressions of territorial behaviour that is easily noticed by the casual tourist in Africa. Bland-Sutton noted this behaviour in 1911, although the hunter-artist Millais referred to the hartebeest's attachment to its scrape or stamping ground as early as 1895. In spite of its more obvious manifestations, the type of territorial behaviour shown by the kongoni and other hartebeests has some similarity to that of the waterbuck, although the latter is not given to displaying itself on the top of termite hills.

The territories of the kongoni differ in not being as permanent as they are in the waterbuck, and also in that the whole area is not equally defended. One area within the territory is more vigorously guarded than the rest, a pattern similar to that found in the reedbuck. Among those hartebeest with a sharply defined breeding season, such as the Lelwel's in northern Uganda, a territory is only held for a part of the year, alternate drought and waterlogging of the soil causing seasonal displacement of the animals. By contrast the kongoni in Kenya breeds throughout the year, but has an annual peak, and as a consequence it remains in its territory year-round. But although these territories are permanent, the bulls still vacate them from time to time for anything from a few hours to several days. This of course leads to their being taken over by another, but they are usually easily taken back again by the original owner, although the turnover in Nairobi Park, where these studies were conducted, was very high.

In this area territories were ranged along river valleys reaching out at right angles up the slope of the valley, so that a range of habitat was covered. The less favourable habitats were occupied by old bulls, ousted from the prime areas, while the bachelor groups were normally excluded from the system, relegated to unfavourable habitat. But if territories bordering water were invaded in any number by bachelors during the dry season, the territorial bulls threw in the sponge and mingled amicably with the invaders. As we saw earlier, the young male in this species spends an extended length of time in the maternal group, so that by the time that it becomes a member of the bachelor group it probably has less than a year to wait before becoming territorial. So it can afford to rough it awhile because of the short period involved.

Mean territory size in the Nairobi Park was of the order of 31 ha, but this was a very fluctuating population; at the time of the study at a high level following recovery after a drought.

As in the waterbuck, the cows had a home range which covered several bull territories through which they wandered at will; but the system differed in that the cows formed small family groups of a mother accompanied by up to four consecutive offspring, rather than associating in random groupings.

Both sexes have a prominent facial gland just before the eye, as well as glands between the toes; but both cows and young have been seen to mark with the facial gland, rubbing it on the ground or on termite mounds.

In spite of the early remarks of Burchell and Cumming on the sentinel-like activities of the wildebeest, the territorial behaviour of this cousin of the hartebeest was only clearly described comparatively recently, from studies conducted in the Ngorongoro Crater in the 1960s. Wildebeest have an extremely sharply-defined breeding season as has been pointed out, and territorial behaviour is centred on this. Sedentary wildebeest have a similar kind of territorial structure to that of the hartebeest, with the bachelors being excluded from the territorial network. But the territorial drive declines in intensity after the annual rut, becoming weakest in the long dry season, when the bulls often quit their territories to feed and drink elsewhere. Where this necessitates crossing another's territory, as with some other species, a bull is permitted to pass without interference provided that he shows the necessary amount of deference to the owner. Some bulls may absent themselves from their territories for up to six months, often associating together in temporary bachelor groups; while when they are on their territories they are often in worse condition than are the bachelors which are excluded from them.

Each territory consists primarily of a 'stamping ground', a small, trampled bare patch, on which the bull defaecates, urinates, rolls, gores the ground and rubs his face, marking with the facial gland. In Ngorongoro Crater, with a density of 46 to 71 bulls to the square kilometre just before the rut, such territories were spaced with distances of from 130 to 160 m between bulls; but during the rut the density of bulls rose to 57 to 85 to the square kilometre, and the distance between them fell to a range of 120 to 147 m. In this we are approaching the type of intensive territorial behaviour shown by the kob, and as in that species, spacing appears to be maintained by visual estimation; while advertisement is by grunting and much displaying.

It has been estimated that up to 45 minutes each day are spent in interactions between neighbours, and although the wildebeest bull is a notoriously cantankerous beast, serious fights are said to be rare. Ritual display, or a brief tussle, usually suffices to decide dominance. But old bulls can often be encountered which have their horns battered to stumps, suggesting that some fights at any rate are serious.

The most sought after areas seem to be those in the centre of a territorial network, and it is here that most displays take place. The intensity of the interactions builds up to the rut, when 80 per cent of the cows are mated within a period of one month. When the cows, most of which are on heat, enter the territories, they are attracted to those in the centre, but as they pass through the encircling ones the bulls in these territories try to herd them to themselves. Activity rises to a frenzy as they strive to keep the cows from moving into another territory, and mate them at the same time; galloping back and forth, grunting and snorting their disapproval at the reluctant cows' efforts to elude them. In the end, many territories are lost through fatigue as the bulls have to bow out to recover.

Little or no mating takes place with the bachelors outside of the territorial network, so there is considerable motivation to enter the territorial arena to participate in the venery. The system thus strongly resembles that of the kob at high densities, the females in heat being attracted to the males, instead of the latter having to search them out. The same system has been confirmed to exist in the sedentary remnant populations of the black wildebeest in South Africa, even though the studies were conducted on a largely 'artificial' or re-introduced population; which serves to underline the deep fundamental nature of these social patterns.

In the Ngorongoro Crater populations, outside of the rutting season when the cows concentrate on good pastures, bulls from outlying territories leave and establish themselves as close to the cows as possible, breaking up the network when the cows move on; thus forming an incipient type of the organisation found in the migratory herds.

The territorial organisation of the Serengeti migratory wildebeest was somewhat more of a puzzle to unravel due to the dense numbers involved, especially during the rut when local densities of over 500 to the square kilometre are possible. The migratory populations consist of mixed aggregations of bulls, and cows with young; the bachelor groups being obliged to remain apart from the cows. When the vast assemblage which is moving across the plain, in some indefinable manner drifts to a halt, this is the signal for the bulls to immediately dash about creating temporary territories around themselves. Within the space of 15 minutes, each bull has cut out and herded together groups of about 16 cows and young, the distance between the bulls being as little as from 1 to 8 m. In this tightly packed scrum, each bull tries to exert his territorial rights for as long as the herd remains stationary.

When the herd drifts on again, the territories are abandoned, although a few bulls linger behind, moving on later. So despite the seeming chaos of these great herds, a similar type of territorial pattern exists to that found among the sedentary sector, attaining intense levels of activity during the rut when the bull continually tries to detain groups of cows among the moving mass, but only succeeds when the forward movement stops. He then herds and tries to mate them all at the same time in the midst of this dense mêlée. In a situation where the bull is denied his familiar dung pile and his identity with a prescribed spot, presumably display is even more important in promoting the image of these transient territories than it is for the more socially secure sedentary wildebeest.

The phrenetic behaviour of the migratory wildebeest is like a battleground, with its bedlam of indescribable uproar and tempestuous movement, and for a more pastoral view of Africa we must turn to the impala. This has always been my favourite antelope, one which is unsurpassed for grace and beauty. Yet although one of the most common of antelopes in East and Southern Africa, taking the place of the kob in the west, and an antelope whose behaviour can be seen almost daily by anyone who visits a game park, for a long time it was thought that the impala was not a territorial species. But longer term studies have shown that it exhibits the same basic territorial traits as are found in other antelope species, the buck becoming territorial in its third to fourth year.

In the Serengeti, where the longer term studies were carried out, during the wet season the impala displays a close territorial network, the size of the individual territories ranging from 2 to 122 ha in area. Through these the does with their young, and the bachelor herds, wander; the does using a home range of about 3 sq km which might cover up to a dozen buck territories.

But unlike other species that we have looked at, the size of an individual impala's territory tends to vary significantly almost from month to month. Smallest in the wet season when the impala need not roam far to satisfy his food requirements and has no need to include a water supply in his domain, they become largest in the dry season. At this time the territorial drive may become very weak, to the extent that the territorial bucks join with the other bucks, as in the wildebeest; but there is always a strong attachment to the original territory, to which the buck will eventually return. The territorial owner also allows the large herds of bachelors to wander over and share his territory, and may graze quite close to them, providing that they are not too close to himself in status, and also provided that they do not engage in any fighting or threat displays among themselves. If this happens he promptly chases them out, as he does also when breeding herds are present. So this is very similar to the tolerance shown by the waterbuck.

In the dry season a fresh flush of grass following burning or early rain in a territory can cause an invasion by other bucks and does, creating densities of up to 300 to the square kilometre. When this happens, as in other species, all attempts to maintain territorial integrity are abandoned as futile. A further factor which has served to cloud the picture of territoriality in this species is that bucks, ousted from their territories, appear to associate loosely together, forming aggregations separate to those of the bachelor herds.

Although the impala breeds throughout the year in the Serengeti, like many equatorial species it has a peak in breeding which is shown at the beginning of March to the end of April by a peak in territorial activity, when the bucks defend their territories against increased competition and spend much of their time trying to herd does in heat. At high levels of intensity territoriality in this species has considerable physiological manifestations; the neck of the buck swells as it does in the rutting red deer, and dark patches develop around the eyes (I feel inclined to add 'as they do in man'), while its forehead gland produces a strong-smelling oily secretion which covers the forehead and much of the neck as well.

With his forehead gland the buck marks his territory, rubbing it on vegetation and also making signposts by thrashing bushes and then rubbing the gland on them. A neighbouring buck coming across these signs of ownership will immediately cover them with his own (perhaps a question of odour-odour being better than war-war, to paraphrase Churchill's famous statement). There is also some evidence that urine and faeces may be used to demarcate a territory, for the buck uses exaggerated postures similar to those of the gazelles and dik-dik.

Not only does the impala buck belie his majestic mien by being very smelly, but he also indulges in the unusual threat display of yawning! When one dominant buck vaingloriously yawns at an inferior, the latter turns or walks away. He is also very vocal, and a unique expression of his territoriality is his roaring, which he indulges with outstretched neck rather in the posture of a red deer stag, but giving utterance to more of a snorting and wheezing sound than a real roar. Nevertheless it is said to be audible up to 2 km away.

Sometimes roaring is also given vent to by bachelor bucks, and watching a large herd of about a hundred of them in the Akagera Park one evening, I was treated to the incredible display of 'mass roaring', as this extraordinary activity has been termed. Suddenly, what was a peaceful grazing

Figure 9.3 An impala buck roars to announce his territory, while the does look on admiringly

herd, sparked off perhaps by an interaction between two of its members, exploded into a ridiculous display of cavorting back and forth in a strange gait like animated rocking-horses, with tails held erect, the white hairs displayed in a fringe like a lavatory brush. Roaring, grunting and snorting, lavatory-brush tails in the air, the whole herd galumphed to and fro, stopping suddenly after about a minute or so almost as abruptly as they had begun.

The Serengeti scientists decided to make a tape-recording of a buck's roars and see what the reaction would be from other bucks when it was played back to them. Having made a suitable recording they took it to the Nairobi Park, where they played it to a number of different territorial bucks. Nearly all of the bucks immediately became alert, and many responded by roaring back. Some marked, while others intensified their herding of does. One however, bolder than the rest, came up to the Land-rover from which the recording was being played, and then walked round it to see if there was someone on the other side! Having discovered that he had been hoaxed, he roared only briefly when it was played again a little later, and then ignored it altogether.

Like other species, serious fighting is rarely seen, but the injuries of the bucks testify to its not infrequent occurrence. With the intensive type of territoriality that the impala undergoes, much of which relates to herding the large concentrations of does, territorial bucks become in very poor condition in the dry season. Even in the wet season they are in worse condition than are the bachelors, most of whom gain in condition at this time.

Impala are very gregarious and there are always many challengers waiting in the wings to take over a territory. If these aspiring bucks cannot supplant an established owner, then some employ methods such as those that we have already seen are used by the waterbuck. For example, squeezing into the boundary zone between two territories. Others may take up a position in the poorer habitat next to the territory which they intend to contest for. The wooded nature of the habitat which the impala prefers, usually acacia woodland, means that the territorial buck cannot see his challenger all of the time, and may often feed within 10 to 30 m of him between bouts of fighting or challenging; where challenging often consists simply of threatening displays with no actual combat.

In southern Africa the species has a more sharply defined breeding season, rutting taking place between mid-May and mid-June, and we may expect territorial behaviour to be more intense at this time; but as yet information is lacking for this race.

Vying with the wildebeest in its dense numbers, at Lochinvar Ranch on Zambia's Kafue Flats, a vast area of seasonal floodplain bordering the Kafue River, the Kafue Flats lechwe, a race unique to this area, reaches densities of over 500 animals to the square kilometre in the flood season, when the rise in water level forces them to concentrate on the periphery of the plains. The other races of lechwe, the black and the red, at one time probably occurred in similar densities, but all are now sadly reduced in numbers, and the Kafue Flats lechwe itself is also threatened.

Of similar size to the impala, but a little larger, territoriality was equally hard to define in this very interesting species. Only one race, the Kafue Flats, has been the subject of a behavioural study, and this has shown that it also has a very pronounced territorial behaviour at the peak of the rut in December to January. At this time numbers of bucks form a lek-type arena similar to that which is found in the kob.

Surprisingly enough, since its area of distribution is well south of the equatorial zone, breeding takes place throughout the year, but there is a peak which coincides with the height of the flooding cycle, when the animals are forced into an even closer association than their habitual dense aggregations. At this time relatively small groups of bucks, numbering about 50 to 100, become organised into small concentrations in conspicuous areas. These areas are usually exposed high ground adjacent to the rising water, of about 500 m in diameter, so that each buck is spaced about 15 m apart from each other. But as is usual with this type of territorial network they are closer together in the centre of the area than they are at the periphery.

In this arena, as we might call it, the bucks indulge in continual ritual displays. Rarely grazing, they stand with head held high in an exaggerated pose, prancing and wagging their tails vigorously, and frequently horning the ground. Swinging the head violently from side to side they fling tufts of grass into the air, often having the debris draped on their horns and neck. The movement of a buck or doe almost anywhere is liable to set off a chain reaction of chases and fights, although fights are much the less frequent activity. Such displays as this have not been seen to take place outside of the breeding season.

Does seek out the bucks on the rutting grounds, favouring as usual the denser central concentrations, where they cluster admiringly around the bucks in groups of ten to 20 or so. But these enviable central positions have a rapid turnover in occupation, so that many of the most vigorous bucks get a chance to breed there. As in other species, there is little mating away from these areas in those where the large mixed herds hang about. There is some tendency for these peripheral herds to associate in groups of similar age and in separate doe and bachelor groups, but probably the dense numbers have prevented bachelor groups from being identified in the way that they exist in other species.

Lechwes have no compound scent glands, possessing only rudimentary pouches of unknown function in the groin; so they cannot mark their territories with scent. It would be rather futile if they could, because the areas are ephemeral, continually retreating before the rising water level. Neither does the lechwe buck announce his presence vocally, since this also would be futile in such dense concentrations. The cacophony of sound that would arise would be meaningless, it would be impossible for a buck to tell from which direction a particular challenge was coming. So they can only advertise their presence by crowding together and announcing their rank by displaying in an exaggerated manner reminiscent of Dickens' absurd Mister Turveydrop, whose sole occupation was to strut down the street in his finery so that he could 'be seen'.

In their undisturbed state the lechwes must have reached concentrations at the limits of social compression, but high concentrations seem to result in the reduction rather than an intensification of territorial drive, which is limited to only a short part of the year. At such dense concentrations continual defensive encounters would soon exhaust all the bucks, and since the habitat is changing all the time they lack something concrete to defend in the way of a territory.

Densities achieved by the lechwe on their arenas are five times those at which a similar type of organisation develops in the kob; the species in which the discovery of territorial behaviour opened the eyes of many to this fascinating world of antelope social organisation. Although territorial behaviour has only been described in the Uganda race of the kob, and there are still questions which remain unanswered in this species, I have seen it among the Buffon's kob on the seasonal flood plains of the Bahr Kameur river in the north of the Central African Republic, and it has been reported to exist in Senegal, the farthest west that one can reach on the continent.

Once you know what you are looking for, it makes one wonder why it took so long to identify such a striking phenomenon, for the posturing and display and the frequent encounters of the arena bucks are very obvious. But we must remember that the Semliki Valley, where the behaviour was first recognised, was up to that date only visited by hunters, whose knowledge is more concerned with the mechanics of shooting rather than the biology of animals. Sir Harry Johnston, who described the area in 1902 in his book *The Uganda Protectorate*, enthused over the waterbuck but made no mention of the kob. But hunting on foot, as was the usual and more sportsmanlike method before the 1960s, also probably had the effect of disrupting the systems before the hunter could appreciate what was taking place, the bucks fleeing from his path. It was obvious enough to me in the Kikorongo region of the Queen Elizabeth Park, but this park was only created in 1952, and most visitors then and now did and do content themselves with a short, comfortable circuit near to the hotel, provided that they can see lions and elephants.

Like other species the kob has a territorial system in which the buck occupies an area which supplies all of his daily needs, except water, and which he defends against other competing bucks. In the Semliki Valley these territories were about 1 to 2 ha in area; whereas in the Queen Elizabeth Park they cover about 25 to 100 ha. But they have some seasonal variation in location, bucks setting up territories on fresh flushes of burnt-off sword grass, and quitting the area when the grass grows up. It seems that where the population reaches a certain density, something of the order of twelve animals to the square kilometre, these standard territories, as we might call them, are in association with a territorial arena. This is an area, as we found in the lechwe, where the territorial bucks crowd together and are sought out by the does in heat, very little mating taking place elsewhere. Breeding takes place throughout the year in Uganda, and there are probably minor peaks as there are for the waterbuck, but no season of rut has been observed.

Unlike the lechwe's temporary rutting grounds, those of the kob are permanent in nature. Although some changes in position may take place, others are known to have existed for over 30 years, and in Uganda are used throughout the year. This obviously cannot be the case in the Central African Republic where they are sited on seasonal flood plains, but breeding here probably follows a seasonal pattern.

In the Semliki Valley the population was divided up into some 15 groups, possibly consisting of 'clans', each of which centres on an arena. In an experiment to determine how attached the bucks were to their particular areas, eight territorial bucks were captured and released at other arenas at distances of from 5 to 23 km away; three being taken across a river which could only be traversed by swimming. Most of them returned to their original areas within one to four weeks, only one taking four months and one disappearing. On their return they either retook their original territory or another territory, or joined the bachelor herd. It is not known how they orientated, but it was probably by visual clues in relation to the position of the sun; although others have suggested that scent may play a part. This experiment served to illustrate two things that are probably fundamental attributes of antelopes; one was that the kob were deeply attached to their areas, and the other was that their surroundings are just as meaningful to them as ours are to us.

The territorial arena, which is the heart of the kob's life, consists of some ten to twenty small worn patches, each of 15 to 35 m across, ranging from circular to irregular in shape, where the bucks display rather in the manner of the lechwe. It appears that the kob has rudimentary facial glands but how they are used is not known, and glands are present in the groin. There is no scent-marking of the territory, and no evidence that it uses dung piles or urine. There are no signposts to warn trespassers away and so, unlike its rather silent cousin the lechwe, the kob makes its presence known by a powerful whistle, which usually results in an answering chorus.

But sound, as we have seen, is an indeterminate means of defining a boundary, so the kob crowds together where it can be both seen and heard at the same time. Mister Turveydrop is present once more as, like the lechwe, the kob swaggers and postures on his little patch, passing the time by displaying to his neighbours and frequently coming to grips with them, fighting vigorously. Fights are recorded as taking place on average once in every two hours, and such exhausting activity means that there is a high turnover rate here also; arena territories are seldom held for longer than ten days in a row. If a buck wants to feed or drink, then he has to run the gauntlet of all of the other territories to get out of the arena. We do not see the same permissiveness that pertains with the waterbuck or the reedbuck, and this also speeds up turnover rate, for a buck may not be able to re-establish himself upon his return, if he finds that his territory has been seized by another during his absence.

As in the lechwe, the doe seeks out the buck for mating. Entering the arena she makes for the central area where the territories are most concentrated. As she passes each stamping ground its hopeful owner prances towards her, stiff-legged and with nose held high in the air; but loses interest abruptly if she crosses his limits into the next territory. If she stays, mating takes place and may be repeated several times, each consummation being announced by a boastful whistle to his neighbours, who respond in a jealous chorus. When the doe is satisfied she may graze or lie down in the territory, and the buck may lie down with her, but quits her instantly to impress another should other does come along.

Thus at these high population concentrations, and the kob does may be in groups of anything from 2,000 to 3,000 head, although 50 to 60 is the most common, the territories lose their role of providing material attractions for the does in the form of food, water and cover, and become instead parade grounds for the bucks to show off in, the does switching their attention to the buck himself.

It has been estimated that about a third of the adult bucks occupy the arena at any one time, the remainder occupying the more conventional types of territories which are adjacent to it. These territories do not seem to

Figure 9.4 A busy kob territorial arena. While two bucks fight a doe looks on and another buck mates with a doe

be resting places for the arena participants, none having been seen to occupy both; neither do they appear to provide an entrée to the arena, for some bucks have been observed to go straight into the arena from the bachelor herd. The bachelor herds consist of both young aspiring bucks as well as deposed arena bucks, and also those ousted from standard territories.

The attitude of the owner of a standard territory towards the bachelor herds is rather ambivalent, some owners ignore them, others chase them out; but if large herds invade the territory then the owner resigns himself to their presence. Proximity to water was not a criterion of choice for these territories, and they were often abandoned in time of drought, or left for several hours during the day in the dry season when visits were made to drink, or to feed near the water.

Interesting as the activities of the bucks are in their arena territories, what most impresses one is the overall universality of the system. From the pugnacious little suni jealously guarding his patch of forest, to the organised chaos of the milling hordes of wildebeest, and finally the macho displays of the bumptious kob performing on his table-top arena. This fundamental organisation must surely have some meaning, but to date its precise significance eludes us. To the parallels that can be drawn with man himself and his desire to possess property, I leave the reader to Robert Ardrey's analysis.

10 Other forms of social organisation – and the reason for territoriality

About 90 per cent of all African antelopes have a territorial organisation. The exception appears to be provided by the tragelaphines, notably the eland. Despite being largest of all the antelopes, the eland is among the most difficult to study due to its extensive, wide-ranging habit and its wary nature. Usually it takes off into the blue long before one can get anywhere near to it; although this applies more to the cows than to the bulls. Studies conducted in South Africa and in and around Nairobi Park in Kenya, suggest that it has a hierarchical type of social organisation, similar to that found in *Bovini*, such as the buffalo; but we will come back to that in a moment.

The other tragelaphines: namely the bushbuck, sitatunga, lesser and greater kudu and the bongo, are all extremely difficult animals to study, due to their secretive and cautious behaviour, or to their inaccessible habitats. From what we have been able to learn of their ways, these species seem to have forms of social organisation which are intermediate between territorial and hierarchic, but some may be more territorial than has hitherto been revealed.

Bushbuck. The bushbuck has been studied both in the Nairobi Park, in Zimbabwe and in the Queen Elizabeth Park, where it is not its more common secretive self. My earliest acquaintance with this animal, around the Aberdare Mountains in Kenya, was with a largely nocturnal creature, only creeping out of the forest edge in the quiet of the evening, although I sometimes came across it in the daytime. Where it is not disturbed, as in the Queen Elizabeth Park, it is just as active during the day as it is at night, temperature permitting, because the bushbuck does not like it too hot. In one small area the density was 26 to the square kilometre, although it is usually much less than this.

Both adults and sub-adults have active groin glands, although their function is unknown; but the ears, face and neck are often scented and oily, suggesting the presence of a gland on the crown of the head, and there is some indication that the bucks mark vegetation with their scent by rubbing their head on it rather like the impala. In the Nairobi Park, adult bucks occupied areas of about half a hectare in extent, while contrary to the usual pattern seen among territorial species, those of the does were smaller than the bucks', being only about half the size. Young bachelor bucks occupied about 2 ha, but in the drier habitat in Zimbabwe much larger ranges are reported, with dominant bucks having areas of almost 6 ha in extent. But all classes, adult bucks, young bucks and does, had preferred areas near to water where they spent the greater part of their time.

There seems to be general agreement that the ranges of the adult bucks do not overlap, but the adult bucks permit the presence of bachelors and does in their areas. This species has a reputation for pugnaciousness in captivity, and deaths and wounding from fighting in the wild have been reported. All of the evidence points to its being territorial, but it has been observed that if an adult buck threatens a younger buck, then the latter threatens another, and so on down the line. Hence it has been suggested that the system may be hierarchical. The most that can be said at the moment is that we do not know.

Sitatunga. At one time, on Nkosi Island in Lake Victoria, you had to hit the sitatunga bucks with a stick to make them get out of the way; and the local missionary had to drive them out of his chapel before he could commence his services. Colonel Meinertzhagen reported stroking them as they walked past him. This was in 1915 and I doubt whether such an ideal situation to study this aquatic relative of the bushbuck exists any longer. Most of the sitatunga's habitat, swamps and dense papyrus beds, is almost impenetrable. The only exception appears to be the Saiwa swamp in Kenya, where relatively dense numbers in a small area have permitted some observations.

But all that seems to be known is that generally the bucks are solitary, but groups of several animals have been seen. I know from my own experience how difficult it is to observe this wary beast in its dense swamp habitat. Once on the shores of Lake George in Uganda, I succeeded in splashing my way clumsily towards a feeding buck whose chocolate-coloured shaggy back and lyrate horns were just visible above the reeds. I was able to do this only because he probably thought that the noise of my approach was made by the huge catfish which were splashing about in the swamp with great gusto at the time. But he twigged before I could get close enough for a photograph, and floundered his way ponderously through the reeds out of sight.

In Kenya's Saiwa swamp I was only lucky enough to see a doe, but studies here have shown that adult bucks may associate with up to three other animals, although more than one adult buck was never seen together; so it looks as if this species may be territorial also. It is very vocal at times, making a barking noise with which it may announce its presence.

Bongo. Just as little is known about the bongo. A viewing point over an artificial salt-lick and watering hole in the Aberdare Mountains had some regular adult buck visitors and occasional strange ones, while yet others were rare or infrequent. We have seen from the way in which territoriality is suppressed in the sharing of water resources that it would be unwise to make any deductions about social organisation from such a situation as this. All that can be said is that most bucks are solitary and appear to avoid one another, although adults are occasionally accompanied by younger ones; and a buck has been seen accompanied by up to seven cows.

The does occur generally in groups with young, and although herds of up to 50 have been reported, they are not cohesive, frequently splitting up and reforming again. Such a large animal has of necessity to cover a wide area in search of food, so we cannot dismiss the idea that the bongo may be territorial, although clearly a territory would be difficult to defend over a large area of forest habitat. The bongo has no apparent scent glands and there is no evidence of marking the habitat; but the buck sometimes clears patches in the earth which are called 'bongo wallows', although he does not wallow in the mud. Strangely enough however, like the hippo which 'sweats blood', the bongo seems to 'bleed' when it rains, the rain washing out a red pigment from its coat. This suggests that it has diffuse glands like the enlarged sebaceous glands of the waterbuck, which also produce a dark pigment; although it is not always obvious and certainly takes more than rain to wash it out.

Lesser Kudu. The lesser kudu, shy and furtive though it is, has been studied to some extent in Kenya's Tsavo East National Park. In an area where the density was probably higher than normal, for much of the animal's preferred habitat had been destroyed by elephants, bucks are considered to have occupied home ranges of about 2 sq km in area, in the range from less than 0.5 km to over 6 sq km. Here adult bucks were either solitary or associated temporarily with doe groups which were mostly up to four in number, but up to 24 have been seen. Sub-adult bucks had larger home ranges than the adult bucks and overlapped with them, while two or more adult bucks apparently use the same area simultaneously. No territorial defence was observed, nor was there any evidence of a hierarchy among the bucks. We may suppose that such ornate horns are designed for display rather than for use, although of course they can be used effectively in fighting, and the skulls of two contestants have been found with the horns inextricably locked together; evidence that fighting certainly does take place.

Greater Kudu. The greater kudu seems to have a similar social organisation to that of its smaller relative. Studies in South Africa showed that the areas of bulls overlapped, and when two bulls met the largest of the two simply presented a lateral display, showing off his horns, the size of his neck and his dewlap (a dewlap is absent in the lesser kudu), and the smaller of them simply withdrew. Perhaps such a confrontation would not have ended so peacefully had the two animals been equally matched, but chasing has only been seen when a smaller bull has taken an interest in a cow.

During the wet season the species is widely dispersed, but bulls have been identified as coming back to the same areas as those which they occupied in the previous dry season. Several were seen to use the same home ranges and in this species also the bulls ranged more widely than the cows; two bulls were observed to have had home ranges of about 11 sq km each, while two cow groups only covered 3.5 and 5 sq km, the ranges overlapping extensively. The cow groups comprised five to six members, consisting of mothers with offspring, the most that were seen together being 15.

Group size changes throughout the year, dropping in the breeding season and peaking after the end of the rains, to fall to its lowest at the end of the dry season. The species has a well-defined breeding season, and after the rut at the end of the South African winter in June, and during August to September north of the equator, the adult and sub-adult bulls congregate in bachelor groups of anything from two to ten animals, all of the bulls associating together at some stage or another. No hierarchical organisation has been seen to exist among the bulls, and competition seems to take place only for the cows during the annual rut.

Eland. We have a little more information about the eland. The species is generally referred to as 'nomadic', but it is perhaps better to think of it as simply having an extremely large home range in conformity with the needs of its size. Certainly it does not wander aimlessly, and I have found giant eland in the same places each dry season in the woodlands of the savannas of the Central African Republic. One hunter here considered that groups had a range of about 150 sq km, considerably less than the 1,500 sq km reported for the Cape eland. Whether the two species have the same sort of social organisation is unknown, as no studies have been made of the giant eland.

In Kenya, the Cape eland was found to occupy overlapping home ranges of up to 350 sq km in the bull, these ranges being about a quarter the size of those of the cows, which may cover a range of as much as 1,500. Some adult bulls tend to live on their own in rather small home ranges for much of the year, joining the cow herds only temporarily during the breeding season, for the bulls apparently prefer more woody vegetation and, in this area of Kenya at any rate, the cows prefer to spend much of their time in the open on the plains.

Figure 10.1   Part of a large herd of Cape eland

While bulls of more than two years old tend to form small groups of 6 or 7, and more commonly 2, the cows and their young may aggregate temporarily in loose herds of up to 200 head, the herd size being larger in the wet season than in the dry. In the 250,000 ha ecosystem of the Akagera Park, I located only two mixed herds, numbering about 70 and 250 animals each; plus a number of small, presumably bull, groups of 2 to 8 head. The young animals seem to have a tendency to associate together with others of similar age, drawing their mothers with them. In the Nairobi area movements of up to 55 km have been reported for the cows, but distances can probably exceed this; although in the Akagera Park I recorded distances of only about 40 km.

In southern Africa there is a well-defined breeding season which culminates in a birth peak in July to September, whereas in the Akagera Park calving peaks appeared to take place in February to March, and again in June to August. But in Kenya the eland breeds throughout the year and seemingly also has a floating peak. Captive bulls experience intermittent periods of aggression lasting for about three weeks, when they become very dangerous to handle; and indeed one such captive bull has been known to kill his keeper. The solitary bulls met with in the wild are not outcasts, but are the breeding bulls, which will mate with any cow that they find on heat within their home range. Fights between bulls have rarely been recorded and have been of brief duration in the Cape eland, but in the giant eland are said to take place in January and February. As with other species we cannot set too much store by this lack of observation, especially in an animal which is so difficult to observe, and I suspect that fights are frequent enough between well-matched bulls.

There is however no defence of territory, and bulls assert their position by means of a rank hierarchy, in principle each one being dominant to those beneath it. This is usually so at the top of the pile; but lower down in the hierarchy X may be dominant to Y, and Y may be dominant to Z, but Z may be dominant to X, so that complicated patterns of cross-dominance occur. To my knowledge however, nobody has clearly established a hierarchical sequence in wild eland. The dominance is achieved initially by sparring contacts among the young bulls in the bachelor herds, which often takes on a unique reversal of behaviour in this species in that the *loser* may tokenly mount the winner. When they get older, dominance may be achieved by sight alone, the thick neck, deep chest and massive dewlap of the older bull serving to sufficiently impress his younger rivals with his immense size.

The important feature which differentiates the truly hierarchical from the territorial is that they are physiologically different. They continue to grow, albeit at a steadily decreasing rate, into mature age, becoming bigger and heavier all the time. In contrast, most species achieve mature size when adult, within about the first third of their lifespan, and any further increases are usually confined to obesity. This suggests that the other tragelaphines, which do not grow continuously, do not have hierarchical social systems, at least not in the true sense as apparently shown by the eland.

Apart from the huge weight and size that the older bulls may attain, they may reinforce their position by smell, for the Cape bull is distinguished by a large tuft of hair on the forehead, much less developed in the giant eland, which changes colour from chestnut to black and which seems

Figure 10.2   A hypothetical example of crossed-dominance in the linear hierarchical system of the eland. The young bull 'A' is dominant to all those below him, as also is 'B'; but 'X' is dominant to 'Y' who is dominant to 'Z', but 'Z' is dominant to 'X'

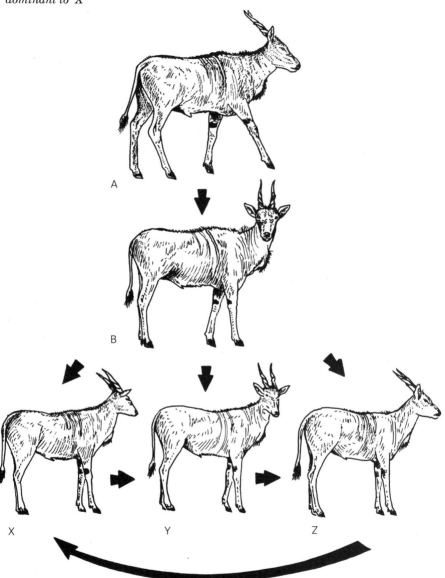

to denote a scent gland (the only other species having a similar tuft is the addax, in which it is also chestnut in colour). But if it does denote a scent gland then the bull is not content with this alone, as he has the rather unpleasant habit of rubbing the tuft in his own urine, liking to cover it with muddy filth. He will also rub it in ordinary mud, and has even been known to do so in elephant's urine. He will also rub it in the urine of a cow on heat, and it has been suggested that this may be to mask the aggressive smell of the bull, which may be intimidating to the cow. Strangely enough, one cow eland will soak her head in the urine of another cow, but not if that cow is in heat.

A further odd attribute of the master bull is his clicking. As he walks he emits a loud clicking noise, said to be made by the sinews of the 'knee' joints of the forelegs only, although I must say that in the captive bull which I observed it appeared to be made by the hind hooves, as is generally supposed. An observer reports a young bull suddenly losing interest in a cow before the dominant bull was in sight, apparently hearing the approach of the clicking noise. Experiments in tape-recording and play-backs of this noise might prove to be interesting.

The picture that emerges of the dominant bull eland reminds me of a photograph that I once saw portraying a typically immensely stout Victorian businessman, puffed up with pomposity, his face covered in beard and sidewhiskers, staring grimly at the camera; with the caption 'The confidence of success'. Consciously or otherwise the sitter was using the same psychological principles as the eland bull, considering that his size and appearance were intimidatory and therefore placed him above the rest. Let us hope that portly Victorian businessmen did not smell like successful eland bulls!

Home Range

In both the descriptions of territoriality and of other systems of social organisation, I have frequently referred to the 'home range', for apart from those small antelopes in which both male and female share a territory, or in which both possess their own, all of the females occupy a home range; a restricted area of occupation where they live, but which they do not defend against intrusion by others. They may nevertheless object to, or prevent, others joining the group, as we saw was the case with the waterbuck bachelor male herd. This would make life uncomfortable for any intruder into a home range, but it would be stretching a point to say that the area was defended. Obviously it is a matter of degree, for the size of an area which can be marked and defended is limited; thus where a species has a large territory there tends to be overlap with adjacent ones, because the owner cannot be in all places at once. As living areas become larger, so the system changes to that of a home range, whether it be that of a male or a female.

Among the waterbuck studied in Uganda, the home ranges appeared to be the property of groups of does, but the does moved about within them as individuals. Does in my study seemed to have very loose associations within the home range, although there was a tendency for some to be often seen together, possibly signifying mother-daughter relationships. An occasional one was never seen in the company of certain other individuals which shared the same home range. The latter situation I observed in the case of a very old doe, grey and gaunt, whose age I estimated after her death by natural causes, at an exceptional $18\frac{1}{2}$ years, compared with an expected maximum life span of 13 years. Out of 15 known individuals (there were others but they were not marked), I never saw her with three of them, whose ages were 3, 5 and 10 years; and only on one or two occasions did I see her with four others. The most frequent association that I saw among the does was that between two of estimated ages 4 and 5 years, suggesting perhaps that they were sisters, rather than a mother and daughter relationship.

No affinity was shown for any particular territorial buck by these does, who wandered at will through several territories, the time spent in any one territory ranging from a few hours up to three months. Sometimes a buck would try and herd the does to keep them in his territory, but this was never seen to be successful. A typical occasion was when a doe started to walk towards a neighbouring territorial buck, the buck in whose territory she was at the time then promptly ran forward and stopped at the boundary of his territory, only some 30 m from the neighbouring buck. Here he turned and confronted the doe, who simply ignored him and continued on her way. The repudiated buck then made a rush at her, head down in threat, but did not follow her across the invisible boundary. The neighbouring buck, who had been standing quietly watching these proceedings, immediately ran up to her. As soon as she crossed the boundary, the former buck simply lost interest and turned and walked away, territorial etiquette being strictly observed. Had the doe been in heat, he might not have given her up so easily.

The total home range of the average doe in my study area was about 600 to 730 ha, equivalent to about 24 ha for each member of the group in the smaller range. But as she gets older, the doe restricts herself to a smaller and smaller range of movement, eventually adopting a preferred spot; and is thus often left on her own by the more active younger animals.

Defining Social Organisation

Patterns of home range occupation among the other gregarious species tend to be similar, the females covering several male territories in their peregrinations; except in the tragelaphines where, as we saw, the situation is reversed. Some species may show tighter bonds among the females than is the case with the waterbuck, or, as with the kongoni, the groups may be familial.

Zoologists have attempted to determine whether there is an underlying pattern to these different forms of social organisation, asking themselves whether they could not be pigeon-holed according to certain characteristics; defining not only why a species has a certain type of territorial organisation, but also what determines group size. Any pattern which might exist is complicated by the large number of antelopes that we have to consider, for they may represent all degrees of pattern from one system to another. But two theories have been proposed to explain their social organisation: one of these theories suggests that antelope social organisation is related to the type of dispersion of the food. It is easy enough to visualise at the one extreme the solitary forest duiker daintily picking at his favoured herbs, and at the other the massed herds of wildebeest mowing their way regardless through the grassland. This divides the antelopes up into five classes based on the size of the animal, its feeding style, group size, anti-predator behaviour and social organisation. Group size is seen as being related to protection from predators concomitant with the food searching pattern, thus species which must spread out to find their food obviously cannot band together as a defence against predators.

The other theory sees their organisation in terms of development in the evolution from an ancestral solitary existence in the forest to a life on the open plains. Herding animals are seen as herding together because for them the bodies of others are substitutes for the cover which their former forest habitat provided.

Neither theory satisfies all of the different patterns of organisation and we cannot say that one theory is more correct than the other, but both agree on the point that social organisation is related to reproduction. Animal societies are organised to enable males to obtain mates and to reproduce their kind. To this end the organisation may centre around a territory which has a food resource to which the female is attracted, thus coming into contact with the male, and where the owner of the resource can mate with the minimum of interference. But where the males are too numerous, the system breaks down, no one male has sufficient to offer the female in terms of resources, and thus the female is attracted to the male himself.

The hierarchical system, which has limited applicability because if the males of small species become too big and cumbrous they would easily be taken by predators, solves the problem for larger species in a sort of establishment manner, by tacit understandings between the males.

This explains why the hierarchical system is perhaps of limited applicability, but does not explain why the territorial system is so universal. Many theories have been advanced to explain this, and one of the most recent sees it in terms of balancing advantages and disadvantages for the animal in relation to reproduction. The male's ultimate success is considered to be dependent upon three main factors: the maximum number of matings that he can achieve; the age span during which this takes place; and the increased chance of death from competition or the extra energy expenditure required to prevent this.

Territoriality is seen as providing the best compromise to produce the most matings, but my personal view is that the territorial system selects for the all-round male. The male is not selected just for his ability to impress other males, as is the eland bull, he is selected – in effect – to provide a 'home' for the female where she can successfully rear her young, and to withstand the onslaughts of predators, disease and drought. In simple terms the territorial system produces a real 'tough guy'; the hierarchical system produces a 'screen image' macho male. Of course this is only my view and others may disagree with it, for when we talk about the functions of territoriality we are on highly contentious ground. Fraser Darling, one of Britain's most distinguished ecologists, avoided the issue by contenting himself with the statement: '... territorial behaviour as a whole is a social phenomenon and it has survival value.'

11 Farming–a future for antelopes?

Why have so few animals been domesticated by man? Almost the whole of our meat and dairy stock stems from only three ruminants; the cow, sheep and goat, all species that are believed to have originated from the region of Asia and the Middle East. Africa, possessor of the world's greatest variety of wild ruminants, has not produced a single domesticated species. There is only some very tenuous evidence from bones found in ancient living sites that some African ungulates may have been domesticated in Stone-Age times, three to four thousand years ago.

That this did not continue may have been due to the fact that African human population densities were probably relatively low until the twentieth century, and with an ample supply of wild animals to hunt, there was no need to develop husbandry methods. Added to this there exists a long tradition of pastoralism among certain tribes, which may date back 3,000 years or more in its origin. This tradition is believed to have originated in the Nile Valley, and to have been spread throughout Africa by the Hamitic peoples who have always remained apart from the hunting Bantu. Their stock having both mystic and prestigious connotations, the pastoralists formed a society which it was never possible for the hunter tribes to become a part of. Thus post Stone-Age Africans seem to have had neither the need nor the inclination to experiment with the domestication of other types of animal; a conservatism which extended to the European colonists, who contented themselves with applying their familiar, temperate zone methods of animal husbandry; while at the same time shooting the game for their meat supply.

Early Experiments

This was not so in ancient Egypt, where a painting in the tomb of Mereruka at Saqqara, dating from about 2400 BC, shows captive gazelles, ibex, beisa oryx, and possibly hartebeest; feeding from mangers and with collars around their necks. An inscription records that one person had 3,988 cattle and 1,135 gazelle, which certainly sounds as if the gazelle were being farmed. In the tomb of Ukht-Hop, dating from 2000 to 1780 BC, a bas-relief shows two small adult male gazelles (perhaps dorcas), and a female beisa oryx in milk with her small calf, being brought as tribute; the oryx being simply led along by a horn. But some of these animals may have

Figure 11.1   Captive (farmed?) antelopes portrayed in the tomb of Mereruka at Saqqara, about 2400 BC. Left to right: unknown species; ibex; unknown; hartebeest and beisa oryx

been kept as no more than curiosities, or for religious purposes, perhaps forming part of an early zoo rather than an experiment in domestication.

Speculation on the use of antelopes as domestic animals has a long history, and from the earliest it is the eland which has caught the imagination because of its ox-like appearance. Filippo Pigafetta writing in 1591 of Angola, suggested that the 'Empalanga', which from his description seems to have been Livingstone's eland, 'might be taught to draw the plough, and also serve in various ways for husbandry'. It was over 250 years later, in 1848, that the subject was raised again, when the prospects of farming buffalo and eland were discussed in South Africa. This seems to have followed the importation into Britain in 1842 of two bulls and a cow eland by the 13th Earl of Derby, for his private menagerie at Knowsley Park; the first elands to be brought to Europe.

Two calves were produced at Knowsley, after accurately recorded gestation lengths of 270 and 273 days; and attempts were then made to cross the bulls with Ayrshire and shorthorn cattle. But as no calves were produced from these unions, the experiments were abandoned. It was recorded that the eland bred with the facility of cattle 'but they are ravenous feeders and appear liable to an epidemic'. Further eland were imported in 1850 and 1851; but the collection was then sold to the embryo Zoological Society of London in the latter year, following the death of the Earl.

By 1855 six eland calves had been produced at the London Zoo, and a bull and two cows were sold to Viscount Hill for his park at Hawkstone. The following year, three calves were purchased by the Earl of Breadalbane

Figure 11.2   Gazelles and a beisa oryx with calf being brought as tribute, portrayed in the tomb of Ukht-Hop, 2000 to 1780 BC

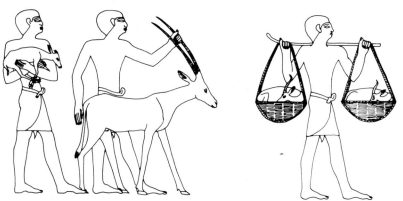

apparently for the purpose of introducing the animal into Scotland. The private herds were dispersed in the 1860s and interest then seems to have waned, despite a letter to *The Times*, dated 21 January 1859, from Dr Owen of the British Museum of Natural History, on the subject of a joint of eland meat which he had received from Lord Hill.

After being hung for ten days and then roasted, this joint was consumed by a 'committee of taste' formed of Dr Owen and three other naturalists. The committee was unanimous that in texture the eland meat was the finest, closest, most tender and chewable of any meat. In taste the first impression was of its sweetness and goodness, without any strongly marked flavour. It was compared with veal and with capon, and finally the suggestion that it was mammalian meat with a suspicion of pheasant flavour was adopted. The committee's final conclusion was that 'a new and superior kind of animal food had been added to the restricted choice from the mammalian class at present available in Europe.'

A description was included in Mrs Beeton's famous cookery book, *The Book of Household Management*, first published in its entirety in 1861, accompanied by the words:

'During the last four or five years a few spirited English noblemen have made the experiment of breeding foreign deer in their parks and have obtained such a decided success, that it may be hoped their example will induce others to follow in a course which will eventually give to England's rural scenery a new element of beauty, and to English table a fresh viand of the choicest character.'

Mrs Beeton noted that Lord Hill's eland 'weighed 1,176 lbs as he dropped ... It was tried in every fashion – braised brisket, roasted ribs, broiled steaks, filet sauté, boiled aitchbone, etc. – and in all, gave evidence of the fact, that a new meat of surpassing value had been added to the products of the English Park.'

However nothing resulted from this seal of approval, and in South Africa itself there were still no serious attempts to husband wildlife. About 1892, the German explorer Dr Carl Peters came across a Boer farmer in Rhodesia who had captured 16 eland to break in for ploughing and drawing a carriage. Peters encouraged the farmer to sell them to Carl Hagenbeck, a famous Hamburg animal dealer, and they were walked to the coast harnessed to buggies, together with zebra, oxen and mules; eventually arriving safely in Europe.

In the same year a herd of eland was founded at Woburn Park with a pair obtained from the London Zoo, to which 17 other imported animals were added, and by the year 1905, 54 calves had been born. Some of these died, some were slaughtered, and others were dispersed. Thus between 1903 and 1911, five cows and six bulls were exported to Australian zoos; one cow however failed to arrive having been 'lost overboard'. Interest in maintaining the herd at Woburn seems to have waned, for eventually we hear no more of it.

Also in the year 1892, four bull and four cow eland were imported onto a private estate in Russia, now the Askaniya Nova Zoo, which proved to be the most persistent endeavour in rearing this species in captivity. The initial animals acclimatised well, and by 1964 had given rise to 408 descendants. Now fully domesticated, the cows are regularly milked.

In Africa itself, prior to the First World War, there were several attempts at farming eland in both Southern Rhodesia and Kenya. In

Kenya a herd was kept on the government farm at Naivasha. But all of these attempts fizzled out, and by 1964 we could point to only one long-term successful attempt, in Russia, at the domestication of an African antelope; although by this time there was a growing development of wildlife ranching in both Southern Rhodesia and South Africa.

Some two to three thousand farms in the Transvaal alone made use of one or two species of game as a source of income; but although frequently held out as the successful practice of game farming, the majority of these farms do not farm game in the true sense of the word. They are primarily cattle ranches, or maize or tobacco farms, usually leasing out hunting rights to people to shoot on their land, or culling a number of animals for meat for their labourers. It has now become sufficiently developed however that landowners will pay significant sums for animals to introduce onto their farms, and rare species are competed for.

Interest has been shown in South Africa in recent years in farming the springbok, which produces a very tasty meat; but this is still on a relatively small scale. Animals are penned and traded, but they are not truly domesticated, and are killed by shooting. The springbok is a very productive species and offtakes of 25 to 30 per cent, and even more, have been recommended. Whether such high yields are sustainable is another matter; it largely depends on the ratio of the bucks to does. But one must remember that in comparison with sheep, apart from the latter's docility and ease of herding, the latter also provides a bonus in wool as well as providing meat.

Beginning in the 1950s, studies purported to show that wild African ungulates existed at much higher densities than domestic stock and without the damage to the habitat that high numbers of the latter create. Due to an error, it was claimed that East African wildlife ecosystems exceeded the most productive domestic stock systems in terms of the weight of the animals that the land could support. In East Africa this was in the range of some 0.2 to 20.3 tonnes per sq km. In fact, the best domestic systems are about ten times more productive, although this may not be true of the nomadic cattle of the marginal areas of Africa; but exaggerated claims of the wildlife potential are still promulgated. If cattle raising is so efficient, why bother with farming wildlife?

Antelopes as Alternatives

Several reasons are advanced as to why wild ungulates (and apart from the buffalo, this means the antelopes) would be better for meat production than conventional stock under similar conditions in marginal areas; one of these reasons being that they make better use of the habitat. Cattle select only a limited number of grass species, in contrast to the much wider range usually chosen by antelopes, which take in addition forbs and may browse on bushes and trees. More important perhaps is their resistance to many diseases of stock, especially trypanosomiasis. That is not to say, as I have already indicated, that wild animals are immune to these diseases, but rather that the domestic stock are more susceptible. However, if wild animals are treated like domestic ones, then they will also require regular treatment against parasites and diseases.

Another of the reasons advanced in favour of antelopes is that they are more productive, that is, they produce a given quantity of meat more quickly. This is because they both breed and grow more quickly on their preferred diet; but the mixed feeders and browsers generally require a richer diet than do cattle.

In the early 1960s a detailed study was conducted in Kenya, in which I participated to a small extent, which compared the carcass and body composition of the principal antelope species with that of cattle, according to butchery criteria. This revealed that the killing-out percentage, or the amount of meat that one gets from the animal, ranged from 50 per cent of the liveweight of the wildebeest, to as much as 63 per cent in the Grant's gazelle; tending to be higher than that of cattle which varied from 40 per cent to over 60 per cent, depending on the fat content.

The percentage of lean meat ranged from 41 per cent in the wildebeest, to 45 per cent in such species as tommy, Uganda kob and oryx; compared with 32.5 per cent in an East African steer. Like deer therefore, the meat of African antelopes is low in fat, for the fat is laid down in pure masses around the internal organs and not in the muscle, so that the marbling effect found in beef does not occur. But whereas European cattle raising has been geared to the production of meat with a high fat content, medical opinion has now shown that this is bad for health, increasing the risk of cardiac disease. The low-fat meat of antelopes could therefore well be the meat of the future.

Finally, in their favour, antelopes have less effect on the habitat than does the same density of cattle, not creating trampling and erosion, due to the fact that they spread out more while feeding and follow narrow paths to watering points.

There are two ways of exploiting this potential for food. One of these is by farming, that is, domesticating or semi-domesticating the animals, keeping them in pens or herding them just as we do cattle. The other method is by 'cropping', more correctly termed 'culling', a controlled offtake from free-ranging populations, sufficient only to stimulate further increase in numbers and not to depress it. This is technically termed the 'maximum sustainable yield'.

Over the years there have been several culling schemes in national parks, mainly directed against the larger animals such as elephant and hippopotamus, but since these have not had the primary aim of producing meat, but were for controlling excessive population numbers, they do not concern us here. Several culling schemes for the production of meat have however been attempted in countries such as Kenya, Tanzania and Mozambique; while during the First World War the Germans tinned the wildebeest in Ngorongoro Crater for rations for their East African troops. None of the culling schemes has persisted, and apart from Mozambique, where the reasons are political, this has often been due to opposition from the vested interests of the cattle industry, and the development of wild meat markets has been largely prevented by the stringent veterinary requirements that are often employed.

Thus game meat is unlikely to appear on the shelves of supermarkets in Britain, for example, because the areas where it originates are not free of foot-and-mouth disease and other transmissible diseases of domestic stock. 'Clean' game meat can only be produced in such areas by rearing disease-free stock in captivity. Of course this does not apply to locally consumed meat, which is often sun-dried or smoked, but rural inhabitants are often unwilling to pay for such meat when they feel that they can obtain it for nothing, even though this may be illegal.

Systematic culling is nevertheless a possibility, but it cannot be shared with poaching; so a certain amount of investment is required to protect the animal populations from abuse if culling is to be sustainable. Culling is not however as easy to practise as people think, antelopes learn very quickly that they are being hunted, often to the point of quickly rendering it impossible to maintain worthwhile offtakes. A further restraint is that the best wildlife areas are usually those which are farthest from human habitation, thus access and transport of the meat all pose difficulties which often render such culling schemes uneconomic. This may not be foreseen at the outset because claims of yields are often grossly exaggerated. A figure of 10 per cent is usually quoted as a permissible annual offtake, but it in fact ranges from about 6 per cent for the large animals, such as the eland, to over 20 per cent for the oribi. The larger the species, the less the number which can be taken.

An example of the dangers of ill-informed culling is provided by the Uganda kob in the Semliki valley; the population where the territorial arena system was first discovered. The total population for the purposes of culling was estimated at 18,000 head, and a quota of 1,000 a year was recommended. As a result, 6,770 head were taken in seven years before culling was stopped due to a drastic decline in the population. Eight years later the population still remained at only 2,700 strong, a figure which appears to be critical for the population's survival. Since a figure of 1,000 head per year would be equivalent to only 5.5 per cent of the population, against an estimated permissible offtake of 15 per cent, one must assume that the original population size was grossly overestimated, and must in fact have been less than 6,000 strong; or the wrong ratios of sexes were culled.

Modern Experiments

Experiments in the farming of antelopes have been less common than culling exercises, but one of the most interesting is that conducted on the Galana Ranch in Kenya. Three wild species, buffalo, eland and oryx, were selected for comparison with cattle. Half-grown animals were preferred for capture, and it was found that if they were kept in the dark for the first week after capture, and then gradually provided with more and more space while becoming familiarised with the herdsmen, then after about six weeks they could be released into the open and herded like cows. Grazing during the day under the eye of a herdsman, they allowed themselves to be herded back to a pen at night in the traditional African manner, where they would sleep around the herdsmen's camp fire. About 10 per cent of the oryx returned to the wild, attracted to passing herds; but the eland stud bull would wander off for three months at a time and then suddenly reappear, to calmly rejoin the domesticated herd as if he had never been away.

In spite of the successful domestication, in this low rainfall area the eland was found to have no advantages over cattle; not being able to search for succulent and dew-laden food at night it required both a richer diet and as much water as cattle. The most promising species was found to be the oryx, which gained weight on grazing that would not even sustain cattle, and it required only a quarter of the amount of water.

Eland do much better in higher rainfall areas, and is the species which has been chosen from the outset for farming trials. This has been said to be

Figure 11.3   Cape eland with Guernsey and Boran cattle on a Tanzanian farm

misguided because it only superficially resembles a cow, its physiology and nutritional requirements being quite different, as well as being an agile, far-ranging species, able to leap a 2 m high fence with ease. Nonetheless it has many characteristics in its favour; it is easily tamed (but it can be aggressive towards strangers and is always potentially dangerous because of its sharp horns) and it produces both a high quality meat and milk. The milk is exceptional in having approximately twice the protein and fat of cow's milk, and in being much richer in calcium and phosphorus, but the sugar content is similar. In Russia it is valued for medicinal purposes and is alleged to be effective in the treatment of gastric ulcers and injuries. Given the right circumstances the eland is more productive than cattle, thus an eland bull may weigh 565 kg at three and a half years, compared with cattle under the same feeding regime reaching less than 500 kg. We have seen that it breeds and thrives in captivity.

One farmer friend of mine in Tanzania had a herd of 22 which he ran with his cattle, and although he had not reached the slaughter and marketing stage, he had tried milking one of the cows. Since the animals were not trained to milking the yield was low, a maximum of 3 l, but in Russia they have achieved yields of 7 l. The experiment in Tanzania collapsed when the farm was nationalised, and other trials elsewhere seem to have failed through a lack of persistence; although there are some currently operating in Kenya, whose main obstruction comes from the veterinary and legal aspects. In Rwanda, a missionary obtained a pair of 3–4 month old eland in 1959 which in the following ten years produced 28 descendants. Of these, 12 were killed for meat, and 6 calves plus one adult died.

Perhaps one should think in terms of such small-scale ventures rather than the large ones which are usually attempted.

The Russians have shown that the eland can be successfully husbanded as a farm animal, and they have also been successful in demonstrating the potential of a sustained yield with one of their own free-ranging antelopes, the saiga. This native of southern Russia, where it once roamed in millions from Poland to the Caucasus and the Caspian, was reduced to a few hundred survivors at the beginning of the century, on account of the demand for its horns by the Chinese pharmaceutical trade. From 1920 it was strictly protected, and by 1960 the original survivors had increased to some 2 million animals, becoming the most numerous ungulate in the Soviet Union. Hunters are now able to take an annual crop of 120,000 to 150,000, producing 6,000 tonnes of meat per year; apart from the leather and other by-products, such as the horns.

The remarkable success of deer-farming introduced into New Zealand in recent years and already an important, high technology industry using helicopters for cropping and capture, shows just how well a relatively timid ruminant can be intensively managed. If the *demand* is there, then man will find a way.

With these successes in Europe and New Zealand, surely something could be done in Africa? It has been said that much of the undeveloped land in Africa is 'rugged in character, easily eroded, covered with bush and with natural watering points often few and far between. Yet in spite of this its potential contribution to the continent's and possibly the world's larder in terms of animal products is considerable.' Game ranching offers a means by which marginal lands could produce food of a high nutritional quality on a sustained basis; but although its potential has yet to be realised, it is not a panacea for Africa's food problems, and certainly not for the world's. I have calculated, for example, that in Burkina Faso (formerly Upper Volta) a country which is classed as among the world's poorest nations, if all of the wildlife areas outside of national parks, totalling 24,700 sq km, were turned over to the production of wildlife meat then this would, at best, add 0.5 kg of fresh meat per person per *year* to the estimated 2.25 kg presently consumed per person from domestic animals.

Looking Ahead

The question is not what contribution antelopes can make to the African's larder, for they already do make a significant contribution through largely illegal hunting, but whether farming could provide a future for them, conferring upon them the status of an asset to be valued rather than senselessly squandered as is the case at present. But do we really want to see wildebeest from the Serengeti being turned into pet food to adorn the shelves of Western supermarkets, and the graceful kudu and impala reduced to the enslaved status of goats and sheep? The history of game preservation in Europe has shown that it is strict preservation alone that has ensured the survival of what wildlife species remain in an intensely populated country like Britain; and therein must lie the future for Africa's antelopes.

Captain Caldwell, one of Kenya's early game wardens, warned in 1926 that it was the commercialisation of game which spelt its demise. The great fauna of South Africa was largely wiped out because of the money which could be made from skins and hides. In 1866 a single firm exported

157,000 blesbok and wildebeest skins, while in 1870–71 Durban exported 485,786 skins of blesbok, wildebeest and zebra. Little wonder that these species were reduced to the point of extinction!

In his 1969 BBC Reith Lectures, Fraser Darling disagreed with the protectionist view. He regarded the future of African wildlife in national parks as confining it to enclaves, or 'at worst, ghettos'; and supported the view that marginal lands should be made productive through the exploitation of their wildlife. But if the production of game meat from marginal lands should become a 'high tech' industry in the future, then the original objective will be lost. Predators and uneconomic species will be eliminated to increase yields and warrant investment; while the wild counterparts of farmed species will be destroyed because of disease risks. Soon, wild nature will be no more than a memory with no place on the profit-motivated farm. Farming or culling are *additional* ways of exploiting wildlife, ways of making it more profitable, but they are no substitute for preservation and the national park ideal.

We want to keep in view that Pleistocene day – either Africa's wonderful antelope diversity is worth preserving or it is not. I see no future for it in terms of a meat resource alone, surely the grace and beauty of antelopes deserve more than that?

Appendix: A catalogue of antelopes

The following synopsis is designed to merely acquaint the reader with the great variety of African antelopes, and is not intended as a guide to their identification or distribution, as these details are readily available in field-guides. Where height, weight and horn length are given, these are maxima. Height is measured at the shoulders or withers. Longevities are those recorded in captivity, which probably exceed the average lifespan experienced in the wild. As indicated in Chapter 1, not all authorities are agreed on the classification.

Tribe *Tragelaphini*

This tribe possesses three living genera and nine species, representing both the most common and the largest of the antelopes. They exploit the widest range of habitat from aquatic, through dense forest and gallery forest to semi-arid. Medium to large in size, the male larger than the female, they have conspicuous ears and long necks; their coats almost always vertically striped in a cryptic pattern. With the exception of the largest members, the eland and bongo, only the males have horns, simplest in the bushbuck and most complex in the greater kudu; they are long and spiralled, always with a longitudinal crest or ridge beginning at the base on the anterior and following the horn's torsion. The two largest genera are characterised by having a tuft at the end of the tail, as opposed to along its length. There is an absence of facial and foot glands, but groin glands are sometimes present. The female has two pairs of teats. They are all browsers and mixed feeders.

Bongo *Boocerus eurycerus*
Height: 1.25 m. Weight: 250 kg. Horn length: 95 cm.

A giant among forest antelopes, the bongo is as furtive as a duiker. Inhabiting dense forest it emerges into the open only at salt-licks in forest clearings, in the early morning or late evening; but mostly it is nocturnal, lying up during the day. The male bears massive, lyrate horns, almost smooth and with unpigmented tips which give the horns the appearance of being tipped with ivory; in the female they are more slender and often irregular in shape. Its colour is a striking bright chestnut red barred with conspicuous white stripes. Solitary or in small groups, it sometimes forms herds of 35 to 50 animals, but nothing is known of its social organisation as, possessed of acute hearing and an extremely wary nature, it is very difficult to observe, and only a few *ad hoc* studies have been made at salt-licks. Two races have been described, a western *B.e. eurycerus*, and an eastern *B.e. isaaci*. Rare in many parts of its range, it is quite common in the dense forests of the Central African Republic, where it also leaves its dense retreats to feed on the fresh flush of grass springing up after a burn. Its longevity is about 18 years.

Mountain nyala *Tragelaphus buxtoni*
Height: 1.3 m. Weight: 225 kg. Horn length: 1.1 m.

A very large antelope, this is an extremely localised species found only in a few highland localities of Ethiopia at altitudes above 2,500 m, where freezing temperatures may occur at night. Resembling the greater kudu, it has similar but shorter and less-convoluted horns. Mainly a browser it inhabits highland forest and thickets, not venturing into the open. The last large living ungulate to be discovered in Africa, it was first made known to science in 1908. A scarce animal, little is known of its habits.

Sitatunga *T. spekei*
Height: 1.1 m. Weight: 110 kg. Horn length: 90 cm.

First made known to science by the explorer Speke, who was presented with a pair of horns by a native king in western Tanzania in 1861, this, the most aquatic of antelopes, has been called an aquatic bushbuck, a species with which it hybridises very easily. It is characterised by its shaggy coat in the male, and extremely long hooves, adapted to walking on marshy ground. Very secretive, it spends much of its time in dense papyrus swamps, but may emerge near the edges in the evenings. The colour varies from drab chocolate-brown to grey-brown in the male, but the female looks like a bushbuck. The horns are more lyrate than those of the bushbuck, and have unpigmented tips. Four races have been described: the northern, western, Zambesi and island; the latter from the islands in Lake Victoria and of doubtful taxonomic status. It lives to almost 18 years.

Nyala *T. angasi*
Height: 1.0 m. Weight: 125 kg. Horn length: 79 cm.

Somewhat resembling the bushbuck, the male is characterised by a very shaggy belly coat, quite unlike other antelope species, and is greyish in colour. The horns have a single, open curve with unpigmented tips. Less localised than the mountain species, it is nevertheless very restricted in range, occurring only in the eastern part of South Africa, where it prefers dense bush, never far from water. A shy species, at one time it was considered to be one of the rarest of antelopes, but strict protection has resulted in a significant increase in numbers. Little is known of its behaviour, nor of the reasons for its restricted distribution. It lives about 16 years.

Bushbuck *T. scriptus*
Height: 94 cm. Weight: 77 kg. Horn length: 55 cm.

A small, to medium-sized antelope and the most widely distributed in Africa, wherever there is suitable dense thicket; it is able to exist close to human settlement with some success. The colouration varies considerably and some 40 races have been described, of which the western and northern forms are the most distinct, the former always having the stripes in a 'harness' pattern. The eastern race is larger and browner with less prominent stripes. Its horns tend to be short, with a single twist. Usually never far from water it is a shy animal unless it is undisturbed, when it becomes more diurnal; otherwise it is crepuscular and nocturnal. The male is said to be dangerous if cornered or wounded. It lives for about 12 to 13 years.

Greater kudu *T. strepsiceros*
Height: 1.6 m. Weight: 318 kg. Horn length: 1.7 m.

A very large, but slenderly built antelope, high withered with a long mane and beard, and magnificent horns in an open spiral. Predominantly grey in colour, some three races are recognised, the southern, which is the biggest; the East African, and the western, which is the smallest. It tends to inhabit rather dry country, often rocky and hilly, where it is shy and retiring, favouring woodland or fairly thick bush. A completely isolated population occurs in the north of the Central African Republic. It is alleged never to have recovered from the effects of the rinderpest plague at the beginning of the century, and today is most numerous in South Africa where some studies have been conducted on it. It lives in small groups of four to five, although up to 30 have been recorded together. Longevity is over 15 years.

Lesser kudu *T. imberbis*
Height: 1.0 m. Weight: 100 kg. Horn length: 89 cm.

A small version of the greater kudu, this is the most slender of all the tragelaphines. It lacks the deep neck with its dewlap and beard of the former but shares the same general form of the horns and coat colour. Water independent, it inhabits thorn-bush country in semi-arid regions within a restricted range in East Africa, but may also have existed recently in Arabia. A timid animal, it is met with in pairs or family groups and is very sedentary, never ranging far; although little is known of its habits. Noted for its prodigious leaps when pursued, it probably lacks stamina and has been observed to be brought down by hunting dogs in fairly thick bush.

Cape eland *Taurotragus oryx*
Height: 1.78 m. Weight: 900 kg. Horn length: 94 cm.

This is the largest of the antelopes and has been described as the 'apotheosis of antelope evolution'. Huge and ox-like in appearance, despite its great size it can leap 2 m into the air with apparent ease. The horns are a tight corkscrew, present in both sexes, the longest recorded being from the female. Several races have been described but only two are recognised, the southern, known as Livingstone's eland, which has the longest horns and lacks the vertical white stripes on the coat; and the East African race which occurs from central Tanzania northwards. Adapted to dry country, it is a gregarious, very shy animal, but easily tamed. Its cattle-like appearance is only superficial, having a specialised diet and adapted to ranging widely in search of food. Gestation is nine months and the calf weighs 35 kg at birth. Longevity is about 20 years.

Giant or Lord Derby's eland *T. derbianus*
Height: 1.75 m. Weight: 900 kg. Horn length: 1.1 m.

This is believed to be even larger than the Cape eland, but few large bulls have been collected so that its exact height and weight have not been accurately established. The horns are much more massive and widely divergent, used by the bull to break branches from the trees to feed on. It is confined to the savanna woodlands north of the equator in areas of good rainfall and is a fastidious browser, its movements reputedly being guided by the presence of the tree *Isoberlinia doka*, whose young leaves appear to be its favourite food, followed by those of the shea butter tree *Vitellaria paradoxum, Lonchocarpus laxiflorus* and the shoots and heavily scented flowers of a species of *Gardenia*.

It was originally named from horns of the western race brought to England from Gambia by Lord Derby's private collector. The western race, distributed between Senegal and Mali, is now rare; but the bigger central race, found from the Cameroons eastwards just into western Uganda, is still numerous in the Central African Republic, where it roams in herds of 50 or more. In spite of its large size and gregarious habit, it moves remarkably furtively through the woodland and little is known of its habits. It is a species which still awaits study.

Sub-family *Cephalophinae*

This sub-family comprises the duikers which are divided into the forest duikers of the genus *Cephalophus*, and the single representative of the bush duiker, *Sylvicapra*. The former are all very similar, mostly small, short-legged furtive animals, with a hunched back and wedge-shaped body suited to diving through the vegetation. The female is larger than the male, and has two pairs of teats. All have facial and foot glands, but groin glands are variable. Horns may be reduced or absent in the female. A peculiarity of the duikers is that in some species the hair on the nape of the neck is directed forwards, and in others backwards. Generally occurring solitarily or in pairs, their habits are little known and several species are regarded as rare. In contrast to the forest duikers the bush duiker has long legs and a straight back, and inhabits bush and scrub, avoiding dense forest.

Blue duiker *Cephalophus monticola*
Height: 40 cm. Weight: 9 kg. Horn length: 9.5 cm.

This is the smallest of the duikers and was at one time regarded as a separate genus. The horns are relatively long, absent in the female of the East African race. The facial gland is prominent but groin glands are absent. Its colour is a bluish-grey in the east of its range, changing to dark brown in the west. It has one of the widest antelope distributions, extending into isolated coastal forest patches in the east, and reaches as far south as the Cape. Twenty-one races have been described among which is one confined to the islands of Pemba and Mafia off the East African coast; and one once known as the 'grave duiker' as it was first found among the graves of the European cemetery on a small island near Zanzibar. It inhabits the moist forests and extends into the Sudanian woodland zone. It utters a sharp whistle when alarmed. No studies have been conducted on the species. Longevity is about six years.

Maxwell's duiker *C. maxwelli*
Height: 35.5 cm. Weight: 5.5 kg. Horn length: 6.5 cm.

Similar to the blue duiker of which some consider it to be just a small variation. Four races have been described, differing mainly in its uniform mouse-grey colour. It is confined to the west African forest block. Both sexes are horned, but in the Liberian race those of the female are vestigial or absent. Some studies have been conducted on this species. It has lived for over ten years.

Black-fronted duiker *C. nigrifrons*
Height: 50 cm. Weight: 18 kg. Horn length: 9.5 cm.

A small species, it has been suggested that the black-fronted duiker may represent the ancestral form of forest duiker from which the red duikers derived which emerged from the forest habitat, the only forest duikers to do so. The colour is a rich chestnut and it is distinguished from other duikers by its black forehead. The hooves are elongated as an adaptation to travelling on marshy ground in the inundated forest habitat where it lives, but it is also found in montane forest, occurring at 4,000 m in the Ruwenzori, where its splayed hooves allow it to move over moss or bogs with amazing rapidity. It is widely distributed in the Congo basin, reaching into outlying forest patches. Possibly only a race of the red duiker, nine variations have been described. Nothing is known of its habits.

Red-flanked duiker *C. rufilatus*
Height: 35 cm. Weight: 13 kg. Horn length: 9.5 cm.

A small species, this duiker is widely distributed in the west African savanna where it is almost as common as the common duiker, but it inhabits forest as well. Its general colour is a bright reddish-chestnut with a dorsal grey-black line and grey-black lower legs. It is restricted to west and central Africa. Nothing is known of its habits, but it is usually seen singly and appears to be diurnal. It lives over six years.

Jentink's duiker *C. jentinki*
Height: 79 cm. Weight: 64 kg. Horn length: 22 cm.

An exceptionally rare duiker, almost equal in size to the yellow-backed of which it was at one time thought to be a variant, but this has now been disproved. It is known only from dense forest in Liberia and Ivory Coast. It is uniquely coloured with a blackish head and neck, a light grey to white collar, and a uniform grey body, making it the lightest coloured of all the duikers, more in keeping with an arid habitat than its moist forest one. The local people call it 'four eyes', believing that its facial glands are an extra pair of eyes. Nothing is known of its habits.

Yellow-backed duiker *C. sylvicultor*
Height: 84 cm. Weight: 63 kg. Horn length: 20 cm.

The largest of all the duikers, this species inhabits the dense forest of the Congo basin and western Africa as far as Senegal. It is absent from eastern and southern Africa. Its colour ranges from a dark velvety brown to jet black, and it is distinguished by a conspicuous triangular yellow flash on the back, broadening over the rump, which develops at five to eight months. About six races have been described but none seems valid. An infrequently seen species, it also occurs in the Sudanian woodland, where it has a predilection for standing on termite mounds. Nothing is known of its habits. It lives for about nine years.

Abbot's duiker *C. spadix*
Height: 66 cm. Weight: 59 kg. Horn length: 10 cm.

A large, rather heavily built species, it differs from the yellow-backed in its slightly smaller size and lacks the yellow dorsal flash. Its colour is a uniform dark chestnut brown. The horns are rather thin and slender. It is of very restricted distribution, occurring only in mountain forests in East Africa up to 3,600 m, being mostly known from Mount Kilimanjaro and the Usambara Mountains in Tanzania. It is said to have a tendency to follow regular runs, but nothing is known of its habits and it has rarely been seen. The popular name is from its discoverer, Dr Abbot, who found it on Mount Kilimanjaro in 1890.

Banded duiker *C. zebra*
Height: 40 cm. Weight: 16 kg. Horn length: 4.5 cm.

This is the most strikingly-patterned of all the duikers, a species recorded only from the mountain forests of Sierra Leone, Liberia and the Ivory Coast. It is marked with about 12 broad, transverse brownish-black bands on a pale background. Nothing is known of its habits, but it is not uncommonly killed for food and is thus probably more numerous in certain areas than it is generally thought to be.

Black duiker *C. niger*
Height: 50 cm. Weight: 16 kg. Horn length: 17 cm.

A medium-sized species with a rather thick coat of a uniformly dark colour ranging from brown to black. The head is particularly long and narrow and horns are present in both sexes. It is confined to the dense forests of the west African coast. Nothing is known of its habits.

Zanzibar duiker *C. adersi*
Height: 32 cm. Weight: 12 kg. Horn length: 6 cm.

A small and little-known species found only on the island of Zanzibar and a small part of the Kenya coast, the former Sokoke forest. It is considered by some authorities to be simply a race of the red duiker, while others attribute it to the Peter's duiker. Its colour and pattern are similar to the latter, and as in that species the hair on the neck is directed forwards, whereas in the red duiker it grows backwards. It is a relatively rare species, but apparently does well in captivity.

Red duiker *C. natalensis*
Height: 50 cm. Weight: 13 kg. Horn length: 10 cm.

A medium-sized species which occurs in eastern and southern Africa. Its colour is a bright chestnut but it lacks the dark dorsal band of the western red-flanked duiker. But the pattern is variable and eight races have been described, the most distinctive of which is the East African Harvey's duiker, which in turn has another nine races. Harvey's has a more vivid colour and a blackish face, while its horns reach 11.5 cm. Red duikers are often found in pairs, and groups of five or six have been seen in forest glades. Its habitat is dense bush and montane forest. It is one of the best known of the forest duikers as it is less secretive than the others and has a wide range, but it has not been studied in detail. It is becoming scarce in South Africa. Longevity is over 15 years.

Peter's duiker *C. callipygus*
Height: 55 cm. Weight: 20 kg. Horn length: 13 cm.

This species inhabits the dense forest of the Congo basin. It is a rather drab brownish fawn in colour, but both colour and pattern show much variation and five races have been named. Nothing is known of its habits, but it is apparently diurnal and appears to be fairly common, often being taken by hunters.

Bay or black-striped duiker *C. dorsalis*
Height: 55 cm. Weight: 20 kg. Horn length: 9.5 cm.

This is one of the most distinctive of the species from west and central Africa, with a bright chestnut colour and a black dorsal band, but also a blackish band edging the belly. Seven races have been described. It is an inhabitant of dense forest but nothing is known of its habits. Longevity is over 12 years.

Gabon or white-bellied duiker *C. leucogaster*
Height: 50 cm. Weight: 18 kg. Horn length: 12.5 cm.

This is lighter in colour than other species but with a contrasting dark forehead, a dark dorsal band and a white rump; the latter distinguishing it from the bay duiker, of which it may be only a race. It is restricted to the eastern and western Congo basin, and although a forest species it enters into the edges of the savanna, but its habits are virtually unknown.

Ogilby's duiker *C. ogilbyi*
Height: 55 cm. Weight: 20 kg. Horn length: 12 cm.

This is a medium-sized species, limited to the west African forest belt and the island of Fernando Po. It is a bright orange rufous in colour with a median black dorsal band. It may be conspecific with the bay duiker, and the mainland race, although termed *C. o. brookei* to distinguish it from the island form, is very similar. It occurs in deep forest, but nothing is known of its habits.

Common, bush, grey or Grimm's duiker *Sylvicapra grimmia*
Height: 66 cm. Weight: 13.5 kg. Horn length: 16 cm.

A medium-sized species, this is the only duiker to warrant a genus of its own. Very different in colour to the *Cephalophus* group it is a grizzled grey, and also lacks the wedge-shaped crouching stance, although it bounds in much the same manner. The horns, which are upright instead of backwardly directed, are present normally only in the male, but sometimes occur in the female. A large number of races has been described, totalling some 25, of which the southern, Angolan, western and East African are regarded as distinctive. Almost ubiquitous in its distribution outside of dense forest and arid areas, it is found regularly in open habitat from semi-arid to high mountain levels; those on the upper levels of Mount Elgon and the Aberdare Mountains in Kenya being characterised by having long shaggy coats. It is very adaptable with a very catholic diet and can survive in fairly densely-settled regions, its ability to breed twice a year enabling it to withstand heavy exploitation. Despite being one of the most common species of antelope, no detailed studies on its social organisation have been conducted and much of the information concerning it is anecdotal. It lives about 12 years.

Sub-family *Reduncinae*

The reduncines form a group of medium to large-sized, stoutly-built antelopes. Only the males bear horns (although females may sometimes carry aberrant ones), which curve backwards and then forwards, and are strongly ridged on the anterior face. There are five main groups in the sub-family: the reedbucks, kobs, waterbucks, lechwes and puku. Facial glands are absent except in the puku and kob, being small in the latter but active, producing a 'sweet and not unpleasant smell'. Groin glands are present but rudimentary in the lechwe, well-developed in the puku, reedbuck and kob, but absent in the waterbuck. A vestigial foot gland is often present in the reedbuck and puku. The reedbuck is also characterised by having a gland below the ear. The female has two pairs of teats. All are essentially grazers or mixed feeders of open country, strongly dependent on water.

Southern or common reedbuck *Redunca arundinum*
Height: 94 cm. Weight: 77 kg. Horn length: 44 cm.

This is the largest of the reedbucks, the female a little smaller than the male. The colour is greyish-fawn similar to other reedbucks, but it is distinguished by its much longer, widely diverging horns. Seven races have been described. It is widely distributed south of the equator, some overlap with the bohor taking place in the north-east of its range. It inhabits open grassland, never far from water, living singly or in pairs, or in small family groups; sometimes forming larger concentrations on open patches of fresh grass. It lives about ten years.

Bohor reedbuck *R. redunca*
Height: 90 cm. Weight: 50 kg. Horn length: 41.5 cm.

A medium-sized antelope with a rather thick coat, of a uniform yellowish or reddish fawn colour. The gland below the ear is conspicuous as a round black patch. Ten races have been described, distributed from Senegal to the Sudan, and into eastern Africa. The Sudan is the biggest. The habitat and social organisation is similar to that of the southern reedbuck. It has the habit of lying still until the very last minute and then suddenly leaping up and running away in a 'rocking horse' gait. Emitting a shrill whistle when alarmed, the tail is held up displaying a white underside. Sometimes confused with young kob, but the rocking gait is different and the coat has a less-sleek appearance. It is mainly a grazer. Bohor is the Amharic name from Ethiopia, but it was first described from Gori Island off the coast of Senegal in 1767. It lives about ten years.

Mountain reedbuck *R. fulvorufula*
Height: 76 cm. Weight: 27 kg. Horn length: 20 cm.

This is the smallest of the reedbucks, with peculiarly short and slender horns, having no forward curve at their tips. The coat is woolly in appearance, greyish-fawn in colour and the general pattern is not dissimilar to that of the common reedbuck, with which it may be confused where the two overlap in range; but apart from the short horns it has a dark nose patch and a reddish neck, lacking in the other. Its distribution is widely separate, one group known as Chanler's occurring in the mountains and hills of East Africa; another, the southern mountain reedbuck occurring at the Cape; while an isolated rare population occurs in the Adamoua massif of Cameroon, over 2,000 km from the nearest known population in the south-eastern Sudan. Its habitat is broken, hilly or mountainous country, living generally in small groups. Longevity is over 12 years.

Common waterbuck *Kobus ellipsiprymnus*
Height: 1.35 m. Weight: 200 kg. Horn length: 95 cm.

A large, stately, easily recognised antelope, the female is lighter than the male. Straight-backed, it has a rather coarse coat with long shaggy hair on the neck. The colour is very variable, most commonly a grizzled grey, but all bear a distinctive elliptical white ring encircling the rump. The horns are imposing, curving slightly backwards and then forwards, sometimes turning in at the tips. Seven races have been described. Almost entirely a grazer it is never found far from water and physiological studies fully justify its name of 'waterbuck' as it cannot survive without frequent drinking, but it is not a marsh species, preferring grasslands and woodlands. The males are territorial and occur singly, young males joining in bachelor groups, while the females generally form separate herds of anything from two to 70. It was first collected by the hunter-explorer Andrew Steedman in South Africa in 1832. The Boers used the thick skin of its neck to make shoes and reins with. It lives over 16 years.

Defassa waterbuck *K. e. defassa*
Height: 1.3 m. Weight: 250 kg. Horn length: 99 cm.

Until comparatively recently the defassa waterbuck was regarded as a separate species, but since it appears to hybridise in the wild in overlap areas, producing forms with an intermediate rump pattern, taxonomists prefer to regard it simply as a race of the common species. It is however readily distinguishable, generally being heavier in most of its range, although in many parts the horns are similar in size. The colour is very variable, ranging from a silver-grey, through bright rufous to a very dark brown; which has led to no less than 29 races being described. Four of these appear to be distinct: the west African, Ugandan, Rhodesian and Angolan. It differs from the common form in having a white blaze on the rump instead of a ring, and is by far the more widely distributed both north and south of the equator; but is above all characteristic of the western northern savannas, reaching into Senegal. It seems to favour a heavier rainfall than the common form, but their habits appear to be more or less identical. The classic example of a territorial species, it has received much attention from researchers. Predominantly a grazer it takes some browse in the dry season. The defassa was discovered by Dr Rüppell in Ethiopia in 1835, and called after its Amharic name. Like the common species it lives about 16 years.

Nile or Mrs Gray's lechwe *K. megaceros*
Height: 94 cm. Weight: 86 kg. Horn length: 84 cm.

Slightly smaller than the southern lechwe, from which it is separated by over 3,000 km. Although similar it has a long rough coat of dark chocolate colour, distinguished by a distinctive white patch on the nape of the neck and shoulders, more conspicuous in the older males; with the female more rufous-coloured. The horns diverge widely. Known only from the Nile swamps its habits are apparently similar to the southern species, but it still awaits study. It lives in large herds of 50 or more but does not approach the dense concentrations of the southern species, perhaps because of its more reedy habitat. It was named by Dr Gray of the British Museum after his wife Maria, at first being known as *K. maria*, from specimens sent home by the British Consul at Khartoum in 1859. But it had in fact already been discovered by von Heuglin, the Austrian naturalist, in 1853, and described as *Adenota megaceros* two years later. The name, 'Mrs Gray's lechwe' has however stuck. It lives about ten years.

Lechwe *K. lechwe*
Height: 99 cm. Weight: 127 kg. Horn length: 89 cm.

A medium-sized antelope with the hindquarters noticeably higher than the fore, giving a crouching appearance; the female much lighter in weight than the male. It has a rather long rough coat of bright chestnut to blackish colour, with contrasting white underparts. The horns are long and lyre-shaped, and relatively thin. The hooves are somewhat long and pointed, an adaptation to its aquatic life for, next to the sitatunga, it is the most aquatic of antelopes, entirely restricted to seasonally inundated flood plains in the vast central basin of Africa south of the equator; spending much time wading in the water. Four races are recognised as distinctive; the red lechwe, which is the type specimen; the black lechwe, distinguished by its significant black colouration; the Kafue Flats lechwe, of very limited distribution; and the Robert's lechwe, now believed to be extinct. Lechwes are characterised by extreme gregariousness and once occurred in vast numbers. Even today the numbers of the Kafue Flats lechwe have been put at 40,000, but this is only a remnant of their former abundance. All races are threatened by excessive hunting, or, as in the case of the Kafue Flats lechwe, the loss of habitat due to a hydro-electric scheme. Longevity is over 12 years.

Kob *K. kob*
Height: 1.09 m. Weight: 95 kg. Horn length: 69 cm.

A medium-sized antelope of graceful appearance, with a short, glossy coat, generally a bright gold fulvous in colour. The horns are relatively short but thick and strongly ridged, curving in an 'S' shape. The female is smaller and her coat lighter in colour. At one time the kobs were regarded as a separate genus *Adenota* from the waterbucks, but since they can be made to hybridise in captivity they are now regarded as conspecific; although they are very different in appearance, social behaviour and physiology. Due to variations of coat colour and pattern 18 races have been described, the most distinctive of which are the western or Buffon's kob (the nominate race, first described in 1777 from a specimen from Upper Guinea); the Uganda kob, called Thomas's in Kenya where it is now virtually extinct; and the Sudanese white-eared kob. The latter is a distinctive race with a dark brown, almost black, back developing in the males, offset by entirely white ears and prominent white rings around the eyes. The latter race undergoes one of the biggest animal migrations still existing in Africa, the annual trek numbering almost a million head. Although confined almost entirely to the north of the equator the kob is one of the most widespread of antelopes, the commonest in central and western Africa. Never far from water, they are entirely grazers, apart from taking some aquatic vegetation. A very gregarious species, sometimes occurring in dense concentrations numbering thousands, although now greatly reduced in most parts of its range. It is noted for its 'lek-type' of territorial behaviour which the male adopts at high densities. It lives for over 16 years.

Puku *K. vardoni*
Height: 81 cm. Weight: 73 kg. Horn length: 52 cm.

This is a species considered by some to be intermediate between the kobs and lechwes. It is similar in size to the former and is much like it in appearance but with a rather longer coat of a bright golden yellow colour. The horns are short and only slightly curved. It could be mistaken for an immature kob but lacks the black markings on the front of the forelegs which are characteristic of the kob, and has a white throat. It is of fairly limited distribution occurring only in the centre of Africa south of the equator. It once formed huge herds, but today is found only in small numbers. Its habits are similar to the kob, a gregarious species with territorial males, but it has not been well studied. It was first reported by Dr Livingstone in 1853.

Sub-family *Hippotraginae*

These are all large antelopes with well-developed horns borne by both sexes, and ranging from the almost straight horns of the oryx to the spiral horns of the addax. There is usually a mane and the ears are large. Facial glands are absent or vestigial, and groin glands are absent but foot glands are present. The female has two pairs of teats. Some authorities consider all of the oryxes to be conspecific, the differences being only racial, but here each is treated separately because of its distinctiveness. One species, the white oryx, formerly occurred in Arabia, but is now believed to be extinct in the wild. The group also includes the now-extinct bluebuck. Gregarious and territorial, the group covers a wide physiological range from woodland to desert species.

Addax *Addax nasomaculatus*
Height: 1.04 m. Weight: 122 kg. Horn length: 1.05 m.

A big antelope of clumsy appearance occasioned by its large feet, the forehead bears a conspicuous thick mat of chestnut brown hair. The rest of the body colour shows a wide range but is predominantly greyish-white in the summer, and changes to light brown in the winter. The horns are spiralled, with ridges at the base; thinner and less spiralled in the female. A true desert antelope of the north of Africa, it once ranged throughout the Sahara, trekking for long distances in search of the pastures which spring up after light rain, which it is said to be able to sense from distances of over 150 km. The desert succulents and night dew provide it with all of its water requirements. A gregarious species it lives in herds of 20 to 200 head, but is one of the most threatened antelopes due to intensive hunting. The present north African drought may well have almost spelt its extinction by forcing it into inhabited areas. Although well-known to the ancients, it was first described in 1816 from a specimen from west Africa. Longevity is over 18 years.

Bluebuck or blaauwbok *Hippotragus leucophoeus*
Height: 1.25 m. Weight: ? Horn length: 62 cm.

This now extinct species was similar to, but smaller than, the roan; bearing similarly backwardly-directed horns, longer but less massive. The body colour was a bluish-grey with a velvety sheen, and it lacked the contrasting facial markings. It is alleged to have fed in woodland and grassy glades. The species is only known to have occurred in the extreme south-west corner of the Cape, and there is no fossil evidence for a once wider distribution. It was exterminated between 1799 and 1800, only 34 years after it was first described; and was the first known African mammal to be exterminated by modern man. Only five mounted specimens are known to exist.

Roan antelope *H. equinus*
Height: 1.6 m. Weight: 270 kg. Horn length: 89 cm.

One of the largest of the antelopes, it has sloping withers accentuated by a short mane; long tufted ears, and a distinctive black-and-white patterned face. The body colour is uniformly dark rufous to reddish fawn, the females and young males being redder than the adult male and resembling the female sable antelope. The horns, fairly thick and heavily ridged, curve backwards. Five races have been described but are not distinctive. Its distribution encircles the Congo forest and it is one of the most common west African antelopes, favouring the relatively high rainfall Sudano-Guinean zone, but is also common in the woodlands south of the equator. A grazer and mixed feeder, the roan lives in small herds of up to 20 head, sometimes forming larger companies. It lives about 14 years.

Sable antelope *H. niger*
Height: 1.4 m. Weight: 250 kg. Horn length: 1.64 m.

Slightly smaller than the roan but with much longer horns curving back in a great arc, the mature bull is perhaps the most magnificent of the antelopes with its beautiful black and white livery. The females and young males are no less attractive in their rich rufous coats. Five races have been described, but the really distinctive one is the giant sable *H. n. variani* of Angola, which carries the longest horns. Found in only a small area the giant race has a doubtful future. The sable inhabits fairly thick woodland and is confined to the eastern half of the continent south of the equator, overlapping in parts of its range with the roan. It lives in herds of 10 to 20 head, sometimes more, and the male is territorial. It is a very specialised grazer, which probably accounts for its restricted distribution. Longevity is over 16 years.

Scimitar-horned oryx *Oryx dammah*
Height: 1.2 m. Weight: 205 kg. Horn length: 1.2 m.

A large, stocky species of a very pale colour with no contrasting markings, the head pattern being brown. The horns are striking, long and thin, curving back in a graceful arc. The hooves are enlarged but not as much as in the addax. A semi-desert species it is confined to the north of the equator, inhabiting the Sahel region and the edge of the Sahara. It is gregarious, living in herds of 12 to 60, but formerly concentrated in large numbers where rain had fallen; like the addax wandering great distances in search of fresh pastures. Now on the verge of extinction. It lives for over 18 years.

Gemsbok *O. gazella*
Height: 1.22 m. Weight: 205 kg. Horn length: 1.2 m.

The pattern of the gemsbok is the most contrasting among the oryxes, the black areas being accentuated and the black tufted tail much larger, setting off the fawn-grey body. The horns, diverging in a 'V' shape, are much longer than those of other species, with the exception of the scimitar-horned; and some females' horns are as long as the males'. Formerly widespread in South Africa in the dry country, it is now restricted to the western region. Gregarious, it is found in groups of 30 to 40, but sometimes congregates in large numbers on fresh pastures. Like its northern relatives it can go without water, but drinks regularly when water is available. It was greatly hunted by the Boers for its tough neck skin to make reins for their ox-wagon teams. First described by Linnaeus in 1758, the specimen was said to have come from 'India'. Longevity is over 18 years.

Beisa oryx *O. g. beisa*
Height: 1.19 m. Weight: 205 kg. Horn length: 1.03 m.

Of similar size to the gemsbok, some authorities consider the beisa to be a separate species *O. beisa*, rather than a race. The pattern is less contrasting and the body lighter in colour. The horns are similar; long, slender and rapier-like, curving only slightly backwards, frequently longer in the female although more slender. Restricted in distribution to eastern Africa, two races have been identified; the beisa oryx from the Red Sea to the Tana River in Kenya, and the fringe-eared *O. g. callotis* which is found south of the Tana into Tanzania, occupying somewhat less-arid country. The latter race is distinguished by its darker colouring and a prominent tassel on the tips of its ears; while the horns tend to be heavier but shorter in length. Although not found in such arid country as the scimitar-horned, these oryxes can exist without water if succulent or dew-laden vegetation is available. Gregarious they are usually found in herds of up to 40 or more. The name 'beisa' is said to be a mis-quotation of the Somali name 'beida'. Longevity is presumably as for the gemsbok.

Sub-family *Alcelaphinae*

These are all large antelopes, distinguished by their sloping backs, the forequarters higher than the hind indicative of great speed; and the long, narrow face, with the eyes tending to be set forwards to give good forward vision. Both sexes are horned, the horns relatively short and stout, in some species ringed at the base, in others smooth. Facial and foot glands are present, but groin glands are absent. The female has one pair of teats. All are very gregarious species, strictly grazers of open grassland and light woodland, with some adapted to arid conditions. They show a marked form of territoriality.

White-tailed gnu or black wildebeest *Connochaetes gnou*
Height: 1.14 m. Weight: 160 kg. Horn length: 67 cm.

A large antelope, dark brown to black in colour, offset with a conspicuous white tail. It is distinguished by a large brush of upright hair on the face, a stiff mane, a short beard and a tassel of hair on the chest. The horns curve forward and up. The female is very similar in appearance to the male. Restricted to southern Africa it once occurred in herds which 'blackened the plains' but by the turn of the century only about 600 remained. Farmers then began protecting small numbers on their farms, and by 1971 the population stood at over 3,100 in protected areas and on private land. A water dependent species favouring open plains, it is naturally prone to migration. Longevity is up to 20 years.

Brindled or black-tailed gnu or blue wildebeest *C. taurinus*
Height: 1.4 m. Weight: 272 kg. Horn length: 81 cm.

A larger species than the black wildebeest, this species has a greyish, rather ox-like body in front with sloping hindquarters and a large head with a long flat muzzle. A scraggy mane and beard with a conspicuous long black tail, complete the picture. The horns curve laterally downwards and upwards, and are smooth along their length. The female is very similar to the male. Ten races have been described of which three are generally recognised: the brindled gnu or blue wildebeest which occurs from southern Africa to southern Tanzania and is characterised by a black beard; the white-bearded gnu *C. t. albojubatus* which is the race found in the Serengeti and Kenya, conspicuously different with its white beard; and the Nyasaland gnu *C. t. johnstoni* found between Malawi and southern Tanzania where it intergrades with the former. At one time the blue wildebeest was given separate generic status under the name of *Gorgon taurinus*. The wildebeest is a southern species only extending just north of the equator in Kenya. It is very gregarious and in East Africa still occurs in vast numbers on the Serengeti plains where it is noted for its remarkable migrations. A grazer, it favours open grassland; although the blue and Nyasaland races occur in woodland. Longevity is up to 20 years.

Lichtenstein's hartebeest *Alcelaphus lichtensteini*
Height: 1.25 m. Weight: 145 kg. Horn length: 58 cm.

A large antelope with markedly sloping withers, the colouration on the back is bright rufous, contrasting with the pale fawn flanks and neck. The horns are short, curving laterally as well as forwards and backwards, with broad bases, and lacking the conspicuous pedicel of other hartebeests. The female, although lighter, resembles the male. Six races have been described but they are not distinctive. Its distribution occupies the area between the limits of the bubal in the north and the red hartebeest in the south, overlapping with the latter in southern Tanzania. A strict grazer inhabiting open woodland, its habits appear to be identical to those of the bubal.

Bubal hartebeest *A. buselaphus*
Height: 1.45 m. Weight: 205 kg. Horn length: 68 cm.

A larger species than the Lichtenstein's, characterised by its sharply sloping back and very long, narrow face, with the horns, which vary widely in their curvature but more or less curve forwards and then backwards in a sickle-shape, perched on a pedicel at the back of the skull. The colour is a uniform sandy fawn with light hindquarters changing to white on the rump. It ranges from eastern Africa, where it extends to just south of the equator, across to Senegal, and is one of the most common of African antelopes, very characteristic of the west African woodlands. Some 70 different names have been given to variations in horn shape and coat colour, but these can be boiled down to 26 races, of which six principal ones are recognised: the Coke's or kongoni is the familiar race of Kenya; the western hartebeest extends throughout western Africa; the Lelwel's occurs from northern Kenya west to the Cameroons; the tora occurs in Ethiopia and the Sudan, and the now rare Swayne's occurs in Somalia and parts of Ethiopia. The true bubal, which was the smallest of the harte-beests and adapted to near-desert conditions, was formerly widespread in North Africa but is believed to have become extinct about 1940. In addition to these races there are several intergrades, such as the Jackson's (a race of the Lelwel's)×Coke's on Mount Kenya. The last survivor of another inter-grade, also intermediate between Jackson's and Coke's, the Lake Nakuru hartebeest, died sometime after 1969. The next most endangered race is the Swayne's, another species which at the turn of the century could be seen in tens of thousands, evidently possessing a type of behaviour not shown by the other hartebeests, but perhaps resembling that of the wil-debeest. Bubal hartebeest are territorial; entirely grazers they are well adapted to forgo water, but drink when it is available. Longevity is up to 19 years.

Cape or red hartebeest A. caama
Height: 1.24 m. Weight: 180 kg. Horn length: 65 cm.

Similar in size and appearance to the bubal of which some consider it is just a race, but it has a more reddish-fawn colour and dark face markings. The horns curve more strongly forwards and are distinguished by a greatly exaggerated pedicel. This is the original hartebeest, apparently so-called by the Dutch settlers at the Cape because they thought it resembled a hart. Another species which in the early days of the Cape settlement occurred in vast numbers, but today the nominate race, first described in 1816, is now extinct. The survivors are those of the Transvaal race A. c. selbornei, which still exists in fair numbers, although it was on the verge of extinction in 1875 when it was accorded protection. The habits are similar to the bubal.

Hunter's hartebeest or hirola Beatragus hunteri
Height: 99 cm. Weight: 73 kg. Horn length: 70 cm.

This is the smallest of the sub-family. It has the general features of a hartebeest but is more lightly built with rather long, thin horns, curving backwards and forwards like an impala's. The colour is a uniform rufous tawny with a distinctive white chevron between the eyes. Some authorities consider it to be congeneric with the Damaliscus group, but the fossil record does not support this showing that the genus probably ante-dates the common Alcelaphus-Damaliscus ancestor. It is restricted to a small region near the Kenya-Somali coast where it seems to have main-tained a niche on an area of isolated grassy plains which have not been colonised by the hartebeest, apparently its competitor. At one time thought to number only about 1,000 animals, air counts in 1973 suggested that the population might be 10,000. But now they are rapidly diminishing in numbers in competition with cattle, and a survey in 1978 revealed only an estimated 2,385, while the cattle population had doubled. It is a strict grazer, living in herds of 12 to 25 head and appears to have a hartebeest-type of territoriality, marking with its facial gland; but it has yet to be studied in detail. This interesting antelope is named after the sportsman H.C.V. Hunter who first recorded it in 1887. Every effort should be made to preserve this rare link species in the complicated pattern of alcelaphine evolution.

Bontebok or blesbok *Damaliscus dorcas*
Height: 99 cm. Weight: 100 kg. Horn length: 47 cm.

A medium-sized antelope characterised by its striking contrasting pattern of white markings on the head, rump and legs, and rich brown body with a purplish gloss. The horns are simply curved and ringed. Once regarded as two separate species, the blesbok is now considered a race *D. d. phillipsi*. It was formerly widely distributed in South Africa but separated into a northern (blesbok) and a southern (bontebok) group. The bontebok, larger, darker and more richly coloured, is probably the rarest antelope in South Africa, and is another species of very restricted distribution. Confined to the extreme south-west of the Cape, a traveller in 1689 recorded seeing more than a thousand of the 'bonte harte bokken' running. By 1835 they were reduced to a few herds strictly protected by law – there was a fine of £37.50 for shooting one without a licence – and by one or two farmers; but by 1927 only 121 survived. In 1931 a national park was created for them and 38 years later their numbers stood at about 800 head on protected and private land. The blesbok was often confused with the bontebok, but was always far more numerous 'covering the plain ... as far as the eye could see' as contemporary accounts recall. Slaughtered mercilessly for its hide its numbers also were rapidly declining until the Boer War in 1899 halted the trade in skins. Although the blesbok began to recover, all of its former habitat was settled so that populations now exist only on private land. But they are once again numerous, estimated in the tens of thousands, and are killed for meat on a large scale. The species is territorial with habits similar to the hartebeest. Longevity is up to 17 years.

Sassaby, tsessebe or bastard hartebeest *D. lunatus*
Height: 1.2 m. Weight: 160 kg. Horn length: 44 cm.

A large antelope, reddish chestnut in colour with a purplish gloss, blackish face and blackish colouration on the lower part of the shoulders and the hindlegs. The horns bend outwards in a half-moon shape and are not on a pedicel. A south African species it is probably conspecific with the topi which it resembles, except in the shape of its horns. But there is no overlap, the two populations being widely separate. A grazer, it occurs in small groups of eight or ten. Although it has the reputation of being the fastest of all antelopes it is probably no faster than other members of the sub-family. Longevity is 15 to 18 years.

Topi *D. korrigum*
Height: 1.29 m. Weight: 130 kg. Horn length: 70 cm.

Similar to the tsessebe, with the typical sloping withers of the group, the face narrow but not elongated and the horns not on a pedicel, ringed and with a simple curvature, turning in at the tips. The coat colour is an attractive glossy reddish-brown, darker than the tsessebe's. The female is similar to the male. A northern species, it extends from just south of the equator in east central Africa, west across to Senegal, with an isolated population on the Kenya-Somali coast. Twelve races have been described of which three are distinct: the Senegal hartebeest or korrigum (the nominate race) occurring eastwards to the Sudan; the topi of eastern Africa, and the tiang of north-eastern Africa. Some regard all topis simply as a race of the tsessebe. A very gregarious species, at one time thought to be the most numerous antelope in Africa, but their numbers have declined drastically in recent years due to competition with cattle. Strictly grazers, they are very specialised in their choice of grass form and although preferring open short grassland are also found in light woodland. It seems to operate a flexible territorial system depending upon whether it is migratory or resident.

Sub-family *Aepycerotinae*

This sub-family boasts a single species, the well-known impala; at one time classified with the gazelles but now placed alone because its evolutionary relationships with other antelopes are uncertain. On the basis of structures in the brain it has affinities with the *Reduncinae*, which group its rumen structure also resembles to some extent. On the basis of fossil similarities another authority regards it as close to the *Alcelaphinae*. Only the males bear horns and the female has two pairs of teats.

Impala *Aepyceros melampus*
Height: 94 cm. Weight: 60 kg. Horn length: 84 cm.

A beautiful and graceful antelope of medium size, lightly built the male is of imposing appearance with long, slender lyrate horns, ridged on their anterior. The coat colour is a bright rufous, dark on the back and lighter on the flanks. The male has a gland in the centre of the forehead, while both sexes have glands between the position of the hind false hooves marked by a tuft of black hairs; but false hooves are lacking. Of widespread occurrence south of the equator, six races have been described; of which the three principal ones are the southern impala, the Angolan or black-faced, and the East African or equatorial impala, which carries the biggest horns. A race termed *A. m. suara*, after the Swahili name 'swara', was found to be based on the skin of a female and the skull and horns of a lesser kudu, so is now dropped. Common where it occurs, it is now extinct in the Cape Region where it was first described in 1812. Territorial and very gregarious, the females form herds of 15 to 20, sometimes many more. It is a mixed feeder of woodland habitat, and is noted for its spectacular leaps of up to 10 m when alarmed. The name impala means 'lyre horn' in Greek. Its longevity is up to 15 years.

Sub-family *Antilopinae*

The 'true' antelopes are small to medium-sized graceful creatures with slender legs and rather long necks. The back is straight but they are capable of great speed. Horns are usually present in both sexes, simply curved and strongly ringed; but they may be reduced or absent in the female. Facial, groin, leg and foot glands may be present. The female may have one or two pairs of teats. Mostly browsers of succulent vegetation they are inhabitants of open dry country, extending into deserts, and many are water-independent. By far the greater number consists of gazelles, of which it has been remarked that the classification is one of the most confused among all mammals. The sub-family extends into Arabia, Asia and India; but only the African species are considered in this book.

Tribe *Antilopini*

Springbuck or springbok *Antidorcas marsupialis*
Height: 90 cm. Weight: 50 kg. Horn length: 43 cm.

A medium-sized antelope characteristic of South Africa to which it is confined. The colour is a bright cinnamon brown with a distinctive dark brown lateral line; there is a tuft of hair on the forehead and, unlike all but the dama, it has a white face. The horns are short and upright, curving slightly but hooked sharply at the tips, more slender in the female. It is unique in possessing a gland on its rump covered by a fold of skin which can be everted when it is excited or alarmed to erect a conspicuous crest of 15 cm long snow-white hairs. Three races have been described of which two, Hofmeyer's and the Angolan (which is the larger of the two) are recognised. Confined today to the open dry plains of the Cape, fossils show that it once had a much wider distribution in Africa. Highly gregarious it is noted for the prodigious numbers in which it existed at the end of last century, undergoing immense periodic migrations. In 1971 its numbers were put at about a quarter of a million still existing in South Africa. It is surprising that no detailed study has yet appeared on this remarkable species. It lives about 10 years.

Gerenuk, Waller's or giraffe gazelle *Litocranius walleri*
Height: 1.04 m. Weight: 32 kg. Horn length: 43 cm.

A large gazelle, the gerenuk is unmistakable with its extraordinary long neck and long, slender legs. The colour is a two-tone milk chocolate brown unlike all other gazelles, and the ears are large and conspicuous. The horns, present only in the male, are short and massive, curving backwards and then forwards and turning in at the tips. The male has prominent facial glands exuding a black substance, and 'knee' glands marked by a tuft of hairs. Two races are recognised, a northern and a southern, the latter somewhat smaller and darker. It is confined to the Horn of Africa and Kenya, with a separate small area of distribution south of the equator in Tanzania. Inhabitants of dry bush country, they live singly or in pairs, and sometimes in small groups of up to seven. A browser, it is noted for balancing erect on its hind legs to feed. It is water-independent. Never common it is said nevertheless to have increased its range in recent times, probably making use of areas overgrazed by cattle. Depicted in bas-relief by the ancient Egyptians about 5600 BC, it was first made known to science in 1878. It has received little study and little is known of its habits.

Addra, Mhorr, red-necked or Dama gazelle *Gazella dama*
Height: 1.09 m. Weight: 73 kg. Horn length: 40 cm.

The largest of the true gazelles, slenderly built with the gazelles' long neck and legs. Like all gazelles the underparts are white, but it has a white face and a distinctive colouration on the back which varies from rufous or chestnut-brown in the western form, to just the neck and shoulders being coloured in the eastern, the rest of the body being white. But colour also changes with age and season, as well as showing individual variation. The horns are short and thick, curving backwards and then forwards, backwardly directed, thinner in the female. A northern desert species, it occupies the edge of the Sahelian zone all around the Sahara. Eight races have been described and it is given different names in different regions. Thus it is the dama in West Africa, mhorr in southern Morocco, red-necked or addra gazelle in the east and nanger in Senegal. It lives singly or in small groups of 10 to 15, but its habits are almost unknown. It has been greatly reduced in numbers in most parts of its range. Longevity is up to 12 years.

Soemmering's gazelle *G. soemmeringi*
Height: 89 cm. Weight: 45 kg. Horn length: 53 cm.

A medium-sized gazelle of a uniformly pale rufous fawn colour with dark facial markings and a white rump. The horns curve gently backwards and then slightly forwards, with inward-pointing tips. Confined to the Horn of Africa, six races have been described of which three are recognised; the Sudan, Somali or aoul and the Borani. The Somali is the largest and until recently it was the commonest gazelle there. It inhabits dry bush and acacia scrub in hilly country, but is also found on the plains, apparently undergoing seasonal migrations, but its habits are almost unknown. It lives up to 14 years.

Grant's gazelle *G. granti*
Height: 89 cm. Weight: 80 kg. Horn length: 77 cm.

A large stocky gazelle, the female smaller than the male. The colour is fawn with a black lateral line sometimes present in the female which has a black outlining to her buttocks. The horns are long, curving backwards and then forwards and turning in at the tips in the typical race, but twisting over and outwards in the extreme Robert's race. They are strong but much shorter and more slender in the female. Small facial glands are present, as well as groin, 'knee' and foot glands. It has a very limited area of distribution, evenly straddling the equator in East Africa, but shows distinctive variations in horn shape, giving rise to nine races, of which the most distinct are the southern, Bright's, Peter's, Robert's and the north Kenya or Rainey's. It inhabits open dry bush country. Probably territorial it has received some study. Longevity probably 10 to 12 years.

Red gazelle *G. rufina*
Height: ? Weight: ? Horn length: 33 cm.

Some regard this as having been a race of the red-fronted gazelle, others as a full species. Its former distribution is unknown, the only two specimens of skin and skull which are in existence having been bought in markets in Algiers or Oran at the end of last century; but it was believed to exist in the south of Algeria. Almost certainly extinct.

Mountain, Atlas, Edmi or Cuvier's gazelle *G. cuvieri*
Height: 68 cm. Weight: 27 kg. Horn length: 37 cm.

A medium-sized gazelle, fawn in colour with a distinct lateral band, it has a thick, rough coat. The horns are rather upright and parallel, present in both sexes. It is the only mountain gazelle in Africa, formerly inhabiting the Atlas range from Morocco to western Tunisia at altitudes up to 2,000 m, where it climbed like a chamois. A recent authority attributes six races to this species, including the red-fronted gazelle and the Thomson's. Once common, it is now rare. It occurs in small parties, rarely exceeding seven head. Nothing is known of its habits.

Rhim, slender-horned or sand gazelle *G. leptoceros*
Height: 66 cm. Weight: 27 kg. Horn length: 40 cm.

Medium-sized, this is the palest of all the gazelles, its pale sandy-fawn colour having a washed-out appearance. The horns are long and almost straight, present in both sexes. The most adapted desert species of gazelle, it has slightly enlarged hooves for walking on sand, and is restricted to true desert regions in the east, occurring also in Arabia. The Loder's gazelle is regarded as a westerly race. It is now considered as endangered. The name 'rhim' comes from the Hebrew Bible meaning a 'wild ox', and is therefore rather inappropriate. Nothing is known of its habits. Longevity about 14 years.

Dorcas gazelle *G. dorcas*
Height: 66 cm. Weight: 23 kg. Horn length: 35 cm.

One of the smallest gazelles with a pale, sandy fawn colour, darker along the flank. The horns are of medium length, curving simply, and present in the female. The 'knee' glands are signified by a tuft of hairs. It is confined to Africa north of the Sahara, also occurring in Israel, Syria and Arabia, and can be said to be the 'original' gazelle, known from ancient times due to its Middle East distribution. Twelve races have been described in Africa, of which the most distinct are the isabelline gazelle of Ethiopia, the Eritrean and the lowland or Pelzeln's gazelle; the latter two sometimes being considered as distinct species *G. littoralis* and *G. pelzelni*. The isabelline inhabits mountainous country up to almost 1,500 m, while the Pelzeln's is restricted to a small area of coastal desert in Somalia, where it is now very rare. Water independent, the dorcas drinks if water is available, but inhabits dry country where it lives in small herds of about 20 head, sometimes more. Possibly migrating in search of fresh pastures, it is also known to eat locusts. Longevity is about 12 to 13 years.

Speke's, plateau, Dero or flabby-nosed gazelle *G. spekei*
Height: 61 cm. Weight: 18 kg. Horn length: 30 cm.

A small species, distinguished by a flabby protuberance on the nose which can be inflated when the animal is excited or alarmed, but may be connected with cooling. The colour is a pale brownish-fawn, with a dark lateral band. The horns are similar to those of the dorcas, curving simply, and present in both sexes. It is restricted to the highlands of Somalia where it lives mostly at an altitude of 900 to 1,800 m, in contrast to the lowland Pelzeln's. Although known to live in herds of 5 to 12, sometimes as many as 20, it is a very rare species whose habits are virtually unknown.

Korin or red-fronted gazelle *G. rufifrons*
Height: 68 cm. Weight: 30 kg. Horn length: 34 cm.

A medium-sized stocky gazelle having a deep reddish fawn colour with a narrow black lateral band. The horns are rather short, only slightly curved, present in both sexes. It is found from Uganda to Senegal in the Sahel and sub-Sahelian zone. Seven races have been attributed to this form, but only one is recognised as distinct, Heuglin's *G. r. tiloneura* of Ethiopia and part of Sudan. It inhabits light woodland and open arid country, but although the commonest North African gazelle its habits are almost unknown. It has been greatly reduced in many parts of its range. Longevity is about 12 years.

Tommy or Thomson's gazelle *G. thomsoni*
Height: 66 cm. Weight: 25 kg. Horn length: 43 cm.

The best known of the gazelles, this moderately small species is a deep sandy fawn in colour on the back with the most conspicuous black lateral line of all gazelles. It resembles closely the red-fronted gazelle. The horns are fairly long and slightly curving in the male, but greatly reduced and very fragile in the female. It is of limited distribution, occurring in separate populations in Kenya and northern Tanzania, but very numerous where present. Some 22 races have been described, but only one is generally regarded as distinct, the Mongalla or Rothschild's *G. t. albonotata*. The tommy inhabits open, well-watered plains, seeking the least arid habitat of all the gazelles. Some studies have been conducted on it. It is named after the famous explorer Joseph Thomson, who first saw it in Kenya's masailand in 1883. It lives for over ten years.

As noted above some now regard the tommy simply as a race of Cuvier's gazelle, thus *G. c. thomsoni* and *G. c. albonotata*.

Tribe *Ammodorcadini*

This tribe contains only a single species of which the precise affinities are uncertain, some regarding it as a highly specialised reduncine; but the structure of the horns does have the appearance of an early gazelline development. Facial and 'knee' glands are present, but no groin or foot glands. The female has two pairs of teats.

Dibatag or Clarke's gazelle *Ammodorcas clarkei*
Height: 89 cm. Weight: 32 kg. Horn length: 30 cm.

A medium-sized species with a coat colour of uniform dark purplish-grey tinged with rufous and face markings like the gazelles. The horns are rather short, curving backwards and forwards like those of the reedbuck, absent in the female. It is characterised by its long neck, although not as long as the gerenuk's, and its long legs. When it runs its carriage is unusual, throwing its head and neck back like an ostrich, and lifting the tail over its back, hence the Somali name 'dabutag' or 'erect-tail'. It is a browser inhabiting fairly open thorn bush country, where it lives singly or in groups of three to nine. Like the gerenuk it stands on its hindlegs to feed. Limited to Somalia it is now rare. It still awaits study.

Tribe *Neotragini*

A fairly large assemblage, this tribe unites several species of small size, with small horns usually borne only by the male. It is not a natural grouping. Facial glands are present (except in *Dorcatragus*), groin glands may or may not be present. False hooves may or may not be present. The female has two pairs of teats, except for *Dorcatragus* which has one pair.

Klipspringer *Oreotragus oreotragus*
Height: 55 cm. Weight: 18 kg. Horn length: 14 cm.

A small antelope, the coat colour shows a wide range of variation but is generally olive-yellow speckled with grey, the coat thick and fairly long characterised by unique air-filled hairs which detach easily. The horns are nearly vertical short spikes, ringed at the base and found in the female only in an East African race. Twelve races have been described but these are not regarded as distinct. The only antelope adapted to a mountainous existence, the best description remains that of Cumming (1850):

'This darling little antelope frequents precipitous rocky hills and mountains, and bounds along over broken masses of rock with the most extraordinary ease and agility: it may often be seen perched, like a chamois, on the sharp pinnacle of some rock or stone, with its four feet drawn up together. Its hoofs are different from those of other antelopes, being solely suited for rocky ground, and are so formed that the weight of the animal rests on their tips.'

Widely distributed in rocky areas throughout eastern and southern Africa, it is absent from the west except for a rare population in Nigeria, isolated by 1,500 km from one suspected to occur in the eastern Central African Republic; in its turn 1,300 km from the next known population in the Sudan. It is territorial, and one of the few species to form permanent pair bonds.

Salt's dik-dik *Madoqua saltiana*
Height: 40 cm. Weight: 3.6 kg. Horn length: 8.5 cm.

A very small antelope, the coat, which is thick, is a grizzled grey colour on the back with bright cinnamon flanks. There is an erectile reddish crest on the forehead characteristic of all the dik-diks. The horns are upright, short and spike-like, present only in the male. It is confined to eastern Ethiopia and part of Sudan. Cordeaux's, from the Ethiopian Danakil region, sometimes regarded as a separate species, is probably a race.

There is a number of *Madoqua* dik-diks confined to Somalia, all of which are very similar in appearance and habits. These are Swayne's *M. swaynei* with four races described; and Phillip's *M. phillipsi* also with four races, and which inhabits the same area as the Swayne's. But the latter appears to differ from other dik-diks in drinking regularly. Dik-diks are generally water-independent, shy and nocturnal browsers, inhabiting dry bush country, living singly or in pairs. All are territorial and have regular dung piles. They make a characteristic 'zik-zik' noise when alarmed, hence their name.

Günther's long-snouted dik-dik *M. guentheri*
Height: 35 cm. Weight: 3.6 kg. Horn length: 9 cm.

One of the smallest of antelopes. The coat colour is a grizzled, greyish fawn and the horns, short upright spikes, are absent in the female. Four races have been described but are not distinct. The species is distinguished by an elongated, proboscis-like snout, probably associated with cooling. At one time these long-snouted dik-diks were placed in a separate genus *Rhynchotragus*. It is limited in distribution to north-east Africa.

Kirk's long-snouted dik-dik *M. kirkii*
Height: 40 cm. Weight: 5.5 kg. Horn length: 9.5 cm.

A bigger species than the Günther's with a less-elongated nose. The coat colour is similar but paler in the drier areas. The horns are short upright spikes, absent in the female. The hooves are characterised by rubbery pads on the post ventral surfaces, believed to be of aid in running over rocky ground. Foot glands are apparently absent or non-functional. This is the common dik-dik of East Africa and the best known species. Eight races have been described, including the widely separated Damaraland dik-dik of Namibia, some 2,100 km apart. Living singly or in pairs it is territorial, its habits resembling those of other species except that it is diurnal, although it rests during the heat of the day. It makes an explosive snort when alarmed. It lives for over nine years.

Beira antelope *Dorcatragus megalotis*
Height: 56 cm. Weight: 27 kg. Horn length: 12 cm.

A small, gazelle-like species, with the female slightly larger than the male. It is characterised by very large ears, relatively long legs and the forequarters lower than the hind. The horns are widely set, upright and ringed at the base, absent in the female. Its coat colour is grey, finely grizzled with a pinkish hue and with an indistinct dark lateral band. At one time it was thought to be a type of klipspringer, inhabiting as it does stony barren hills, and possessing well-developed pads on the hooves; but is now considered to be close to the dik-diks. It lacks a facial gland but foot glands are present. It is restricted to a very small area in northern Somalia and is now very rare with the status of an endangered species. Apparently a mixed feeder, it is water-independent and occurs in small herds of up to seven animals, but almost nothing is known of its habits.

Oribi *Ourebia ourebia*
Height: 66 cm. Weight: 20 kg. Horn length: 18 cm.

A small, slenderly built antelope, with a straight back slightly dipping at the forequarters, and rather a long neck. The coat is silky to the touch, ranging from bright sandy rufous in colour to brownish fawn, contrasting with the white underparts. The ears are relatively large and pointed and the horns are fairly short, upright and ringed at the base, absent in the female. It has almost a full complement of glands: one below the ear signified by a circular black patch as in the reedbuck, facial, groin, foot and 'knee' glands; the latter marked by a tuft of hair. It flares a white rump when excited. It is distinguished from a young reedbuck by its upright flight, often stotting, and its small, black and white patterned tail. Thirteen races have been described, the most distinctive being Haggard's oribi from the Kenya and Tanzania coastal areas; named after Jack Haggard, British Vice-consul at Lamu in 1885, the brother of the adventure writer H. Rider Haggard. This race has laterally compressed horns and its colour is clay-like. The oribi is the only grazing neotragine, widely distributed in grasslands and wooded grassland, and particularly characteristic of the west African savannas, less common in the lower rainfall East African region. Territorial, it lives in pairs or in small family groups up to five. First recorded from the Cape in 1783, its numbers there are now greatly reduced. It lives about 14 years.

Steenbok or steinbuck *Raphicerus campestris*
Height: 55 cm. Weight: 13.5 kg. Horn length: 16 cm.

A small species with a coat of uniform bright rufous fawn, it is distinguished by a lack of false hooves. The horns are smooth, upright spikes,
absent in the female. Twelve races have been described, but are not
distinct. It has a discontinuous distribution, occurring in East Africa just
reaching north of the equator, and in southern Africa. Its habitat consists
of open bushed plains or light woodland, and although fairly common in
places, it is never numerous perhaps on account of its very specialised food
habits, selecting only certain forbs. Territorial in habit, pairing apparently only takes place for breeding; but its habits are not well known. It is
said to make use of old burrows to rest in. A chin gland, apparently unique
among antelopes, has recently been discovered in this species.

Cape grysbok *R. melanotis*
Height: 56 cm. Weight: 11 kg. Horn length: 11 cm.

Similar in size to the steenbok but with a long, coarse coat of a rufous-
brown colour grizzled with white hairs. It has almost vertical horns, absent
in the female. It is restricted to the extreme south of the Cape, where it
inhabits scrub-covered flats. A mixed feeder it is territorial and solitary in
habit. Some studies have been conducted on it but it is not very common.

Sharpe's grysbok *R. sharpei*
Height: 50 cm. Weight: 11 kg. Horn length: 5 cm.

Similar in size and appearance to the Cape grysbok but with much shorter
horns. The colour is rufous brown speckled with white, giving it a grizzled
appearance. It forms a link between the grysbok and the steenbok, having
the grysbok's colour, but like the steenbok, lacking false hooves. It is
sometimes called Sharpe's steenbok. It occurs south of the equator in the
central eastern part of the continent down to South Africa, occupying
stony, hilly country. It is territorial and solitary and, like the steenbok,
apparently uses old burrows to lie up in.

Royal or pygmy antelope *Neotragus pygmaeus*
Height: 25 cm. Weight: 4 kg. Horn length: 3 cm.

This is the smallest African ungulate, the size of a rabbit. Its colour is a
bright rufous-fawn, darker on the back. The eyes are large and the face
snub-nosed. The horns are smooth, backwardly directed, and absent in the
female. A concentrate feeder, it inhabits the dense west African forest from
Guinea to eastern Nigeria. It is said to live in pairs, and to bound through
the forest in great springs when flushed. Although known of by William
Bosman in 1691 to 1705, who reported that the natives called it the 'King of
Harts' (possibly suggesting a very pugnacious territorial temperament), it
remains virtually unknown.

Bates' pygmy, dwarf or Congo dwarf antelope *N. batesi*
Height: 30 cm. Weight: 5.5 kg. Horn length: 3.5 cm.

Slightly larger than the royal antelope, which it strongly resembles except
for a darker colour and the tiny horns being ringed at the base. It could be
confused with the western blue duiker but has no crest between the horns
and has a more snub-nosed face, a hunched body and rounded ears. An

inhabitant of dense forest, it has an apparently discontinuous distribution, occurring in the northern Congo forest into the Cameroons, with a separate population in the eastern Congo forest, where it has been termed Harrison's. Its skull structure is more akin to that of the suni than to that of the royal antelope. The habits are unknown.

Suni *N. moschatus*
Height: 40 cm. Weight: 8 kg. Horn length: 11 cm.

Slightly larger than its pygmy relatives, this is still one of the smallest of antelopes, standing on very short legs. The colour is a dark chestnut and the horns are flattened and ridged, pointing backwards. They are absent in the female. It is confined almost entirely to the south of the equator, inhabiting forest along the eastern side of the continent as far as South Africa, where a more richly coloured and larger race is found known as Livingstone's. Three other races have been described, including one from two small islands near Zanzibar, where it was first discovered in 1846. It is really the pygmy antelope equivalent of the drier forests. Territorial, it appears to live singly and although rarely seen, is fairly common in some areas, but its habits await study. The prominent facial glands emit a strong musky odour, from whence it gets its name *moschatus*. It is regarded by some authorities as being in a separate genus of its own termed *Nesotragus*.

Sub-family *Peleinae*

This sub-family contains a single species considered by some to be an aberrant member of the *Reduncinae*, but it lacks facial and groin glands, although foot and preputial glands are present. Only the male is horned and the female has two pairs of teats. It is placed in a sub-family of its own because of its uncertain affinities.

Grey or Vaal Rhebuck or rhebok *Pelea capreolus*
Height: 76 cm. Weight: 23 kg. Horn length: 29 cm.

A slender, moderately long-necked species, with a brownish-grey coat colour, the underparts slightly paler. The horns are the most upright of all antelopes, set at an angle of 90 degrees with the skull, forming straight spikes, ringed at the base. A grazer, it is confined to the Cape where it is still fairly widely distributed, inhabiting grassy hills in mountainous districts, descending at night to drink and graze. Its habitat overlaps with that of the mountain reedbuck, which it is said to kill occasionally, as well as sheep and goats, indicating that it is strongly territorial. The male usually lives with a female group of 5 to 12, and a bachelor group. A very wary species, fleeing in a rocking-horse gait, it is not well-known, despite being first described in 1799.

Select bibliography

Ardrey, R. (1967) *The Territorial Imperative*, Collins, London
Beeton, I. (1861) *Mrs Beeton's Book of Household Management*, reprinted 1982, Chancellor Press, London
Bell, R.H.V. (1971) 'A grazing ecosystem in the Serengeti', *Scientific American*, Vol. 225, 86–93
Bere, R. (1970) *Antelopes*, Arthur Barker, London
Bland-Sutton, J. (1911) *Man and Beast in Eastern Ethiopia*, Macmillan, London
Brocklehurst, H.C. (1931) *Game Animals of the Sudan*, Gurney & Jackson, London
Cronwright-Schreiner, S.C. (1925) *The Migratory Springbucks of South Africa*, T. Fisher Unwin, London
Cumming, R.G. (1850) *The Lion Hunter in South Africa*, 2 vols., John Murray, London
David, J.H.M. (1973) 'The behaviour of the bontebok, *Damaliscus dorcas dorcas* with special reference to territorial behaviour', *Z. Tierpsychol.*, Vol. 33, 38–107
Dorst, J. and Dandelot, P. (1970) *A Field Guide to the Larger Mammals of Africa*, Collins, London
Estes, R. (1969) 'Territorial behaviour of the wildebeest (*Connochaetes taurinus* Burchell, 1823)', *Z. Tierpsychol.*, Vol. 26, 284–370
Haltenorth, T. and Diller, H. (1980) *A Field Guide to the Mammals of Africa including Madagascar*, Collins, London
Jarman, M.V. (1979) 'Impala social behaviour, territory, hierarchy, mating and the use of space', *Advances in Ethology 21*, Verlag Paul Parey, Berlin and Hamburg
Kingdon, J. (1982) *East African Mammals. An Atlas of Evolution in Africa*, Vol. III, Parts C and D (Bovids), Academic Press, London
Leuthold, W. (1977) *African Ungulates. A Comparative Review of their Ethology and Behavioural Ecology*, Springer-Verlag, Berlin, Heidelberg, New York
Millais, J.G. (1895) *A Breath from the Veldt*, Henry Sotheran, London
Moore, A. (1938) *Serengeti*, Country Life Limited, London
Sclater, P.L. and Thomas, O. (1894–1900) *The Book of Antelopes*. 4 vols., R.H. Porter, London

Spinage, C.A. (1982) *A Territorial Antelope: The Uganda Waterbuck.* Academic Press, London

Taylor, C.R. (1969) 'The eland and the oryx', *Scientific American*, Vol. 220, 89–95

Tinley, K.L. (1969) 'Dikdik *Madoqua kirki* in South West Africa: Notes on distribution, ecology and behaviour', *Madoqua*, Vol. I, 7–33

Von Richter, W. (1971) *The Black Wildebeest (Connochaetes gnou)*, Nature Conservation Orange Free State, Bloemfontein

Walther, F.R. (1966) *Mit Horn und Huf*, Verlag Paul Parey, Berlin and Hamburg

Walther, F.R. (1969) 'Flight behaviour and avoidance of predators in Thomson's gazelle (*Gazella thomsoni* Günther, 1884)', *Behaviour*, Vol. 34, 184–221

Walther, F.R., Mungall, E.C. and Grau, G.A. (1983) *Gazelles and their Relatives. A Study in Territorial Behaviour*, Noyes Publications, New Jersey

Index